MY MAD MAGICAL MOROCCAN JOURNEY

A Memoir of Sex, Drugs, Rock and Roll, and Spiritual Enlightenment 1970–1973

May all beings
be happy
Steven Antler

By Fred Zola with Steven Antler

ISBN 978-1-63784-509-7 (paperback)
ISBN 978-1-63784-510-3 (digital)

Hawes & Jenkins Publishing
16427 N Scottsdale Road Suite 410
Scottsdale, AZ 85254
www.hawesjenkins.com

Printed in the United States of America

He who travels far will often see things
Far removed from what he believed was true
When he talks about it in the fields of home,
He is often accused of lying.
For the obdurate people will not believe
What they do not see and distinctly feel.
Inexperience, I believe
Will give little credence to my song.

—Herman Hesse, *Journey to the East*

CONTENTS

ACKNOWLEDGMENT

My memoir would not exist without the inspiration and hard work of my dear lifelong friend Steven Antler.

We shared a year and many adventures together in Morocco during the early 1970s. We have maintained our friendship for fifty years, and our adventures continue.

When I told Steven that my friends were telling me to write a memoir of my Morocco years, he leapt to the project and made it happen.

Thank you, Steve, we have shared a spiritual journey and had lots of fun along the way.

FZ

Fred Zola 1971

Steven Antler 1971

AUTHOR'S NOTE

This memoir is written from the Tangier Prison where I was confined.

The prison portions are the first and last sections of each chapter.

In between are flashbacks of how I came to be there.

PROLOGUE

Give Peace a Chance

Why should they ask me to put on a uniform and go ten thousand miles from home and drop bombs on Brown people in Vietnam while so-called Negro people in Louisville are treated like dogs and denied simple human rights?

—Muhammad Ali

On May 27, 1969, I received this letter from my draft board, "Greetings, you are hereby ordered for induction into the Armed Forces of the United States. Report to the Military Processing Station, Milwaukee."

In 1969, the war in Vietnam occupied every young man's mind. Daily television coverage showed American soldiers wounded and dying. I opposed the unjustified and immoral war and participated in the protests at the 1968 Democratic Convention where I chanted Om with Allen Ginsberg and barely escaped a brutal beating by the Chicago police.

Because my 2S student deferment ended upon graduation from the Northwestern University School of Business, I anticipated being drafted and applied for conscientious objector status. Denied. I tried to join the peace corps. Rejected. Sweden and Canada offered political asylum, but that option meant no return to the States and permanent separation from my family.

Determined to avoid going to Vietnam, I entered the large downtown building for my physical examination. I reconciled myself to serving the two-and-a half-year federal prison sentence I would receive for refusing military induction.

The process began with a sergeant barking orders, yelling at us to sit on the benches and listen.

I thought, *I'm going to jail, so why listen to this guy?* I stood on the bench and yelled, "Fuck you!"

The sergeant walked up to me. He put his face close to mine and shouted again, "Sit down!"

I replied, "What are you going to do? Put me in jail?" I had nothing to lose.

When the physical exam began, we lined up to be weighed. I would not get on the scale. At the eye test, I couldn't see anything. At the hearing test, I couldn't hear anything. I refused to allow the blood draw and returned the urine sample bottle empty.

Beginning the mental/psychological tests, the first paper to sign called for me to swear I was not now, and had never been, a member of the Communist Party. The rumor at school advised not signing this pledge would result in an FBI investigation, which could delay induction six months. I left it blank.

The army booklets reminded me of college entrance exams. While the others struggled to answer the numerous questions, I wrote on every page, in large black letters, "Thou shalt not kill."

Late in the afternoon, I could hear most of the other men gathered together reciting the pledge to enter the army. A sergeant told me, "Sit on the bench with those four to see the shrink." The others had thick file folders with letters and reports from psychiatrists, psychologists, and counselors documenting their mental issues. I had no papers, only my rage.

One after the other, the men entered the office.

The first guy came out cheering. He shouted, "I'm classified 1-Y, a one-year deferral!"

Each of the next three received the same result, happily leaving the psychiatrist's office. They considered it a victory; the war might be over in a year.

When my turn came, the psychiatrist asked, "Have you ever taken drugs?"

"I drop acid every day." At this point, I had never taken LSD.

"Have you ever thought about suicide?" he continued.

"Yes, every day."

He asked a few more questions; I responded with the craziest things I could think of.

After reviewing my forms, he finished my paperwork and told me to take it to the soldier at the desk outside his office. I saw, stamped in large red letters, "4-F"—unfit for military service.

I turned to cheer my good fortune to the now-empty hall. I walked out the front door into the sunlight with the chains lifted. I floated to the street light as a feather. Free. Maybe I would travel. I had always wanted to spend a year seeing Europe.

Fred on the road to Morocco, Summer, 1970

CHAPTER 1

On the Road

Ye who enter abandon all hope.

—Dante's *Inferno*

My day had come. I had an audience to smoke hashish with Hassan II, the king of Morocco. Lying stretched out in the back of the speeding vehicle as the driver raced through traffic lights with the siren blasting and lights flashing made my heart beat fast in anticipation of getting super stoned. The king had a reputation as a connoisseur of hash, and now he wanted to share his good hash with me.

We screeched to a stop outside a gate guarded by machine gun-carrying soldiers who lifted the barricade and let us enter under an arched gateway into a courtyard surrounded by a high wall. The building did not appear palatial. I expected a statelier venue for the king. However, I realized our meeting required secrecy at a discreet location to avoid publicity about the king entertaining the hash supplier to The Rolling Stones.

The driver and attendant opened the back door and lifted out the gurney. The attendant unlocked the straps holding me, and the driver pointed to the ground and said something in Arabic.

I thought, *I should be wheeled into my audience to impress the king*, so I crossed my arms and said, "No."

The driver yelled in French and Spanish, but I refused to get up. Finally, the driver started pulling me up, but I grabbed the sides of the gurney and wouldn't let go. Extremely angry, the two men maneuvered the gurney up the ramp and down a dim hallway. After opening a thick wood door, they pushed me inside and overturned the gurney, dropping me onto a metal cot covered by a thin mattress.

"Fuck you," the driver said as he raised his middle finger and slammed the door behind him.

I looked at my surroundings, a bare gray room with a pail in one corner and the cot. A shaft of sunlight shone through the bars of a small window in the wall high above the bed while a burning single light bulb hung from the ceiling.

The door swung open. A man wearing a white vest over his brown djellaba entered the room. Without saying anything, he turned me onto my side and pulled down the back of my jeans. He stuck a large needle into my butt, and everything went black.

Opening my eyes, I wondered how much time had passed. My clothes were gone. I wore only a thin, short hospital gown barely reaching below my genitals. I lay with my arms behind my head, looking at the cracks running across the ceiling. I had to pee, so I got up, and as if moving through cement, I stumbled to the door and turned the knob. It turned, but the door didn't open in or out. I pushed and pulled a few times.

Frustrated, I slammed my palm into the wood and screamed, "*Necesitar baño!*" Using my closed fists, I pounded louder, "Come here!" and finally, "Help me."

I got no response. Nearly bursting, I limped to the corner to use the pail.

Unsteady, I sat on the cot and sank into the fetal position. Images rushed by and cartoon characters appeared talking distortedly as through water. Various women's names, *Lora, Michelle, Gerri, Jan, Gail, Mina* kept repeating like a mantra until I put my hands over my ears so I wouldn't hear them anymore.

To escape my rushing mind, I got up and stood on the cot. On my tiptoes, I looked out the small window into a circular courtyard surrounded by a high wall, topped with shards of broken glass. In the yard, a few men in torn djellabas were standing or sitting idly.

The sun's late-afternoon angle meant that a full day must have passed since I entered my unknown place of confinement.

I heard the metal sound of a key in the lock and turned to see a wizened, wrinkled man enter, carrying a tray with a bowl of thin broth with a few peas floating in it, a glass of mint tea, and a small loaf of Spanish white bread. Showing his broken teeth, the man pointed to a paper cup containing three pills and, raising his hand to his lips, indicated I should take the pills.

"Where I am?" I asked first in English but quickly said, "*Donde esta?*"

The old man just pointed to the cup of pills and motioned I should swallow them.

I continued to ask questions, but the man's only response consisted of silently pointing at the pills. I grabbed the cup and took the pills in one gulp, washing them down with the mint tea.

The man turned around, taking a key from the ring tied around his waist. I could hear him locking the door from the outside. He hadn't uttered a word.

I started spooning mouthfuls of the broth and ate the unappetizing bread until I became dizzy and lay down again. I tried to focus. I remembered vaguely becoming one with the universe, the enlightenment I had studied and worked for.

Back on the cot, I recognized the fantasy of my meeting King Hassan, but where was I, and how had I gotten to the point of being confined here? I thought I'd review my time in Morocco to orient myself. As the pills took effect, I drifted back to my arrival in Morocco in December 1970.

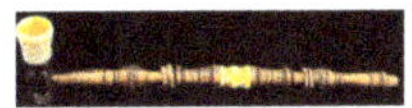

I saw the white walls of the Tangier Casbah rising above the harbor as the ferry from Malaga docked. After nine months of traveling in Europe, I was on the hippie "hash trail" that stretched from Amsterdam to Kathmandu. Tangier was a stop on the trail.

Tanned with my long, wavy, thick brown hair, parted in the middle, flowing to my shoulders, and my orthodontia white teeth smiling from behind my full beard, I walked down the gangplank. I proudly wore my suede-fringed vest over a Rolling Stones T-shirt I picked up when I saw the Stones in Amsterdam. Also, I had on my denim blue-and-red striped bell-bottom jeans and desert boots. A seashell I picked up from the beach of Ibiza hung on a leather strap around my neck.

A pack of ragged boys surrounded me, shouting and gesturing. "Hash to sell, good place to stay, follow me." Some boys reached out and touched my pant legs. Malaga hippies warned me about the street hustlers and advised avoiding them. I started walking uphill toward the nearby terminal travelers recommend for catching a bus to the campgrounds on the outskirts of town.

A boy with a shaved head and bright, dark eyes jumped in our path and said, "Can I guide you, sir? Where are you from? English?"

I shouted, "Fuck you!"

The boy answered in good English, "You come to my country and you say, 'fuck you.' Is this the proper way to enter my country?"

Shaken by this encounter, I quickened my pace, ignoring all the boys.

At the terminal with my cousin Mike, his two-year old son Emanuel, and Mike's British girlfriend Sarah, we caught a bus.

After we checked in and established our site, where I put my sleeping bag on a tarp in the open air, I walked to the bathroom from the campsite. I heard someone shouting, "Fred! Yes, Fred, you hippie!" I turned to see GI John, who along with five other recently discharged US soldiers, had picked me up when I was hitchhiking through France on the way to Southern Spain in September.

We hugged.

"You take the acid?" were the first words out of John's mouth.

"Yes, I did and watched the full moon over the clear Spanish sky. It was far-out. What's up with you and the others?" I replied.

"Last day in Morocco. Tomorrow back to Spain. We visited Katama where they grow the plants and where the kief is extra powerful. We couldn't even smoke up what we bought," John said. "Come over to our campsite, number thirty-four. Meeting you here today, crazy, man, and perfect."

At campsite thirty-four, the GI's van, a little more dented and covered with dust, brought me back to my wild ride of acid and wine with these guys. The five others greeted me warmly, but they let John do most of the talking.

"Sit down in one of the comfortable chairs," John said as he motioned to a stuffed recliner. "We're leaving this chair. You want it?"

"No, thanks. We don't even have a vehicle. We're just getting our bearings. We plan to move to Tangier. We just arrived today," I said.

"Check out the Pension Miami in Tangier. We've stayed there twice. It's got a safe, friendly vibe, and you can communicate with the owner in Spanish," John said as he sat down next to me.

Now two joints were moving around the circle in opposite directions, both heading toward me. I took a hit and began coughing.

"I should have warned you. Kief is marijuana mixed with black tobacco. It takes getting used to," John said in a kind way, although he had a smile on his face, as did the others.

I took my second hit more carefully and let the smoke out slowly. My heart was beating faster, and I felt dizzy.

John continued, "You smoke kief in a pipe called a sebsi. Here, take this one." He took out a pipe made of a wooden shaft as long as one's outstretched arm and handed it to me. "A small clay bowl attaches to end. Buy plenty because they break easily. A hash bowl is larger. Get plenty of them too. The sebsi cools the smoke and detaches in the middle to fit in a pouch."

I saw it worked like the pool cue I used in Chicago, although my mind drifted as I looked at the two large palm trees at the end of the row of campsites and thought about dates and eating the fruit and having dates with women.

John continued describing their two months in Morocco. "Don't miss the square in Marrakech. Storytellers, fortune tellers, camels, monkeys, see it now before it gets commercialized."

As time passed, I thought Mike would start to worry when I didn't return from the bathroom for hours. Had it been hours? What time was it?

"Got to go," I said and stood up swaying.

"Hold on, partner, I've got something for you." One of the other ex-soldiers brought out a burlap bag wrapped around a sheaf of long-stemmed marijuana flowers and handed it to me.

"There's black tobacco in there too. Have fun smoking it," John said and gave me a hug.

"I feel the USA is safer now that you guys aren't in the army," I said, and I walked back to my campsite carrying the package like a bouquet.

When I arrived, Mike called out, "Where the hell were you? I was ready to report you kidnapped by Moroccan slave traders."

"I ran into GI John from my ride to your place outside of Malaga. They're leaving tomorrow. He gave me a present." I handed the bouquet to Mike.

The smell hit Mike, and as he unwrapped the burlap, he exclaimed, "Allah be praised.

After I smoked a few pipes with Mike and Sarah and feeling somewhat disoriented, I said, "I'm going for a walk."

I left the campsite along the path, which circled, through and around the campground. A half-moon's light made it easy for me to follow the path as I gazed up at the palm trees and other flowering shrubs. I walked by the last occupied site and farther along a dirt road. The thick trees, bushes, vines, and tall grasses on both sides of the path formed odd shapes with dark shadows.

"What did you say?" I called out as I heard a voice talking from the side of the path. "Who goes there?"

There was a rustling in the bushes.

"Who goes there?" I repeated, upset at getting no reply.

I heard a scrapping noise from the other side of the path, and beginning to get frightened, I yelled, "Is anyone out there?"

No reply, but I could see the shapes of two figures standing among the bushes.

Now very frightened, I said again, "Who's out there? Come out. What do you want?" I thought I saw the figures begin to move toward me with hostile intent. I took a defensive boxing stance and said, "Come out. Face me in the open." I heard movement on the opposite side of the path, and thinking I was surrounded, I ran as fast as I could back to our campsite.

I ran without stopping or turning around, my lungs bursting until I doubled over gasping. I still heard the footsteps behind me, and when I looked back, I could see shadows coming after me on both sides of the path. I was stumbling and forcing myself to move forward as my life now depended on my escaping the hostile men pursuing me.

I rushed into the campsite and dropped to my knees outside Mike's tent. I screamed, "They're going to kill me! I'm being attacked! Help, help!"

There was a rush of activity in the tent, and Mike unzipped the door and got out while pulling on his pants.

"What the fuck's 'appening?" Sarah called out from inside the tent.

"Moroccans attacked me on the path near the campground," I blurted out, still trying to catch my breath. "There were men in the bushes waiting for me, chasing me."

"Calm down. You're stoned," said Mike. "I doubt anyone attacked you. You just got paranoid."

"No, no, I heard them. They were on both sides of the path. I could feel the threat," I said.

"Did you actually see anyone?" Mike asked as he adopted his rational, lawyerlike approach.

"No, I heard them. They were in the bushes, I couldn't see them," I replied. "I'm frightened."

"You coming back in 'ere or I'll have to finish myself," Sarah called out.

"I need to talk to Fred. Do what you have do," Mike called back as he wrapped his arm around my shoulder. "Calm down, let's go back down the path. I'll get the flashlight. I know there were no people hiding in the bushes, and I'll show you. You just got paranoid from the kief. Sarah said you were hitting the pipe heavy." Mike reached down for the flashlight and led me out along the path. "Your mind can play tricks on you when you're stoned. Everyone here has been friendly. Are you getting more relaxed?"

"How could I imagine people? I heard them and was afraid they wanted to hurt me," I said, following the route I had taken.

As we approached the place where I heard the sounds and saw the movement in the shadows, my body began to shake, and pointing to a large tree, I shouted, "I heard them under this tree!"

Mike shined the flashlight into the thick brush and stepped off the trail toward the tree. "No one's here. See how thick the vines and bushes are." Mike continued to shine the light to show me no one was there. "You just had a paranoia attack. Just relax. I'm the one who has to worry about Emanuel, but no one wants to hurt you. Remember when Grandma Minnie had her bout of insanity and she ended up in an asylum for a while?" Mike asked. "Little moments of insanity happen in our family. This is nothing to worry about. I can see you're already snapping out of it."

I shook my head and said, "I guess you're right. A little moment of insanity, drug induced, nothing to worry about."

Before I could hear Mike's reply, the sound of the key in the door lock brought me back to the present. The old man entered, carrying my food and pill tray.

I got to my feet and asked him, "*Donde esta?*" but looking at his unchanged, nonresponsive face, I understood continuing to question him would only increase my frustration.

The light coming through the small window meant I had slept for a full night. Now I began my second or third day locked up. Once I swallowed the pills, the man left. I could hear him locking the door. I decided to keep track of the passing time as I remembered a scene from the movie *The Count of Monte Cristo* and scratched a line on the wall.

I fell asleep again with images appearing and fading, most of which meant nothing to me. I saw my deaf parents with worried looks on their faces and heard my mother say, "Fred, you were such a good boy. What happened?"

CHAPTER 2

I'll Follow the Sun

Occasional collisions unexpectedly encountered
determine the direction of a lifetime.
—Elias Canetti, *Auto du Fe*

I woke up disturbed by my dream about my first days in Tangier. I knew the medications helped me calm down, but my inner agitation still came and went. I hadn't seen any staff and did not know the nature of this facility but my guess, "a prison for the insane." I recognized the difference between my fantastic visions upon entering and the cold reality of my foul-smelling room. My meeting the king of Morocco had been a delusion.

My door opened and the silent gnome, as I had named my keeper, entered with the same daily tray. He handed me the cup of pills, and I took them with a sip of tea. He held up a key and shook his head from side to side. He handed me a brown paper bag containing my red-and-blue stripped bell-bottom jeans and the T-shirt I had been wearing when I arrived. I stripped off my skimpy gown and put on my hippie threads. Even with my heavy legs and my mind cloudy, I wanted out of my isolated, locked room.

I hesitantly opened the door and looked down to the end of the narrow hall where I saw daylight. Opening the door, I stumbled into a large courtyard. Sunlight and the heat of the late-August air stunned me as I wandered forward on shaky legs.

I stopped to rest and surveyed the scene. A circular ten-foot-high perimeter wall topped with broken glass, which I called Moroccan barbed wire, surrounded the courtyard of loose dirt and dead grass. The building in the center had several entrances.

Older Moroccan men with blank expressions sat against the high wall. A few younger men with the same expression and heavy gait were trudging slowly around the yard. I looked for someone who appeared to be in a position of authority. I walked up to three men wearing ragged brown wool djellabas standing together, leaning against the wall. Two were older and one who looked about thirty. They did not turn to me when I walked up.

I said, "*Donde esta?*" in a loud voice.

As soon as I spoke, the three men moved slowly away without responding.

Gathering myself, I approached a man standing alone. In English, I pleaded, "What is this place? Where are we?"

The man had a vacant look in his eyes, and he just stared back at me. I sensed if I asked again, he would walk away too. Confused and saddened, I couldn't get anyone in the yard to respond. I noticed the one entry gate with the guards carrying machine guns and vaguely remembered entering through it.

Not finding any staff and not getting any response to my inquiries, I thought I'd be safer and more cared for in my locked room. I went back to the central building and walked down the hallway to the room where I had been confined. Unable to open the locked door, I started to cry. The room I had been so desperate to get out of only hours before seemed like a safe haven, but I couldn't get back in.

An older Moroccan man wearing a white coat came out of one of the other rooms.

I tried through broken Spanish and gestures to beg him to let me into the room. He made a sour face and pointed for me to leave the hallway then turned his back and walked away.

I returned to the courtyard and sat against the wall, absorbing the dry heat. Feeling the effects of the sun combined with my morning pills, I drifted into a vivid dream. I saw myself in the Blue Door Commune, which I had joined a week after arriving Tangier.

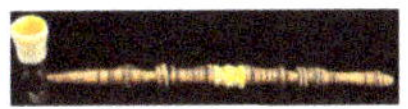

On my first morning in the commune, I woke up to Eldon, an American hippie and longtime Tangier resident, squatting next to me with glass of water in his hand. Yesterday he brought ten hippies, six men and four women, together to live in a rented concrete house at the top of a hill above the casbah overlooking the Mediterranean Sea.

Eldon said, "Wake up and drink this."

I asked, "What's up?"

To which he replied, "I filled this bottle with ten glasses of water and mixed in ten tabs of acid. I'm giving one glass to each person living in the house. I thought we should start our lives in this house on LSD."

As the acid hit, we ten strangers drifted to the windowed upstairs room with a view of the Rock of Gibraltar. We began getting acquainted, telling stories of our lives. While tripping into a higher consciousness, we melded into a family. We smoked hash festively, and the group burst into joyous laughter for no apparent reason. The group started saying, "We're in the 'magic room,'" and would burst out laughing again.

As the sun set, Eldon placed a crate of oranges on the low Moroccan brass table in the center of the room. George, his almost always-silent companion, began squeezing fresh glasses of orange juice. Eldon filled a pipe, which went from hand to hand around the table, each person smiling and making eye contact with the next person as she, or he, passed the pipe. English Jan, one of three single women who were part of the group, rolled a fat joint, which circulated around the table too.

As I sat back super relaxed, Eldon picked up a thick hard-covered book and said, "I'm going to read a song from the great Tibetan Buddhist yogi, Milarepa, the patron saint of Tibet. 'Things in the outer world are all illusion. The inner mind is that which I observe.'"

I was raised in a Jewish family and had a Bar Mitzvah but considered myself an atheist. I never heard of Milarepa. His songs featured in the stories Eldon read, focused on gaining enlightenment, which Milarepa had achieved after receiving instruction in Mahayana Buddhism from his guru Marpa. Using the teachings, he meditated for years in isolation in caves in the Himalayas. Milarepa's teaching of compassion underlay our newly formed hippie family, with which Eldon directed our spiritual quest. My quest centered on sex, drugs, and rock and roll.

Just at sunset, I smelled a vegetable stew, mint tea, and lingering hash odor permeating the magic room. On the table were two large bowls, one filled with couscous and the other with a steaming vegetable stew. An assortment of plates, flatware, teacups, and some colored cloth napkins lay ready for use. Candles illuminated the room. A bright poster version of a Tibetan Tanka showed a white-clad yogi, seated in the lotus position with his hand to his ear. I figured it represented Milarepa, who only wore a light cotton robe even while traveling through the high mountains.

Eldon said, "We offer this food and the strength we get from it to enhance the welfare of all sentient beings. Now dig in."

I sat next to Dolores, an attractive dark-haired woman from Vancouver, and said, "Help yourself. Ladies first." I made a gesture with my hand and bowed slightly.

"A real gentleman. I like to be treated special," Dolores replied as she took spoonfuls of the stew and couscous.

Eldon continued, "In this house, we will function as a hippie commune. To each according to their need, from each their contribution according to their skills and finances. Share and share alike. Our next important activity is to resupply our stash of hash. Everyone here should put money into the pot, what you can afford, but remember the more we buy, the better deal we get. I see this as a group of heavy smokers. Tomorrow I'll go to my dealer with the money and bring back some more of this good hash. We'll take a third and make it the 'magic room' stash and otherwise share it according to the amount each person contributes."

I decided supplying hash could be my contribution to the commune. I turned to Eldon and said, "I'll go with you if that's okay." Acting on an impulse, I took a twenty-dollar bill and handed it to him.

Eldon didn't answer, but a discussion of hash and obtaining it followed.

After everyone had spoken, I learned the others—excluding my cousin and myself—had come to Morocco for the purpose of smuggling hash back to England, Canada, and the US.

In a righteous way, I said, "I'm a pure hash consumer. I don't intend to take it across any border, but I do intend to stay here and smoke plenty."

Eldon turned to me and said, "Tomorrow morning you can come along. I'll introduce you to Mustapha." Eldon lit the hash pipe and passed it to me as he began to read another Milarepa story, "If one continues searching for the nature of mind, he will see it fully in end."

The next morning, I got up early enough to ensure Eldon would not make the hash deal without me.

In the kitchen, Eldon said, "I met the bigger Tangier hash dealers while in jail. After spending time with them, I now know the hash scene from the inside. There are three main dealers. Mohamed at the low end in terms of quality and price whose front business is a chicken farm. Achmed, who we call Achmed Gold Pipe, is the most expensive. I hear The Rolling Stones and Hendrix are among his customers. His front business is a high-end women's clothing boutique. My supplier is Mustapha, who sells good quality hash at a medium price we can afford. Mustapha owns the Café Royale, a nightclub with music nightly and entertainment provided by dancing boys." Eldon turned to me and said, "Let's go. 'There is no idleness in the life of a devotee.' Do you remember the line from Milarepa?"

I answered back, "I'm a devotee of hash and I'm ready."

As we walked toward the center of town, I asked, "What was it like to be in a Moroccan prison?"

"Not too bad once I learned the ropes. I knew I'd be out in three months, the maximum sentence for possession of small amounts of hash. I adjusted and adapted. I had to sleep on the floor because of the overcrowding, but you'd be surprised how much warmer putting newspaper under you can make the concrete. As an American, I got special treatment. I ended up smoking hash with Mustapha. It's strange, but there are even some hustlers who like to spend the winter in jail, where they have a roof over their heads and it's relatively warm. The food's crap, but if you have money, you can buy other food. There's absolutely no shortage of kief and hash. I got high nearly every day and read my Milarepa book," Eldon replied.

This upbeat description of jail didn't ease my anxiety. Three months maybe I could handle, but I hoped it would never happen.

The large, red "Café Royale" sign hung from the white stucco wall of the two-story building. Under a white canopy, tables on the sidewalk surrounded the entrance. Although a sign on the door said closed, open at 7:00 pm, Eldon just walked inside. A few men were working inside—one sweeping the floor, another stacking glasses, and a third who appeared to be checking on the stock of tea.

A fourth man wearing an embroidered white caftan approached us from behind the serving counter. He was about five feet six tall with a stocky build and had bushy dark eyebrows and friendly, large, dark eyes.

"*Labas*," the man said and touched his hand to his heart.

"*Coltree Labas*," replied Eldon as he made the same gesture with his hand.

"How's it going, Eldon?" the man said in good English.

"I re-rented my old house, and I've got a group of hippies to share it with me. This is Fred who's part of the group." Turning toward me, he said, "Fred, meet Mustapha, the owner of this fine establishment."

I said, "*Labas*," and Mustapha returned the greeting while Eldon said, "We came on business to make a purchase."

Mustapha said, "Come upstairs to my office," and led us to the back of the café and up a flight of stairs.

We entered a room that looked like an office in a typical business establishment with an old typewriter on one table, a big desk, a phone, and several filing cabinets. Mustapha did not pause in this room but walked through it and gestured us into another room.

For a minute, I flashed back to San Francisco's Haight Ashbury because black lights and dayglow posters hung on the walls. The Jimi Hendrix tune "All Along the Watchtower" was playing on a good sound system. Even without much light, I appreciated the room's psychedelic decor.

Mustapha touched an intercom and said something in Arabic. "I just ordered us some mint tea. So how much do you want to buy?" Mustapha inquired as he took a piece of hash from a decorated wooden box. He heated the hash and put some in a large clay pipe bowl, lit it, and took a deep drag before handing the pipe to Eldon.

After Eldon took a hit, he passed the pipe to me and said, "Same good quality." He reached into his pocket and put all the money he had collected on the table. "I want what this much money can buy. Ninety US dollars' worth."

Mustapha reached forward and quickly counted the money and took it off the table.

A waiter came into the room with a tray and the fixings for mint tea and left without saying a word. Mustapha ceremoniously put two tablespoons of gunpowder tea leaves into a teapot with boiling water. Next he added a dozen sugar cubes and more boiling water. As the tea steeped, he got up and went into another room. He returned with three and half pieces of hash, each about half the size of a hardbound book.

"This is 456 grams. It's one pound, a little less than half a kilo, which is what ninety dollars buys," he said.

Eldon picked up the hash and moved his hand up and down as if judging the weight and looked at it and said, "This is one pound?"

Mustapha replied, "Yes, my friend. In fact, it's slightly more because I'm glad you're set up again. The price is the same for you and your friends." Adding green mint tea leaves, Mustapha poured more boiling water from a height into the teapot.

He filled the cups and we each took a sip.

I said, "I can't believe this room, where did you get all the decorations?" as the hash had relaxed me. I wanted to establish a personal connection with Mustapha, so if necessary, I could buy hash on my own.

"Friends bring me presents from London and the States. This room shows Westerners I'm in tune with them and their world. I just got a new tape of the *Easy Rider* soundtrack. Would you like to hear it?"

"Seeing the movie *Easy Rider* changed my life," I replied. "That movie inspired me to follow the hippie movement."

I laughed at the warning in the first song on the tape "The Pusher" by Steppenwolf when I caught the line, "The pusher man don't care if you live or if you die."

When "Born to be Wild" came on next, I thought, *My theme song.*

After finishing the tea and smoking another pipe, Eldon picked up the hash, put it in the fringed leather purse he carried, and got up. "*Shukraan*, I hope I'll be bringing you lot's more customers," Eldon said with a slight bow.

"*Inshallah*, may God will it, my friends," Mustapha said as he walked us down the stairs to the café door.

In the background, I heard Dylan singing, "He that is not busy being born is busy dying."

Back at the commune, I went to my cousin Mike's room. Sarah and Dolores sat in one corner, talking and looking over some astrological charts and books. Emanuel was playing with some blocks on the floor near them.

"How'd the hash deal go?" Mike said as he greeted me with a hug.

"Groovy. Eldon bought a little less than half a kilo for ninety bucks. We get a third, which should last us a while. Mustapha has a hippie room upstairs at the Royale where the deal went down."

"Now that we have a hash connection, we need to figure out how to refill our kief supply," Mike said.

I replied, "Eldon told me that kief is available at a backstreet café called Baba's."

Mike said, "Here's thirty dirhams. Tomorrow see if you can score a stash for us."

Sarah called, "Fred, please come over 'ere, we've got a question to ask you."

I walked over to the corner and dropped down on the straw mat next to Dolores.

"What are the date, time, and place where you were born?" Dolores said, "I want to make a chart to see if we're possibly compatible."

"September 1, 1946, at six a.m. in Chicago. I hope the stars line up in the right way because on the earthly plane, I feel there's something between us."

"Listen, I've got a boyfriend in Vancouver, and he's supposed to be in Tangier in a few weeks. So he and I can buy hash and take it back. God knows a few weeks can be a long time without any action. I feel something too, but the stars must affirm our harmoniousness," Dolores said as she consulted her charts based on the information I had given her.

I had my fingers crossed the stars would be on my side. *Stars, please, support my connection with Dolores*, I prayed to myself.

The next day, I decided that I wanted to blend more with the local men most of whom a wore a dark-brown, woolen, hooded outer robe, which extended to just above their shoes, called a djellaba. I went to a casbah shop, where I bargained for more than an hour with an old merchant who sold djellabas. I walked away from the purchase feeling just like the store owner wanted me to, that I robbed him blind, although I knew he had made a good profit. I felt warm and happy wearing my authentic djellaba. Elated, I proceeded to purchase some kief.

Eldon told me to go uphill to the end of a narrow street above a house owned by the heiress Barbara Hutton. I walked past whitewashed cement walls to where a small sign in English and Arabic said, "Café Baba."

I entered a smoke-filled room where only men were sitting at tables with pots of mint tea in front of them. I could see that some men had marijuana flowers on their tables, which they were cutting and sorting.

A short bearded man in a djellaba and *taqiyah* (skullcap) greeted me, saying, "*Labas*."

To which I replied, "*Cochee Labas*."

The man touched his hand to his heart and said in perfect English, "I'm Rocky, please come over here and sit down," as he motioned to a table near the back of the café.

"I'm Fred, Rocky. I'm a friend of Eldon's, and I'm out of kief."

Rocky said, "Would you like some mint tea? You have come to a place where your need can be satisfied," and signaled with his hand for the waiter to bring the tea before I could reply. "Are you the type of American like Eldon who enjoys the traditional relaxant of us Moroccans?" Rocky asked.

"Yes, I'm more than a tourist. I respect kief and the traditions that surround it. I love to get high, but I want to experience my high the way the Moroccan's experience theirs," I said as the waiter brought and poured two cups of tea.

"Good, very good. It is wise for a person to respect the traditions. In the Moroccan way of smoking, the leaves are thrown away. They give you headaches. Of course, we discard the seeds. There's a trick to rolling the knife when chopping the tobacco and flowers, always separately," Rocky said as he seemed to enjoy having a student who wanted to learn about the culture of kief.

Rocky stood up and said, "I'll be right back," and went through a curtained door at the very back of the café.

I sipped my tea and looked around. I could see several men sitting alone at tables, working a knife back and forth on cutting boards, and another man at a separate table dumping a pile of cut flowers and tobacco into a leather pouch. All the men were wearing djellabas, which made me feel at home.

"Here," Rocky said, handing me a cone-shaped package folded from one sheet of white paper about a foot long.

I took the cone and put it on the table as Rocky sat down opposite me. Rocky picked up the cone, undid the wrapping smoothing out the paper, which contained about twenty seeded Moroccan marijuana flower tops and three thin strips of black tobacco that looked like pieces of bacon.

"I sell these like this. They're called *rabitas*. Each *rabita* costs seven dirhams." At that moment, Rocky reached under his djellaba and took out two narrow leather pouches, from one he withdrew and assembled his sebsi. He dipped and filled it from the other.

Striking a match, he took a hit and handed the pipe to me, and I took a hit and handed the pipe back.

Rocky took the third hit and blew out the ashes. "I just cut my mixture this morning. I cut it fresh every day or so. Look at my blister." He held up his right index finger, which had a hard large callus at its base. "Let me see your knife."

I took out my French fisherman's knife with its round wooden handle, opened it, and gave the opened knife to Rocky, who said, "This is a good kief knife. Its blade's rounded. Keep it sharp so you don't mash the flowers." Rocky picked up one of the flower tops and held it up, gazing at it approvingly. "Straight from Katama where the farmers grow our product. You pick off all these big leaves first," he said as he went down the stem and pulled off any leaves that weren't tiny. "Throw these away," he said, pointing to the leaves he pulled off. Rocky brought out a rough cardboard shoebox top resting by his chair and began popping the seeds out of the flowers onto it. He shook the top a few times to get all the seeds to roll to the bottom. He then carefully picked any flowers' petals off the top of the box and started making a pile on one side of a cutting board that he pulled from a dark corner next to his chair. "You know it's the tobacco the government is concerned about because it's not taxed. They don't give a damn about the flowers," Rocky said as he picked up the tobacco and started cutting it. "You cut away the hard stems from the center, and if a leaf has big veins, discard them too. There's more tobacco here than you'll need. People say the best rough formula is one-part tobacco and two-parts flowers. I personally prefer slightly less tobacco."

"Thanks for the information, but I'm a little dizzy now. Can I come back another time for a review session?" I said as I picked up the five *rabitas* Rocky said I could have for the thirty dirhams I told him I brought. I put the *rabitas* on the bottom of my straw basket and covered them with my shirt and above that a bunch of vegetables I had bought on the way to Baba's, anticipating this moment.

"Very nice meeting you, Fred. Give my regards to Eldon," Rocky said and stood and walked with me to the door of the café.

It seemed that not one person in the room was paying a bit of attention to us. I looked around and saw that in a separate area of the café, men were sitting on the floor, playing Parcheesi, smoking sebsis and drinking mint tea.

As I walked downhill and across the upper streets to the commune, I felt blessed with fabulous kief and hash connections, a great cheap place to live and the wonder and excitement of Tangier before me.

Two days later, I looked up from my green sleeping bag as Dolores, dressed in a flowing robe, entered my room. She lay out a sheaf of papers and charts in front of her.

"You're in luck," Dolores said, looking over at me as she dropped her robe to the floor, leaving her standing naked. "The stars say I can't conceive today, so let's fuck like mad before Eldon starts reading the Buddhist songs in the magic room."

After our hot fucking, Dolores still basking in her post orgasm glow, I took a deep hit of kief and thought, *This is heaven*, as the rush hit my brain and made my heart beat faster.

Life in the commune revolved around our dinners together and the reading of Milarepa songs. I connected sexually with Dolores when the stars permitted.

The next morning, I walked into the kitchen where I saw Dolores boiling some water.

"Join me in mint tea and a walk to the fountain to refill our water containers?" she asked, reminding me our house had no running water.

"Sure, be glad to," I smilingly said as I had woken up in a cheerful mood, and seeing Dolores with her wild curly hair and slim figure improved my mood further.

We walked down to the fountain that supplied the neighborhood with water. After one container was filled, I took the empty one Dolores had been carrying and put it under the faucet. When the second container was filled, we each took one and looked back up the hill.

"Let's take our time. I like to take my time in a lot of things, and walking up this hill with this heavy container is one of them," I said as we slowly started back to the commune.

Eldon, the acknowledged leader of the commune, set the pace of life by organizing acid trips, visits to the communal baths, the hammam, and walking tours of Tangier. Although everyone in the house had our separate daily activities—shopping, cooking, café sitting, buying, and selling hash—in the late afternoon, we gathered for a hot vegetarian dinner prepared by Linda and English Jan.

My cousin Mike decided to leave Morocco because he feared for his son's safety. Mike told me, "I can't relax. This is not a good environment for a young blond boy." He and Emanuel took a flight to the Canary Islands, but Sarah stayed at the commune.

One afternoon while Eldon was reading a Milarepa song in the magic room, English Jan looked down through the window above the front door and saw a man wearing a uniform knocking with his fists.

She started screaming, "We're being raided, and there's a cop at the front door! Quick, let's get rid of all the hash!" She ran to the hash bowl in the center of the table, grabbed the hash, and threw it out the window onto the hillside below the house where goats grazed in the shrubbery.

Eldon said calmly, "Don't panic. Everyone go get your hash and toss it out the back window. I'll talk to the officer at the door."

I rushed to my room and threw my three pieces of hash away as did all the others.

After emptying the house of hash, we returned to the magic room.

When Eldon came back, he sat down and said, "That man was just a collector from the electric company. We haven't paid our bill. Electricity is very expensive, and we've had that single bulb burning day and night. I told the guy we'd bring the money to the office tomorrow so everyone pitches in. Now let's get down that hill and retrieve our hash."

We burst out the door scrambling through the shrubs on the hillside, picking up pieces of hash before the goats could eat them.

Eldon was again reading Milarepa as we smoked joints and pipes and laughed at our reaction. What a joke, just a utility collector.

A few days later, while carrying oranges from the kitchen, I heard a loud knock. Dolores went to see who was at the door.

When I entered Dolores' room, a tall American woman shouted, "Fred, Fred! I knew the tarot never lies!" She ran over and gave me a hug.

Gail was referring to a dramatic tarot reading during a Halloween party in Steve and Gail's flat in El Palo. The tarot cards designated me as the "hermit" and Gail as the "star."

Steve and Gail lived outside of Malaga in El Palo, where I had spent two months living with Cousin Mike. Mike and Steve had worked as lawyers together at the San Francisco legal services program. I spent time with them, exchanging books, occasionally smoking pot, and discussing philosophy and religion.

I asked, "What are you doing in Tangier, and how did you find me?"

Gail responded, "We're here on a week's vacation without Patsy (their four-year old daughter). We're staying at the Miami, and Mina told us she thought you and Mike and Emanuel went to the Canary Islands. A hippie we met in a café told us you lived in this commune and gave us directions."

As we talked, Dolores dipped her sebsi into her kief pouch rounding out the top, took a hit, and let out the smoke slowly. After waiting a heartbeat, she took another hit and blew the ashes into an ashtray. She refilled the pipe and handed it to Gail.

I said, "It's got some tobacco, Gail, so just be warned."

Gail took a deep inhale and exploded in a wild coughing fit. Three puffs later, she was smiling widely as she handed the pipe back to Dolores.

"Just like Timothy Leary said at that lecture in Berkeley, 'Life is about time.' Are you using your time in the most beneficial way for yourself and others?" Gail said, apparently reflecting on whether she was using her time in the most satisfying way.

I said, "I saw Leary too. I read about Leary and LSD in his *Playboy* interview. He came to Northwestern in the spring of '68 when he was on the 'Tune In, Turn On, Drop Out' tour. People were pushing and fighting to get in. I thought they might pull the doors to the lecture hall off their hinges. Leary came out in a white robe and sat alone on the stage in the lotus position. He said that every minute that is passing, we are losing brain cells, and therefore we have to make the most of every moment. When I left the hall that night, I decided to follow the path that Leary had outlined."

Steve answered, "We almost didn't get to hear and see Leary because our babysitter came late. When we got to the hall, it was packed. People were sitting in the aisles and every seat in the theater was filled. Gail and I stood in the back. Just as Leary began, someone wended their way through all the people in the aisles and walked up onto the stage. It was a very attractive blond woman, who took off all her clothes and stood facing Leary and the audience naked. She was coming on strong to Leary, but he was saying, 'Rosemary won't like this and let's talk privately.' Leary talked the woman off the stage and gave his lecture. After we left that night, Gail and I talked long and hard. We saw we weren't using the minutes, hours, and days of our lives in ways that satisfied our souls. I think it's safe to say we wouldn't be here now if it weren't for that Leary talk."

Gail said, "That's another thing we have in common, we're followers of Timothy Leary, but I've never taken acid."

"I love acid. I've taken acid in California, Amsterdam, Chicago, and Spain. I'd be happy to guide you on your first trip when I can score," I said.

Steve looked rather uncomfortable and mumbled, "I've never taken any acid either."

I said, "The commune is gathering in the magic room. It's our daily ritual, and everyone will be glad to have you join us. Follow me."

Linda and English Jan sat against the right wall wearing loose-fitting robes with colorful scarves and broad belts around their waists. In front of them, a round table held Gauloises, several pipes, cigarette papers, and matches. I placed a large bowl of cut oranges on the table. A bearded man, Holy Harry, was sitting in the lotus position, hands on his lap with his eyes closed.

I walked along the opposite wall to Eldon, who sat in front of the large window. "Eldon, these are my friends, Gail and Steve from Malaga." Turning to Gail and Steve, I said, "This is Eldon, the elder of our commune. He rented this house and got the group of us together."

"Pleased to meet you," said Gail, extending her hand, but Eldon did not reach out his hand in response.

Instead, he said, "Any friend of Fred's is welcome here. We are now going to read from *The Hundred Thousand Songs of Milarepa*, the patron saint of Tibet and an eleventh century yogi who teaches the wisdom of the Buddha through songs and stories. May all who hear his words heed them and use them to seek their own enlightenment."

I motioned to some pillows against the wall opposite the two women and the meditating man and said, "Sit down here, near Eldon." I moved next to Dolores, dropping two pieces of my hash into a ceramic bowl, which already had five or six pieces of hash in it. "You have any hash to contribute?" I asked Steve.

He replied, "I do have some hash, but I'm not carrying now. I'll bring some next time. Good shit."

Another man entered the room, dropped some hash in the bowl, and sat down as Eldon cleared his throat, took a sip of water, and picked up a thick hardback book with a design of a woman in Indian garb petting a peacock.

He opened the book and started reading, "*The Enlightenment of Rechungpa.* Having circled Di Se Snow Mountain, Milarepa and his disciples…"

A large burning joint was circling the table from hand to hand. Steve took a hit and touched Gail, so he could pass the joint onto her on his right at the same moment Gail turned to him and passed him a long pipe with a large bowl of hash burning at its end. Steve and Gail exchanged the joint for the pipe, taking hits off each.

"Like a wild beast creeping along low ground, happy it is to practice yoga in solitude…" were the words which seemed to vibrate in the air.

Steve's head nodded toward his chest as Gail tapped him again and handed him a new fat joint Eldon managed to puff and pass to her without altering the cadence of his reading.

Everyone seated in the room was smoking from the pipes, and joints were moving in both directions around the table. The two women across from us reached forward and started to roll a joint each, taking hash from the ceramic bowl and mixing it with black tobacco, although at least one pipe and half a joint were still circulating.

My mind wandered from Eldon's reading as I thought about Gail's reference to the tarot reading, which associated me with the hermit. At a Halloween party with Gail dressed in flowing scarves, harem pants, and ten silver bracelets on each arm, she took the center of the room.

She called out, "Gather around and I will read your fortune. I use the tarot cards, an ancient system of wisdom, codified in Fez, Morocco, in the twelfth century by scholars and holy men from all over the world. If a person has the gift and studies the cards, a reader can guide people. A good reader can bring wisdom to someone's actions. If you follow the cards, you'll progress in harmony with universal forces. I've already read part of Arthur Waite's famous book, *The Pictorial Key to the Tarot*," she said, holding up a maroon hardcover book. Gail raised her voice a little louder and said, "Fred, move that table to the center and bring in that chair. Now everyone sit in a circle."

"Pay attention!" Gail yelled. She took the tarot cards and unwrapped them from a silk scarf, and looking at me, she continued, "I will read your future and tell you what will happen. Move your chair closer to the table. Fear not, the truth will make us free."

I became more apprehensive and said, "I pass. I don't think I'm ready to know what the future holds for me."

"You have no questions. What are you, a man or a mouse? You fear to learn the truth. What are you afraid will be revealed? Move your chair forward now!" Gail ordered and I did. "Begin to compose a question that the cards can assist you in answering," she continued. "The cards never lie. Open your soul."

I felt drunk but put extreme concentration in placing the cut deck face up on the table. Every eye focused on the spot. The first card I chose had the picture of a bearded man in a robe holding a staff and carrying a lantern. The card read, "The Hermit."

Gail said, "Your first tarot card is the hermit. Funny. The hermit is the Virgo card. I'm a Virgo."

I replied, "My birthday's September first. I'm a Virgo too, but I'm from the big city, Chicago. I don't think I'd make a very good hermit."

"No, the hermit not only lives alone in isolation, but he is also the source of all and the goal of all. All endeavor aims at the union of personal consciousness with the cosmic will. The hermit looks within for answers," Gail intoned as if reciting a holy text that she had committed to memory.

Just as Gail finished, a loud knock on the front door stopped the reading. As a man and woman came in, my eyes stayed fixed on an absolutely beautiful young olive-skinned teen girl with dark hair hanging below her waist wearing a light, opened, cotton blouse. She wore a large silver crucifix.

The woman named Anna said, "Roma, learn to tell fortunes by the cards from childhood. I can do an expert reading for you, Juana." When Anna saw the hermit card, she said, "The hermit. In the future position means that you and the hermit, whoever that indicates, will spend some important time together or have an encounter that will be extremely significant for your life."

With Gail turning up in Tangier now, I wondered about the truth of the tarot prophecy.

Eldon closed the book and said, "I bow before the holy gurus. May all beings be happy and at ease."

I had my arm around Dolores' shoulder, and she was leaning on me, staring at the bowl of oranges when she said, "Pee break." She stood up and turned to Gail, who was staring straight ahead with her back rigid, a disturbed look on her face.

Without saying a word or changing her expression, Gail tried to uncross her legs and stand up. It took her three tries to get to her feet, and when she did, she wobbled after Dolores out of the room.

"What do you think?" I said to Steve, who was also having difficulty getting to his feet.

"I need a pee break badly, too, if I can stand up," Steve replied. "This hash is blowing my mind. Where has this been all my life?"

"Are you enjoying the songs of Milarepa?" I persisted.

"Yes, very much. I especially liked the line, 'A good Buddhist is one who conquers all bad dispositions.'"

Steve stretched his arms above his head, saying, "Sitting on the floor is tough when you're used to chairs. It's dark now so we must have been sitting for almost two hours."

"Come back to Dolores' room. Are you hungry? I've got some crackers, peanut butter, oranges, and some figs we can snack on before Eldon starts reading again," I said. As we entered the empty room, I put out some food.

"I don't want to eat. Food makes me less high," Steve said as he stretched again.

I said, "Milarepa travels freely from place to place with no fixed home. He just walks in the Himalayas singing and spreading the teachings leading to enlightenment. He stays and meditates for long periods in one place where he develops and deepens his realizations. From his long meditations in solitude, he gains the insights to teach others. 'Happy it is to practice yoga in solitude,' that's from the story Eldon just read. Every day he reads a story. They are actually poems since Milarepa sang his teachings. It is said Milarepa had the most beautiful voice sounding like an angel."

Steve said, "While Eldon reads you and the others smoke hash until you can't stand up. 'I like it, I like it,'" the last words said by Steve in an imitation of Jerry Lewis' old comedy bit.

When Gail came back with Dolores, she and Steve left, but they returned each of the next two days, smoking hash and listening to Eldon read. I told them I had to visit Malaga in February to renew my visa, and they offered me a place to stay there with them. Before they departed Tangier, Gail said we should keep in touch and she would write to me at *poste restante.*

Soon after the New Year began, one evening while the pipe was being passed, I said, "I'd like to know more about Achmed Gold Pipe. I've heard he sells the best hashish in Morocco. What's his story?"

Holy Harry spoke up, "We call him that because his sebsi has a gold bowl, rather than the ceramic bowls we use. He's known as a ladies' man. His women's clothing boutique gives him the opportunity to meet Western women."

"Far-out. Even if I can't afford his hash, I want to smoke that gold pipe," I said.

While laying on my straw mat in my room later that evening, I continued to think about Achmed Gold Pipe and came up with a plan.

The next morning, I went to Sarah and said, "Remember what Holy Harry and Eldon said about Achmed? My idea is you and I go to Achmed's boutique, pretend we are newly arrived tourists looking for dresses for you. Since he loves the ladies, hopefully he'll hit on you. Let's use that to try and get close to the gold pipe."

"Brilliant Fred," Sarah said. "I'd like to smoke that pipe, but I hope I don't have to fuck him."

Entering the French Quarter, we walked up a hilly street off Rue Amerique Du Sud to the boutique. Achmed came out of the back office and began talking to Sarah. Of medium height and slim with his olive skin, a thin sharp nose, great smile, and slick black hair, I understood why he had success with Western women.

After chatting with Sarah for a few minutes, Achmed invited her to his office for mint tea.

Aha, I thought. *My plan is working.*

Achmed ignored me, but as he and Sarah entered the office, she grabbed my hand so we could go in together.

Fine Moroccan carpets, pillows, and artwork covered the floor and walls. An elaborate silver tea set was on a nearby table. Radio Cairo played in the background.

Achmed sat at his large, dark wooden desk and motioned for Sarah to sit next to him. Ignored, I sat on a nearby chair. On the desk was a pile of the whitest kief flowers I had seen. Achmed reached into the desk drawer for the wooden shaft of his sebsi. To my delight, he opened another drawer and took out the gold bowl. Filling the bowl, Achmed took a hit and passed the pipe to Sarah. She took a hit, and instead of returning it to Achmed, she passed it to me.

I took a hit from the pipe, holding the gold bowl in my hand. *Hendrix, Jagger, and Richards held this bowl,* I thought. Since the bowl only held two hits, I sucked in a mouthful of ashes, but I didn't care. I smoked the gold pipe.

Achmed focused on Sarah, inviting her to join him for dinner.

She declined and said, "Thanks and goodbye," and headed for the door.

Elated, Sarah and I skipped back to the Blue Door commune.

Many days I'd sit in cafés talking to travelers and other expatriates. One day drinking mint tea, I was conversing with a couple of longtime Tangier residents. The English wife, Lizzie, had distinctive bright-red curly hair and a fair complexion. She didn't say much and left most of the talking to her husband, Hans—a short, sturdily built Austrian who spoke English rapidly with a heavy accent.

Hans raised the subject of dealing hash and other drugs to tourists visiting Tangier. "You're a friendly, nonthreatening guy with a big welcoming smile. You'd be doing hippie tourists a favor supplying them with real hash at a reasonable price. Otherwise, they get camel shit from the street hustlers. You'd be performing a public service by selling them hash. I'll front you the hash. You sell it. We split the profit," Hans said.

With Mike gone, I had begun to think about how I could earn some money to keep myself afloat. I replied, "I don't know. I'm just a consumer. After all, Eldon and others have gone to jail, and I don't want to be locked up in Morocco."

"Think it over. Your risk would be very small. You meet American or Canadian tourists, talk to them, and just say, 'I have strong hash, and I can sell you some.' They'll jump at the chance, and like I said, you'll be doing them a favor. I scare a lot of tourists because they think I'm German, but you're a natural," Hans continued as Lizzie sat silently, looking through a copy of *Vogue* magazine from July 1970.

"It could work," I replied. "Tourists often approach me and ask for all kinds of information, including where and how to score drugs. Just a few sales and I'd make enough to cover my expenses. I'll think it over." Although the thought of jail made me uneasy.

Later that night, at the Café Royale with the men from the commune, listening to music, smoking kief, and drinking mint tea, Hans came table-hopping and sat next to me.

"Did you think about my offer?" Hans said to me in a low voice.

"Yes, I decided to do it. There's not much to lose, and if I make three sales a week, I'll have enough money to continue living here without difficulty. Let's do it, partner," I said.

"Good. Come back to my pension, and I'll give you the hash I have packaged. It's weighed and wrapped and ready for sale. I know it won't be any problem for you," Hans said.

Being connected to Hans whose vibes made me uncomfortable unnerved me, but selling hash seemed a perfect opportunity.

After leaving the café, Hans and I walked through the streets, stoned and happy, feeling the bite of the wind on the January night. Entering the Pensione Paris, which provided even more dilapidated rooms than the Miami, I felt excited but also apprehensive.

Once inside Hans' room, where Lizzie sat on the bed wearing a flowered nightgown, reading *Elle* magazine, Hans unlocked a trunk, removed the top shelf with clothes on it, and withdrew three plastic bags.

Opening one, he removed five small squares wrapped in aluminum foil. "Here, these are weighed. Each square sells for twenty dollars, split fifty-fifty. If you meet a hippie wanting hash, sell them these. If they want a larger quantity, you can set them up to meet me, and I'll pay you a finder's fee depending on how much they buy. Simple, clean, and easy and you stay solvent, stoned, and happy," Hans said with an evil smile.

I looked at the five squares and, unwrapping one, saw that it contained dark hash that I could tell was of good quality. "Okay, why not? I'll try it and see how I feel being a dealer."

I happily walked out of the pension. I'd solved my financial problems with a "job" that fit perfectly into my lifestyle. I began to walk faster and faster and then broke into a run. When I reached the bright-blue door, I was sweating and breathing hard. Hitting my sleeping bag, I couldn't fall asleep, and in the candlelight, I sampled my wares, got very stoned, and passed out.

The next day, I walked over to the Petite Souk and sat down for a café au lait at the time I knew was just after the ferry from Spain arrived. I watched the people passing by and spotted a short attractive blond woman carrying a bright-blue nylon backpack standing in the corner, looking down confusedly at a white piece of paper. Glad to see a hippie woman, I thought maybe I could score or make a hash sale.

I walked over to her and said, "I've been in Tangier a while. Do you need some help?"

She looked up and said in a Midwest accent, "I'm looking for the Pension Amar."

"You from the Midwest? I grew up in Milwaukee. What makes you want to go to the Amar?" I replied.

"I'm from Urbana. A friend who visited Morocco last year told us about the Amar. I'm Betsy," she said and held out her hand. "This is Brad, my partner." She turned to a dark-haired man coming out of the store carrying two sebsis and some other purchases.

"Fred," I replied as we shook hands, "pleased to meet you. The Amar's a real dump. If you're looking for a cheap pension, I'd suggest the Miami, which is three blocks down the street across the Souk to the right. Check it out. I always stay there."

"Thanks for the suggestion," Brad responded. As he dropped his voice, he asked, "Do you know where I can score some dope?"

"I just bought a small amount of hash yesterday, but I'd be glad to sell you some of what I've got. Twenty dollars for twenty grams of strong, pure hash that will blow your mind," I said.

Without any hesitation, Brad reached into a pouch he wore around his neck and handed me a twenty-dollar bill.

I took a wrapped package of hash out of my straw basket and put it in the pocket of his jacket and said, "Do you plan to stay in Tangier a while?"

"Yes, we'll be settling in to make some purchases and send items to the States," Betsy said.

"Thanks so much. It's lucky we ran into each other," Brad said as he felt the packet in his pocket.

"Glad to be of service. See you around," I answered as we walked off in different directions. I had just earned my month's rent in the commune.

I continued to cultivate my hash connection with Mustapha and accompanied Eldon to Mustapha's three times. Eldon had schemes involving hash smuggling in full operation. Eldon went to Gibraltar and bought radios. He put pieces of hash into the radios and mailed them to friends around the world. He built a hydraulic press and was able to press the hash paper thin and insert it in envelopes. He also hid it in book covers and put it into the soles of leather shoes.

He recruited Sarah to be a mule to carry hash on her body to London. After Eldon took her to a French beauty parlor in the European Quarter and bought her new clothes and high heels, she looked like a straight high-class woman. The night before her flight, the members of the commune helped by sewing hash into the corset Sarah would be wearing under her clothing when she flew to London.

Eldon hosted a party to celebrate the work of preparing Sarah for her journey. He dissolved twenty tabs of acid into freshly squeezed orange juice, and everyone drank a glass. I invited Hans and Lizzie and Brad and Betsy, who I had spent some more time with in cafés.

Tripping and hallucinating, I went to the roof to look at the night sky. While sitting, leaning back against the wall, my mind cleared. The acid erased the perpetual haze from my kief and hash smoking, and I experienced a moment of clarity. Grabbing the moment, I thought about abandoning the hippie/dealer life and returning to the States.

As I reflected on my life in Tangier, the door to the roof opened and out stepped Hans, holding a big joint. He knew I sold all the hash he had given me without any difficulty. "I have ten more packets of hash for you to sell, and I think we can increase the price," Hans said as he held out the joint to me.

In the starlight with shadows behind him, Hans reminded me of Satan with his devious smile. I took the joint, and with a big hit, the moment of clarity passed. My thoughts of returning to the States went up in a cloud of smoke. I'd continue my life as a hash dealer in Tangier. Hans removed a plastic bag from his jacket pocket with ten packets and handed it to me.

At first, when I joined the commune, I only cared about the hash, but night after night of hearing Milarepa's teachings began to have an impact. As I lay in bed with my kief pipe, I thought about Milarepa, Leary, acid, Buddhism, the tarot, astrology, and the path I was traveling. Was I traveling a path? Was Milarepa right, the world was an illusion, and by transcending it through Buddhist meditation practice, a person could become enlightened and free from suffering? Once enlightened, was it the seeker's task to help all other living beings find peace, happiness, and enlightenment? With these questions floating through my brain, I passed out each night.

Life in the commune developed into a well-established routine. I tried several times to initiate sexual encounters with Dolores, but my success depended on the mercy of the stars. The word from the ephemeris saying "yes" or "not today" controlled. The stars determined whether Dolores could become pregnant and whether it was a good day for fucking in general. Some days, Dolores entered my room with a smile, saying, "Come on, big boy," and inviting me to join her in her room, always a pleasant surprise. I didn't mind this arrangement, but some days, it was frustrating when Dolores said, "The stars say no today."

I knew Dolores was enjoying our encounters as Sarah, who had become a close friend of Dolores after Mike and Emanuel left, said to me, "Thanks for making Dolores so happy."

The second week in January, I went into Dolores' room to see if the stars would give a thumbs-up to a sexual encounter. When I parted the curtain doorway to her room, she was rolling on the bed, hugging and kissing a dark-haired man with a ponytail. Quietly closing the curtain, I understood Dolores' long-awaited boyfriend had arrived from Canada, and my affair with her was over.

While sitting in a café, I was reading a letter from Mike in the Canaries when Brad and Betsy came by and sat down with me.

"You look like a happy camper," Betsy said with bouncy, playful energy that I found attractive.

"I've got to go to the *pharmacia* and pick up some diarrhea medicine. You two wait here and I'll be right back," Brad said as he walked away slowly.

"I guess we can't call it Montezuma's revenge in Morocco. Maybe Mohamed's revenge," I joked, "or maybe just bad colon karma."

Betsy laughed and said, "He's been useless lately. Can't be away from a bathroom and all he wants to talk about is the state of his bowels."

At this moment, two lost-looking men with short hair, wearing patched jeans and embroidered shirts, sat down at the table next to us.

The taller one turned to us and said, "You two look like an American couple, and I see you're married. Have you been here long? We need some advice." He rubbed his hands through his short brown hair.

"Sure, what would you like to know?" Betsy said, not correcting him about us being a couple.

"Do you know a good place to stay? We rented a room at the Pension Amar, where we were led by some boy from the ferry, but it's a dump and we're paying too much."

I said, "Pension Miami. It's five blocks down from here. It's clean, well run, and friendly, and you'll pay less than they're charging you now. Listen, I'm going that way, I'll walk and show you." I recognized this encounter as a hash sale opportunity. Turning to Betsy, I said, "Hope to see you again soon."

Betsy laughed and said, "No problemo. I've got a feeling we'll meet again."

That evening after dinner and Eldon's reading Milarepa, I was lying on my sleeping bag with two candles burning, reading a story in *Rolling Stone* magazine about Jimi Hendrix when the curtain covering my doorway parted and Betsy came through, saying, "May I come in?"

Surprised, I stumbled as I got up but said, "Welcome, welcome, welcome," and made a bow and a sweeping gesture with my arm. "Sit down. Would you like to smoke some hash?"

"You bet," Betsy said as she arranged herself on the floor near me using my pillow as a backrest. "I came here especially to see you. You made me smile today, and now I want to fuck you."

I continued preparing the pipe and said, "What about Brad? I thought you two were married."

Betsy puffed twice to get the hash burning and took a long, slow drag, exhaling slowly. As she handed me the pipe, she looked directly into my eyes and said, "Brad and I are not married, and we have an open relationship. You seem so happy. I'd like to get close to that. In fact, I'd like it inside me."

The enthusiasm Betsy showed for our sex lifted me higher since I had not had any sex since Dolores' boyfriend arrived. I enjoyed sex combined with drugs and thought of the line from The Rolling Stones, "Let's spend the night together / I'll satisfy your every need / and now I know you will satisfy me."

After Betsy raised herself off me, she turned and said, "Do you have any water?"

"Drinking or washing?" I replied and handed her a plastic liter bottle half full.

I rose up on my elbow and looked at her now on her hands and knees as she reached and took the bottle.

Seeing her with her breast hanging down got me excited again, but she said, "That was great, but I've got to get home."

I never saw her again.

February 14th, Valentine's Day, was when I came into the magic room, and I picked up on a troubled vibe. No hash circulated, and Eldon did not have his Milarepa book open. He sat in a lotus posture with his eyes closed.

He opened his eyes and, seeing me sit down, said, "I have an announcement to make. I've decided it's time for me to go to India and Nepal. I have confidence the remaining members can continue without me here. Fred knows the ropes for getting hash. George can do the marketing, and the rest of you can continue living here until you return successfully to your country with hash. Yesterday I paid one month's rent in advance, and George knows how to continue to pay it. I love each and every one of you, and it's not easy for me to leave Morocco. But spiritually, I'm a Buddhist, and I need to go to an environment appropriate to my spiritual path."

He recited, "Think ye' thus of all of the fleeting world, a star at dawn, a bubble in a stream, a flash of lightening, a flickering lamp, a phantom, and a dream." He continued saying, "All of life is constantly changing, and we should never become attached to any person, place, or thing. Attachment is the cause of suffering as Buddha made clear 2,500 years ago in his *Four Noble Truths*. Tonight we'll smoke some of Achmed Gold Pipe's special hash, and together we'll experience the same high as The Rolling Stones." Eldon took a chunk of hash darker than what we usually smoked, lit a pipe, and passed to me. He handed the remainder of the hash to Linda and English Jan, who began rolling joints.

After three hits, I slumped down as my mind drifted. I thought about Dolores, who already left with Greg for Canada having shipped five kilos of hash pressed into the walls of tooled, leather boxes. Next my mind jumped to my visa, which was expiring in two weeks. I planned to go to Spain and return again to Tangier, but would the commune even exist when I returned? Only English Jan, Linda, George, and Holy Harry remained, and I doubted we could keep our scene together without Eldon.

I snapped out of my dreams when Eldon touched my arm and said, "Fred, tonight would you please read the Milarepa story?" and handed me the open book.

I looked down at the print, cleared my throat, and began to read aloud, "Obeisance to all gurus…to be born a human being is rarer than a star that shines by day. Many will waste it by running after pleasures, but few can tread the path of dharma…"

The next morning, a pall hung over the house due to Eldon's immanent departure. Five residents planned to remain in Tangier after March first. Eldon had been our leader, and I knew no one could replace him. I lay on my sleeping bag checking through my desires, options, and choices. I kept going back to what would Milarepa do if he were faced with the same type of situation.

Three evenings later, the atmosphere in the commune had not improved, but I had resolved to make the best of the situation.

As the group gathered after dinner, Eldon sat with a pile of dates and a piece of hash about the size of the book in front of him. "I have my plane ticket to Delhi for tomorrow's noon flight. I plan to bring this hash with me by taking the pits out of these dates and replacing them with hash and carrying the dates on board the plane. I'd like some of you to start removing the pits and others breaking the hash into pit-sized pieces." He held up a small piece of hash to show everyone the size he was describing. He took several other pieces of hash from his leather pouch and, handing them to English Jan, said, "Let's make this our joyous farewell party. Remember when Milarepa went to meditate on Lashi Snow Mountain? Well, Eldon is on his way to go there now for the same purpose."

The next day, the commune members accompanied Eldon to the airport. English Jan cried. I had a sinking feeling. At the airport, Eldon showed his passport and prepared to board the plane. From the observation deck, we waited to wave a final goodbye. After about ten minutes, Eldon emerged from the customs checkpoint and walked across the tarmac to the plane. At the top of the stairs, he turned and waved to us. He reached into a paper bag holding the dates, plucked a date from the bunch, and put it in his mouth and laughed. I imagined how stoned Eldon would be on the flight, eating dates with hash pits.

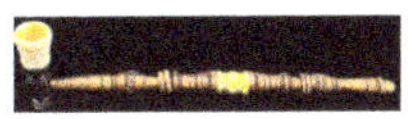

The ringing of a gong brought me back to my present reality, sitting outside, leaning against the yard wall. A huge man wearing a white coat came out of the central building rolling a steaming vat. Most of the Moroccan men were shorter and thinner than me, but the man rolling the cart was at least six feet four tall and 240 pounds. Another taller man in a white coat was rolling a table with mint tea and a basket of small loaves of Spanish white bread.

Gathering from around the courtyard, the men lined up to the left of the table. From another table, each man took a clay bowl and a small loaf of bread. The huge man ladled soup into each bowl held out to him. With their other hand, the men picked up a plastic glass of mint tea. At the end of the line, another man in white coat gave each person a paper cup with three pills and watched as they swallowed them.

Hungry, I walked across the courtyard and joined the line near its end. What was set out for everyone was the same soup and bread I had been given in my room. I took the bowl, but the basket of bread was empty. I didn't get any. I observed; the bigger, stronger men stood at the front of the line and the weaker, smaller men got their dinner last.

The men in the white coats represented of some sort of authority, and I asked, "*Donde Esta?*" I tried English too, saying, "Where am I? Who's in charge? Can I speak to a supervisor?" But from the angry expressions on the men's faces, I didn't press my inquiries.

CHAPTER 3

Good Vibrations

To visit Morocco is like turning the pages of some illuminated Persian manuscript embroidered with bright shapes and subtle lines.

—Edith Wharton

A short time after my first meal, as the sun was setting, a blind old man in a white jacket walking hunched over came out of the main building holding a ring of keys. Gliding his fingertips over the keys, he picked one and opened a door to the building. Some of the men were filtering into the unlocked building, and I followed them inside.

In the sleeping area, I waited to learn where my assigned sleeping place would be. I waited on the bench outside the sleeping rooms, but I was ignored. I held onto the thought that there would be rules. I had not received anything like a coherent instruction or explanation from anyone. No one had told me a thing since I entered the facility. I was completely isolated, alone, and uncared for. As I sat waiting for some directions, I drifted off thinking about the turn my life took as the Blue Door commune dissolved.

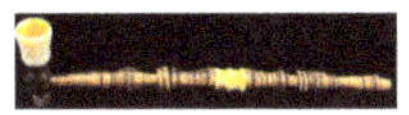

Because my three-month Moroccan entry visa expired in February 1971, I had to leave the country, but after a short stay in Spain, I planned to return to seek new adventures.

I looked in the mirror on the Malaga ferry and saw my long dark hair flowing halfway down my back and my full beard. My smile showed my white teeth. I reread Gail's inviting postcard, "Steve and I are moving our household to Morocco," and "I have someone here to satisfy your desires."

When I arrived in El Palo, I told Gail, "I feel lucky and can't wait the meet this attractive, sexy American you wrote about."

Two days later, a gracefully thin woman in her midthirties greeted me with a hug at her front door. The fresh smell of her short hair and the clear look in her blue eyes appealed to me, so markedly different from the long-haired, colorfully dressed hippie chicks I usually met. She looked healthy, fit, clean-cut, and very sexy.

Gail introduced Jan, who said, looking directly at me, "I'm so glad we planned for you to come today because my daughters have gone with friends for an overnighter. We can party together from this afternoon until dawn."

We did.

Over the next days, I moved in. We ate at quaint cafés, took long walks through the countryside, held hands, hugged, and kissed. We were together every minute.

A week later, next to Steve's VW Camper, I held Jan's hand and looked into her eyes and said, "This is not farewell but rather hasta la vista, until we meet again. Come join me in Morocco as soon as you can get it together."

Jan kissed my neck and whispered, "Hasta la vista."

I jumped into the back with Patsy to begin the five-hour ferry crossing to the Spanish port of Ceuta on the North African coast, a short drive from the Moroccan border.

Later, as we drove off the ferry in Ceuta, I said, "I'm a little concerned about crossing the border into Morocco. I hear the government won't let hippies with long hair into the country. I've got long hair I don't intend to cut. I'll tuck my ponytail into my shirt. Hopefully, the border guards won't notice."

Steve said, "You mean you'd rather keep your hair long than continue to smoke the cheap hash and kief in Tangier? We'll put you in the back with Patsy, and they probably won't look too closely at a family in a new VW Camper. But if they don't let you through, would you return to Spain? How?"

"I've got to let my 'freak flag fly,' as Crosby, Stills and Nash sing. Wouldn't Milarepa want me to stay steadfast in my principles?" I said as I patted my copy of Milarepa's songs.

Gail chimed in, "Do you know today's date? March 4th, 1971. March fourth. We're marching forward today into a new life. I want to celebrate. I'll always remember this date and this ferry trip and the changes happening in me. I feel moving to Tangier is just what the tarot cards predicted. The death of one phase of my life and the start of my magic life."

I agreed.

A large sign said, "*Fontera de Marroquin, cinco kilometros*," and an arrow straight ahead with the same phrase in English, "Moroccan Border, five kilometers," and a bunch of Arabic letters, which obviously said the same thing. A fence stretched out on both sides of the road from the toll booth-like buildings indicated the dividing line between countries. Steve pulled up behind several vehicles in line at the Moroccan entry booth.

As we waited, a man in a dark suit with a hostile expression sporting a shoulder holster with a pistol clearly visible came up and said, "*Pasaportes*."

Steve said, "We're Americans," and smiled.

"Passports," the man repeated in a louder voice.

Steve handed his, Gail, and Patsy's passport through the window and said in a friendly way, "We're a family coming to Morocco for our vacation."

The man looked at the passports and walked to the van's side window and looked in the back where I sat. The officer pointed at me and said, "You, outside," indicating I should open the back door of the van and get out.

Steve attempted to hand him my passport.

"Outside," the agent repeated in an even louder and more hostile voice.

I stepped onto the ground in front of the man, who reached behind my head and took out my long ponytail from inside my sweatshirt. Staring at my hair, the agent yelled, "You, no. Others, okay. You, no enter!"

Gail said, "Ridiculous. He's an American and we want to enter together. Let us through."

The man responded with anger, saying, "No more talk, no."

As the car in front of us pulled forward, I said, "Let's turn around and I'll get a haircut in Ceuta."

As we drove back into Spanish territory, we saw a European man with long hair hitchhiking.

Steve said, "Hop in. We're going back to a barbershop in Spain, and I bet that's what you're doing too."

Etienne, a Belgium lion tamer, needed his haircut to rendezvous with his companions who crossed the border without him.

I said, "I do not want to cut my hair, period."

It was siesta time when we arrived in front of a closed barbershop, so we parked and relaxed for the two hours until it reopened. At 4:00 p.m., an older man entered, raising the blinds and dusting off the barber chair.

Etienne sat in the chair and said in passable Spanish, "Cut my hair and make it short. I must be able to enter Maroc."

I looked at myself in the mirror and moved my hair to the top of my head. I said, "Look, I can put it on top and have the barber trim my neck. I'll fake getting a haircut."

Gail stepped forward and rolled up my hair from the bottom.

When the barber was finished cutting Etienne's hair, he shaved my neck, combed the top flat, and sprayed some fixer to hold the whole arrangement in place.

I said, "March forth," with a nod to Gail as we climbed back into the camper.

Etienne, who looked completely straight, sat in the front passenger seat.

Smiling and very calm, I said, "Milarepa would not be cowed by arbitrary rules or restrictions. He would persist on the path whatever obstacles he encountered. He probably had long hair too, and I'm sure he wouldn't have cut it."

At this time of day, there was no line at the Moroccan border station, and we drove right up to the window. Steve brought the passports to an uniformed soldier seated behind the window.

The soldier, looking at the passports, said, “Four American, one Belgium,” and handed Steve five white entry cards. “Fill these out and bring them back.”

When Steve returned with the completed cards, he hardly looked at them but stamped a three-month entry visa in each passport. He waved to another soldier carrying a machine gun, who raised the metal gate.

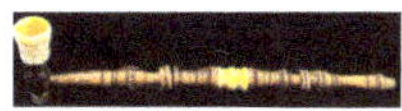

The image of a machine gun-carrying guard raising the gate at the border jolted me back to my present captivity. I surveyed the scene; the building contained three sleeping rooms radiating from a central circular sitting area like spokes from a wheel. A single light bulb hung in each room, illuminating ten metal-framed cots lined along the wall facing an aisle running to the back of the room. Each cot had four metal legs with a thin mattress over a wire frame. There were no blankets or other linen over the bare mattresses. There were no windows, and the stucco walls reeked of dampness and mold. The disgusting body odor of the men filled the air.

Looking into the rooms, every bed was filled with two men sleeping on each cot head to toe, some men lay on the tile floor under the beds. Just as in the food line, the smaller, weaker men slept on the floor. I saw there were far fewer cots than inmates.

Sitting, waiting to be assigned a place to sleep had left me isolated with no place to sleep. I hadn’t encountered anyone to answer my questions or provide me with any assistance. As far as I could tell, no non-inmate controlled any aspect of the institution.

No roll for dinner and now no place to sleep. Angrily, I thought, *Every man for himself.* I needed a bed even if I had to fight to get one. I started to scream and walk in the aisle next to the beds in the first room. Using my limited Arabic, I began yelling, “*Ana Kabir!* (I am big!)” in my deepest voice and puffing myself up.

The men began sitting up in their beds.

I added, "*Ana Mzien Bezaf!*" (I am very good!), which I screamed in Arabic.

If I wasn't going to get a bed, I'd make sure everyone knew the crazy American was big and good. I'd cause a disturbance and keep everyone awake until I got a bed. I walked up and back and continued screaming in Arabic. I did the same thing in the second room and proceeded to scream in the third room. I repeated the process again in each room, feeling angrier but also aware no one was stopping me.

After walking down the aisles in each room twice, when I returned to do the same thing for a third time in the second room, a short thick-necked man stood halfway down the aisle, blocking my way. When I approached, he reared back and punched me directly in my chest. I stumbled backward from the force of the blow. It hurt and I got the message I should not continue screaming in that room. With my palms up, I gave the man a sign of acceptance, and I backed out of the room.

Returning to the first room, a young strong man came over to me and, with gestures and Arabic words, indicated I could join him and another man. They pushed two beds together and showed me I should sleep head to toe between them as the two beds were able to accommodate the three of us squeezed together. The men sleeping under the beds got up and readjusted their positions as well. I had accomplished getting a place to sleep.

Even with the two other men's feet close to my face, I fell asleep. My dreaming picked up from where it had ended while I waited to establish my sleeping place.

CHAPTER 4

Catch the Wind

Our normal waking consciousness is but one special type of consciousness
—William James

As I fell asleep, I willed myself to think about something positive and remembered moving to my sanctuary, our tranquil house in Khemis Sahel.

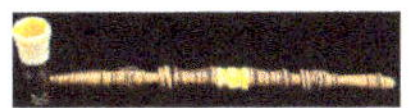

After our successful crossing the border, we went directly to the Pension Miami, which was like returning to a welcoming home. The smell of split pea soup, the high-pitched Arab women singing through the radio, and Mina's welcoming arms.

Mina approached Patsy and hugged her with intense affection. "Welcome, Juana, Don Estaban, Fredrico, and *esta linda nina* (this beautiful girl)."

Gail and Mina reconnected and talked together in a somewhat conspiratorial manner as Mina doted over Patsy. I went to the Blue Door commune, which was in the process of dissolving. Six commune members had scored hash and returned to England and Canada with it hidden in shoes, books, and in their clothes and on their bodies. Only English Jan, Linda, and Holy Harry remained.

Gail and Steve did not intend to live for long at the Miami with their possessions in their van parked outside on the street. They wanted a house of their own and began inquiring about rentals in neighborhoods in and around Tangier where a family could set up housekeeping. A couple in a café suggested renting a house in the Malabata area.

In the evening, sitting in the vestibule at the Miami with Mina, Gail, while looking at a map on the coffee table, said, "Tomorrow we'll check out Bella Malabata."

Mina squawked, "Malabata. *No, no, no, no, es no sano. Muchos ladrones. No puedo vivir en* (No, no, no, it isn't safe. Many thieves. You cannot live in Malabata)"

Gail replied in Spanish with feeling, "I need a house. Love you, Mina, but I can't live in one room in a pension. I want a house and I'd like something in the country."

Mina said (in Spanish), "Would you live in a small village in the country? Not too far from Tangier, forty-five kilometers south? Near Larache. Whole house, completely safe, with my family. You could be very happy in Khemis Sahel."

Steve jumped at the idea and said in Spanish, "Let's go see the place. When can we drive there? Mina, we'll take you in the Camper."

Gail warmed to moving to primitive conditions in a small village even though with no electricity and water hand drawn from a well. Gail said, "I'll become a Moroccan country woman. This has to be for all of us, including Fred. The cards said we'd live together."

I liked the idea too as the simple life appealed.

Mina said (in Spanish), "I'll find out when we can go and meet with the owner. You cannot live in Malabata, *muchos ladrones*."

Two days later, after an hour ride south on the coastal highway, Mina leaned forward, saying, "Turn left, just before the small store."

Steve swung the Camper off the highway into a narrow dirt drive and slowly drove forward between dirty white stucco walls about eight feet high. From a door in a metal gate, a prosperous-looking man wearing a finely made robe stepped forward. Mina greeted him formally in the traditional manner and with a hug. After a short conversation in Arabic, Mina called to us and introduced each one by name to the man whom she called, "*El dueno* (the owner)."

No other foreigners lived in the village, and the conditions were primitive. Entering a courtyard, I saw a well with a pulley device, rope, and bucket to draw the water.

The landlord walked ahead and opened the door to a white concrete house, saying, "This is the house, come in and look around."

The clean, empty house consisted of a front room with a small window on each side of the door and another larger room toward the back without any windows. Tiles covered the floor. I saw a staircase and asked the landlord about it.

"Go up, look at the roof, the highest place in town," the landlord replied.

I ascended to the flat roof surround by a three-foot-high wall. As I stood at a corner and looked over the rooftops and courtyards of the village, I viewed a peaceful scene from the Middle Ages, time travelling back hundreds of years.

Gail came onto the roof and said, "I can live in a place like this, and I feel drawn here. Let's rent it and move in."

I said, "Bargain, remember you've got to bargain. We don't want to pay too much."

Downstairs again, the landlord led us out the front door and said, "This next building is the kitchen." He opened the door to a room with storage shelves and a concrete counter. He said, "Separate kitchen, market every Saturday, vegetables cheap."

Steve asked, "How much to rent this house?"

The landlord replied, "How much are you willing to pay?" He used the old bargaining technique of having the other person set the price to start the bargaining.

Steve replied, "Maybe we'll try it for a month. How much for a month?"

"What do you want to pay?" the landlord repeated.

Steve hesitated a moment and said, "I'm willing to pay sixty dirhams (fifteen dollars) a month."

The landlord smiled and said no and asked for eighty dirhams ($20).

Steve replied, "How about eighty dirhams for the first month and sixty dirhams each month after that?"

The landlord extended his hand and said, "Welcome. You can move in any time." He took out a large metal skeleton key and gave it to Steve.

Steve extended his hand to shake with the landlord and said, "We'll move in four days from now," and took eighty dirhams and handed it to the landlord, who counted the money and put it in his pocket.

"*Bueno,*" said the landlord with a smile on his face.

Back in Tangier, we organized for the move, buying food, art supplies, propane bottles for our stove, and a poster of Shiva. Steve bought a clay tagine cooker to use over a charcoal fire. With ten packs of six-volt batteries for our portable radio/tape player, we could listen to our two cassettes, Jimi Hendrix' *Electric Ladyland* and The Rolling Stones' *Flowers.*

With my backpack holding a pound of Mustapha's quality hash, twenty *rabitas* of kief, and three tabs of acid I intended to share with Gail and Steve, the house in Khemis seemed perfect. At the same time, Gail's behavior concerned me. Her talk about the magician and her need to "connect" with the magician made me feel she wasn't planning on settling in the Moroccan countryside but rather had other ideas and perhaps even plans.

Once in the house, we established a toilet area behind the house protected from rain by the eaves and completely private. We'd dig holes and cover our waste with a small shovel of dirt and use toilet paper we kept in a tin can.

Later, while sitting on the roof, Steve asked, "Do you think Gail is behaving strangely?"

I responded, "Perhaps. I wouldn't worry if I were you. As Milarepa says, 'How laughable to fight and quarrel with your wives and relatives.'"

Before dinner, Gail returned from visiting some neighbor women, saying, "This afternoon, Fatima and the other women told me the landlord's wife is expecting her fourteenth child. Most of the women have had eight children or more."

"I'm not ready for one child," I said and continued, "I'd rather read a Milarepa story tonight, instead of tuning to Radio Luxemburg to hear rock and roll."

We had gotten away from reading Milarepa and spent each evening listening to rock and roll from the pirate radio station.

"The radio is our only connection to the outside world. It takes forever for letters to arrive. There's no way to phone, and I know certain people want to communicate with me," Gail said, emphasizing "certain people" so it had an almost-ominous connotation.

Two days later, Steve told me Gail wanted to go back to the States to see her father and family because she picked up a "vibration" her father needs her.

"What bull!" he said. "In the last letter, her mother said her dad's health had actually improved. I think she wants to stop to see a man in London."

Listening to Radio Luxemburg that evening, the announcer said, "Now for our fans listening in North Africa and places south, this song is dedicated to you." The music started with Judy Collins singing, "When every fairy tale comes real / I've looked at love that way…"

After the song, Gail said, "Did you two hear that? The magician is calling to me. He's asking me to join him."

The next day, Gail announced, "The neighbor women are painting my hands and feet with henna. Then I want you to drive Patsy and me to Tangier. My father needs me, and I'm going to get a plane ticket to London and fly onto the States."

As Gail walked out the door, Steve said, "Hash, I need something strong right now. Look, my hands are shaking," as he held his hands in front of him.

After a period of quiet, I said, "What are you going to do?" I worried our short happy life in Khemis was about to end. Where would I go?

The days of the Blue Door commune were over.

Steve replied, "I don't know, I don't know. I can't believe Gail would just leave me and take Patsy away. What should I do? I want to stay and continue my spiritual growth, but my family is all I know."

I replied, "Stay here with me when Gail goes. We can drive to Tangier tomorrow, and you and I can come back here and live until we learn what our future will bring. Remember what Milarepa says about the ways that lead to liberation? Good discipline, solitude, and meditation. We can live Milarepa's instructions for determined, persevering practice."

The next day, the temperature dropped sharply, and a hard rain began to fall. Steve told Mina that Gail and Patsy were going away for about a month. He said he and I would live in Khemis.

I said, "We love the place, thank you so much for finding it for us."

I walked around Tangier thinking my world had been thrown into a state of turmoil. What would happen if Gail came back, or what would happen if she didn't?

I walked past one of the many shops selling secondhand books and stopped to look over the titles displayed in racks on the street. I saw one, *Yoga Self-Taught*, that I wanted to add to our Khemis library. I picked up the copy of *Yoga Self-Taught* and offhandedly, without seeming to care, offered half the marked price. The proprietor said a slightly higher amount. I accepted and walked away happily with the book in my hand. The second half of the book, which showed hatha yoga and asanas (physical postures and breathing exercises), had attracted me, but I saw the first half was devoted to yoga philosophy and meditation. One phrase jumped out at me, a devotional exercise of "radiating friendliness over the entire world."

We spent the night at the Miami, and the next morning, Gail took me aside in the hall and said, "Please take care of Steve in Khemis. He really fell apart last night, and I don't want to see him end up in a mental hospital, especially not a Moroccan nuthouse. He's extremely vulnerable, and I'm afraid he'll go crazy. Whatever you do, don't give him the LSD you offered as a birthday present."

I answered, "I'm not looking forward to caring for someone having a mental breakdown," which I sensed was a possible, maybe even probable option, but answered, "I'll keep him out of the asylum."

At the airport as I hugged Gail and Patsy, I said, "Have a safe trip. I hope you'll honor the teachings you've heard here and think about what Milarepa says, 'The law of cause and effect, karma, is e'er supreme,' so try to practice awareness and kindness."

Gail kissed Steve and said, "I know you love and need me but don't despair. There's a small chance I might return." She walked away through the gate.

Tears formed in Steve's eyes. He was crying gently, trying to not let anyone see, but his sobbing increased. "This is a disaster. It's the worst day of my life. I know I'm losing my daughter and my wife, and I can't do anything to prevent it."

"Remember Milarepa says, 'Think not that all suffering is ill,'" I said as we began a silent ride to the cold, damp, stone house in Khemis.

The rain continued to fall and we bundled up, even wearing socks on our hands as gloves as we sat and smoked hash.

Steve said, "Our circumstances are a disaster, but maybe we can turn it into something useful."

I replied, "I have those acid tabs that were your birthday gift and which I thought I'd use to guide you and Gail on your first LSD trip. Now Gail's gone, but you and I can trip here. Are you game?"

"Great. We're free and I want to turn on," Steve responded.

"I'm a master at creating the positive atmosphere that contributes so much to an enlightening and mind-blowing experience. Let's do it on a sunny day so we can get outside. When the rain stops, we'll do it," I said.

"Right on, brother. Half of Milarepa's songs are about looking into your own mind. Isn't that what Leary said LSD does? Bring it on, I'm ready and excited," said Steve.

I dropped acid over ten times and liked the idea of guiding Steve on his first trip and opening his mind. I didn't care that Gail warned me against giving Steve the acid.

We had been smoking kief all day when I remarked, "Before you got out of your sleeping bag this morning, you reached for the pipe and pouch."

"Remember the Moroccan saying, 'A pipe of kief in the morning makes you as strong as a hundred camels in the courtyard,'" Steve answered, referring to the title of a book written by Morocco resident Paul Bowles.

"The way you smoke kief, you'll be as strong, or maybe as weak, as a thousand camels," I said with a laugh.

"My pouch is almost empty. Let's get a *rabita* and cut some more kief, so we can refill our pouches before we run out. I don't want to have to go into withdrawal," Steve said, laughing.

The *rabita* consisted of several stalks of kief flowers and a couple of leaves of black tobacco. It took us about an hour to remove the seeds, remove the leaves, devein the tobacco, and chop the two components separately.

"We need to experiment with the mixture we want. Not too much tobacco or it will be harsh. Not too little or it won't burn well. Moroccans pride themselves on their mixture," I said while I mixed the proportions of flowers to tobacco.

"I'm glad we follow Moroccan customs and throw the leaves away. Besides, the stronger the mixture, the higher the high," Steve said.

Lighting our sebsis at the same time, we each took a hit and acted like connoisseurs sampling a fine wine.

"Perfect, you've got the touch. If pot ever becomes legal in the States, you can be a kief brew master," Steve said, complimenting my work.

The next morning, the sun was shining and a mist was rising from the concrete patio in front of our door. I heard birds chirping above.

Swallows, I thought as the birds flew in circles and darted under the eaves of the houses. Without a clock, I looked at the height of the sun in the March sky and estimated it was about 10:00 a.m.

"If it's sunny tomorrow, we could take our acid trip," I said.

"Why not right now?" Steve inquired.

"First of all, one never eats before a trip. An empty stomach is important. Secondly we need to prepare ourselves mentally. Tonight we can do some reading and reflecting. Also, I'd like to cook a pot of vegetables today, so when we come down, we'll have a meal ready as we won't have eaten anything for the whole day. I'll orchestrate this trip. Your first LSD experience needs to be special. I'd like to have everything under control," I said authoritatively. "The key to a great acid trip is 'set and setting.'"

The next morning, I woke Steve and said, "Acid, the sun's shinning, the mind should be shining too. Wake up and see the universe."

Steve sat up slowly and automatically reached for his kief pipe but stopped and said, "Is it good to smoke kief before a trip?"

"No, just pee, wash your face and hands, put on some clean clothes, and I'll prepare a short ritual to project us into the right frame of mind to drop acid," I replied.

A little while later, Steve sat opposite me on the straw mat, three round pills on the plate between us.

"May this day be auspicious. May this acid open our minds and hearts to universal wisdom. May what we do today contribute to the welfare of all beings," I said. As I poured two glasses of water and handed one to Steve, saying, "We'll take one tab each as I haven't taken this acid before and don't know how strong it is. Later we'll see about sharing the other half tab."

Steve replied, "I say, let's just take the extra half at the start. We want to blow our minds, don't we? Later we might forget about the extra half. Let's go whole hog, full speed ahead!" And he reached and picked up a pill and a half.

"Okay, down the hatch. You'll never be the same again, and I mean that in a good way," I said.

After swallowing, we sat facing each other in silence. Soon, I began to feel slightly nauseous, and my vision and hearing got clearer. In the courtyard, I heard some noises just beyond the well and saw a Moroccan man and woman carrying poles. They seemed to be preparing to build something.

Their presence, so close to the front door, unnerved Steve, and he went outside and said, "Whatever you're doing out here has to stop. Not today. No work today."

The woman came toward him, and Steve saw she had hands coming out of her shoulders but no arms.

"Go, leave now, no work here today," Steve repeated. "Right now stop," Steve said as the women's hands flapped from her shoulders.

The woman spoke to the man in Arabic, and they both turned slowly and left. Steve walked back to the house confused. I could tell interruption made him paranoid, and the vision of the woman's armless hands remained in his mind as he sat down again on the straw mat.

With the acid hitting, a change of scenery after that confrontation would improve the vibes, so I said, "Let's get out of here and go for a walk in the countryside. Being immersed in nature is calling to us."

We walked down a narrow dirt path in the direction of the ocean. The path descended past bushes and trees; nature was flowing harmoniously together in changing patterns. As we came around a turn, we saw several small pieces of white paper on the ground, and Steve bent over to pick them up. The papers were parts of a letter he received from his mother and thrown away several days ago. After an unsuccessful attempt to clumsily reconstruct the letter, all he could make out was the phrase, "We are incompatible." At first seeing the letter and the phrase shook Steve, but he told me this liberated him from his mother's negative remarks and threw the letter away.

A little farther along, we stopped to watch a man plow his field with a team of two donkeys. He was singing as he worked, and the happiness he exuded doing a simple task in rhythm with his animals added to the symmetry of the scene. It reminded me of the biblical phrase about earning one's bread by the sweat of one's brow. Since he was plowing a field of wheat, the activity brought that verse to life. Two horses grazing on the hillside above and a twisted unusually shaped tree near us reminded me of a medieval painting I saw in a museum.

When we returned to the house, the acid hit even harder.

We sat and lit our pipes and began smoking. Steve told me he was seeing shapes and colors changing around him. The walls were cartoons and movie announcements, but he couldn't clearly decipher any pictures. We ascended to the flat roof. Steve took off his clothes and lay naked in the sun. Later he told me he was so alive in that moment he had a spiritual connection to every part of his surroundings.

I left Steve on the roof and went downstairs, my brain on a roller coaster. In the kitchen, I took a sharp knife and sliced oranges. I wondered if I just cut the oranges, or did I cut off a few of my fingers? I panicked, looked at my hands, and counted, relieved to see I still had ten. I carried the orange slices to the sitting room to share with Steve.

In the sitting room, Steve told me I looked like Jesus Christ. "Can we smoke some hash now?" he asked.

"Sure, it will keep the hallucinations coming," I told him.

We smoked a big pipe of hash and entered an acid/hash high surrounded by psychedelic colors and spinning shapes.

Steve returned to the roof as the sun was setting. He told me he felt immersed in "universal goodwill without measure," a phrase from our yoga book.

I learned later that after dark, Steve became uncomfortable and began to have a paranoid fantasy. He told me the man and woman we saw earlier were constructing a site to perform a ritual sacrifice on him, which Gail had planned from the start. When he again returned to the roof, he saw men in djellabas with hoods over their heads, carrying lanterns, walking through the village's narrow paths, and became frightened the ritual was about to begin. Overcome with fear and paranoia, he struggled to find his center. He calmed himself by thinking about me. Steve realized I could never be part of any plot to hurt him. Reassured he returned to the room with a new confidence having conquered the paranoid thoughts, he now considered demons attempting to unbalance his mind. When I heard his tale, I hugged him, glad he got through the paranoia, aware I was on his side.

Later my mind went to Timothy Leary's description of the ecstasy of LSD, and now I understood what Leary meant. I had been in another dimension beyond the physical world.

Steve took his sleeping bag to the roof and, under a blanket of stars, drifted to sleep. Steve described being unburdened and touched by unseen energy.

I retrieved our cassette player and played our Hendrix tape. The song "All along the Watchtower" blew my mind. *A Dylan song performed by Hendrix far-out*, I thought.

"There must be some kind of way outa here / Said the joker to the thief / There's too much confusion / I can't get no relief..." Was I the joker or the thief?

I heard this song in various states of consciousness—straight, high on pot, high on kief, high on hashish—but it was a different song on acid. The lyrics spoke to me when Hendrix sang, "There are many here among us who feel that life is but a joke / but you and I / we've been through that / and this is not our fate so let us stop talkin' falsely now the hour's getting late..."

When I opened my eyes, I saw the men getting out of their beds and leaving the sleeping area. As I walked out, I saw the old blind man with the keys locking the door to the now-empty rooms.

With our sleeping quarters locked, the serving of the morning meal began. In rolled the large vat being pushed by the same huge servers as yesterday. These few inmates in white coats acted like "trustees," who I surmised came from their long stays within the institution or some other quality, which increased their status.

The inmates lined up to the left of the table. We shuffled forward like a depressing conveyer belt of dirty men, each receiving a small loaf of white bread and a glass of mint tea. Soup was reserved for dinner, our only other meal. After each inmate received the bread and tea, a white-coated inmate gave each a paper cup containing three pills and made sure we swallowed them.

The stronger men were at the front the food line. I decided to use my size and physicality to make sure I had enough food to eat. I screamed in English, "I'm an American!" and went right to the front of the line.

A few imposing men stepped out to challenge me. Something in the stare of these men with a wild look in their eyes and the way they held themselves sent a chill down my spine. I backed off because I didn't want to be punched again. I went down the line still screaming, and finally two men moved apart so a space opened, and I stepped in. My place was near enough to the front, so I didn't have to worry about the food running out. I now had secured my spot in the food line and in the sleeping area.

After I walked around the yard a few times, I sat down in a sunny spot.

CHAPTER 5

And the Beat Goes On

Life flees fast. Soon, death will knock upon your door.
It is foolish, therefore, one's devotion to postpone.

—Milarepa

The first time I needed to defecate, I approached several inmates trying through gestures to communicate my need to shit. I needed to find the bathroom. A very thin man with a kind face took my hand and walked me to a side door on the outside of the central building.

Walking down a few stairs, I opened the door and felt a stab at the back of my throat. The horrific smell nearly caused me to vomit right there. The toilet facilities consisted of two holes to squat over. A water faucet about a foot above the ground on the left of each hole served for wiping and cleaning.

As I squatted over the hole, I heard scraping noises coming from below. I feared the rats in the holes might jump out at any time and bite my balls or ass. Despite my fear, I squatted over the refuse hole and did my business. Finishing, I turned on the faucet and ran some tepid water over my left hand and used it to clean myself. I splashed water on my face too. I hadn't known how to obtain water. Now I knew.

The toilet faucets provided the only running water inside the compound available to the inmates. When I left the room, I bent over and scooped a handful of water to drink out of my right hand.

Gagging from the dirt and smell, I hurried to get outside air in my lungs.

I struggled to take a short walk but quickly ended up sitting with my back against the concrete wall. I couldn't recall why I was put in this place. I strained my brain, but as thoughts of my earlier days in Morocco came back, I followed them back to happier times.

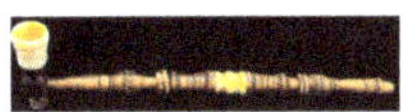

After Steve's acid trip, the weather turned rainy and cold. In the evening, I could see the vapor from our breaths as we exhaled. Steve added another layer of clothing including a pair of white sweat socks on his hands as we passed the hash pipe, refilling it twice.

Just before he nodded out, Steve said, "You know Gail took the tarot deck. We don't have any cards or the Waite book to interpret them. Shit, I'm lost. I want to put my life in tune with the mystical forces that surround us, and I'm screwed without a tarot deck. No woman, no child, no tarot, no hope."

"Didn't you hear what I just read?" I said and repeated Milarepa's advice, "'No hope and no fear is the assurance of accomplishment.' We'll figure out a way because I know the tarot is important for us."

After I smoked another pipe of hash, I passed out too.

A loud explosion shocked me into consciousness as flames shot over the straw mat. Pieces of burning material hit my djellaba, and I rolled over several times to put it out. Using a nearby towel, I started to smother other fires starting on the straw mat. Steve began tamping down the flames with his sock-covered hands. After franticly crawling around the straw mat, we extinguished the burning areas.

"What the fuck was that?" Steve said, checking the area to make sure nothing was still burning.

I looked around and said, "What happened to the candle that was on top of the clay jug?"

Steve picked up the jug and looked inside. "The candle is gone."

The kerosene lamp was the only light in the room.

"When the candle burned down into the jug, it exploded and the wick flew out onto the mat. That's because of the air in the jug," I said.

"Let's remember to put candles on flat plates from now on. That was scary," Steve said, regaining his composure as he saw no danger from the fire remained.

It was still black and raining outside as Steve reached for his sebsi and said, "Want a pipe?"

"We just passed out. It's the middle of the night, and you want to start smoking dope again?" I said. "Of course, pass the pouch. I need something to relax me after that booming alarm clock."

The next morning, I arranged notebook-sized paper in a pile on the straw mat and said, "I've considered our situation, and I know we need a tarot deck. So why not draw one ourselves? We can draw the twenty-two cards of the major arcana from memory. We've been studying the cards a few months now. Once we draw the deck, we can use it to see what's happening and connect to universal forces."

"What a great idea. This deck will have our vibrations in every card. It seems like we'll be sitting on this mat day and night anyway and drawing a deck will give us a meaningful art project, adding the wisdom of the tarot to our other studies. You're a genius. I'm going to break tradition and say let's smoke a pipe of hash right now to give our activities an auspicious start," Steve responded.

"I'll draw the hermit. I've thought a lot about that card since it came up at your Halloween party. I've even dreamed about it," I said

"The fool, that's the card I can draw. Remember, there's a small dog beside him as he stands on the edge of a cliff. I think he has a flower in his hand," Steve said, listening to the rainfall as he sat back against the wall.

"What do you think?" I said, holding up the nearly completed hermit card. "Did I forget anything?"

"Perfect. You got everything I remember, the beard, the lamp, the staff, and he looks like he's wearing a djellaba. You've got artistic talent," Steve said.

Taking a break, I decided to get the rope and can to draw water from the well. The words printed on the can read, "Cooking oil. Gift of the people of the United States." I strung the rope over the pulley and slowly lowered the can to the water about fifteen feet below. I watched the young girls from the other households in the courtyard get water and learned from them. They laughed, seeing a man doing a woman's work.

On my first try, the can landed flat on its bottom and just floated on the surface. I had difficulty tipping an edge of the can under the water so it would sink and begin to fill. After several attempts, I filled the can and pulled it up hand over hand. I poured the water into our plastic container and lowered the can again. It took three cans to fill the container.

When I returned, I said, "I want to send postcards and aerograms to my family and friends and let them know where I am and what I'm doing. I need to send people my new address, so they can write to me. We should probably go to the post office at the other end of the village and get our address correct so we can receive mail. I want to write Jan, so we can plan her upcoming visit."

"Good thinking. When we left England last fall, Gail and I spoke to an Australian woman, Gerri, who we knew in Malaga. She was talking about coming back for a visit, and I'd like to let her know I'm living in Morocco. She probably knows about it from Gail as Gerri is in London now," Steve said.

"What's the story with you and Gerri? Sounds like you have a thing for her," I said as I began writing.

"We're just friends. She is an attractive natural blond with a sweet disposition. She babysat for Patsy in El Palo. If I had been the type to cheat, I could have gone for her, but I was into being faithful. Looks like maybe I was a fool."

A pile of completed postcards and four aerograms lay in the center of the mat.

Steve said, "Please walk over to mail these after you make sure our return address is correct."

"I wonder if Jan could take this place. It might be a bit primitive for her, but we could travel south," I said. "I know that like the New Yorkers who go to Miami Beach in the winter, the hippies in the north of Morocco go south for the winter. Some hippies in Tangier told me of a beach in the south, Taghazout, where the people dance naked under the moon and smoke hash as they watched the sun set over the Atlantic. Maybe when Jan comes, it would be a good time to go there." I took the letters and postcards and put them into a straw basket. I put on my Moroccan slippers and said, "I'll get our address, mail these, and pick up our daily bread at the store too."

I walked out the door into the sunshine in a happy mood. I continued across our private courtyard into the larger compound then out the compound gate and down the alley toward the highway. As I went by an open gate, four aggressive dogs came running toward me, snarling and barking. I bent down and grabbed a rock and made a throwing motion as I saw the Moroccans do. The dogs scurried back out of the roadway.

On the highway, I turned south and walked passed a line of high white walls, some topped with broken glass that marked the outer walls of other compounds. Every few hundred feet, an alley leading to another compound ran off to the left. One larger two-lane road went left to the field where the weekly market, called a *souk* in Arabic, was held. As I approached the store that doubled as the post office, I saw two men sitting outside, looking over a board and playing a game of checkers.

Standing next to them, I said, "*Salaam alaikum* (PEACE be upon you)."

The men looked up, and the younger one replied, "*Mualaikum salaam* (Peace be also upon you)."

I stood watching and, after a while, reached into the straw basket and took out the letters and postcards and, holding them up, said, "Mail here?"

The younger man got up and led me inside the store, where he looked at each aerogram that already had the stamps printed on them, and after counting the postcards, he said, "Five dirhams," and held up the five fingers of his hand.

I took out a five-dirham note and said, "Address here," and pointed to where the return address needed to be written on the letters.

A few minutes of confusion followed in which we each tried to make the other understand using a combination of Spanish, French, Arabic, English, and hand motions. I finally brought a piece of paper and pen out of the straw bag and showed the man I wanted to have him write the name of the town and how a letter should be addressed. The man acted as if a light had just gone off and, nodding, took the pen and wrote in a small scrawl, "Derb Chorfa, Khemis Sahel, Maroc."

I said, "*Shukraan*" (Thank you)," wrote the return address on the mail, and took the piece of paper and left.

On the way back, I stopped at the small store on the highway near our house, where I picked up a loaf of the round whole-wheat brown bread baked daily by the shopkeeper's wife.

When I returned to the house, I announced, "We live in Derb Chorfa, Khemis Sahel."

Two days later, after having eaten our couscous breakfast, I said, "We need to finish drawing the tarot deck so the cards can tell us what's happening."

Steve said, "I'd like to start some attempt at meditation. Part of *Yoga Self-Taught* covers this. We should have a time each day when we just sit silently and meditate. After all, Milarepa meditated in caves for twelve years, eating only nettles. He always starts his disciples on a meditation practice. We're his disciples, too, eight centuries later."

Opening the book at random, I looked at the page and read, "Lay down your doubts and meditate. He who relies on the true teachings will never go astray."

The next day was the weekly souk. Although we were told that Khemis Sahel translated as Thursday Market, the market was held on Saturdays. Stalls were set up in a large dirt soccer field, where the boys played during the week. Next to it was a lot filled with the farmers' burros. The farmers brought onions, leeks, turnips, potatoes, and other seasonal produce to sell. Wearing our djellabas and carrying straw baskets, we did not attract any undue attention.

On one side of the field were tables displaying fly-covered chunks of meat, including an occasional cow or goat's head. If we had not already given up eating meat, one trip to the souk would turn any Westerner into a vegetarian. As we walked slowly among the other shoppers, we watched what the locals were paying as the sellers weighed their vegetables on balance scales. The prices seemed so low it was hard to believe that several pounds of just-harvested potatoes could be brought for only a few pennies.

I saw Steve being tapped on his shoulder by the woman he saw on our acid trip with hands coming out of her shoulders.

She greeted him warmly, saying in Spanish, "*Coche bueno ahora* (Your car's good now)." To protect the van, she and her husband built a carport at another location for us.

Steve smiled back at her and said, "*Si, muy bueno. Gracias por su trabajo* (Yes, very good. Thank you for your work)."

The woman continued smiling and said, "*Muy bueno zanahorias ahi* (Very good carrots there)," and pointed one of her shoulder/hand fingers to another vendor.

"*Gracias, querro compare zanahorias* (Thank you I want to buy carrots)," Steve replied as he was now accustomed to the woman's birth defect, which didn't seem to inhibit her spirit or activities, although seeing her did flash him back to their encounter during the acid trip. I walked over, and the woman moved on.

"I just bought some salt and some cumin from the spice vendor. Tonight we'll have a special tagine. I can't believe the prices," I said, holding up my basket full of vegetables. "All this cost less than three dollars, and with what you have, we can feast for a week."

Back at our house, we each began drawing a tarot card.

"I counted ten completed cards yesterday. Twelve more and we'll have a deck we can use," Steve said.

I said, "I'll draw the tower next, just to keep our quest in perspective." I started sketching the lightning bolt blowing the top off a burning tower and two figures apparently falling to their deaths.

The following week went along smoothly as we concentrated on drawing the tarot deck along with our routine of reading Milarepa in morning after breakfast and meditating in the late afternoon. Hash was reserved for heavy smoking at night when we read sections from *In Search of the Miraculous* before we passed out with the candles still burning. This book taught the teachings Ouspensky received from Gurdjieff.

We kept notebooks, writing poems, our dreams and other thoughts, and occasionally a resolution. Steve wrote a vow dated April 8, 1971: "I will never help anybody buy drugs." I told him that I didn't agree. I argued that my selling good quality hash at a fair price was helping everyone, including the Moroccans as well as hippies. I was spreading the love.

Before going to the souk the next Saturday, Steve said, "Let's not buy too much food. I think we should drive to Tangier. I need to bathe with hot water. We need to get some supplies, and I'd like to see if there's any mail from Gail. I'm spending too much time speculating on what happened when she arrived in London. When she left, we asked her to write care of *poste restante* Tangier."

"I was thinking about going to Tangier too. Jan will be writing me at *poste restante* before she gets my letter giving her the address here. Also, we're out of acid, and from your reaction, I expect we'll want to trip some more," I said.

Steve said, "Using a washrag and cold water isn't enough. You were telling me about the hammam, the Moroccan bathhouse you've gone to in Tangier. It sounds like a fun and a necessary place for us to visit."

"We can drive to Tangier this afternoon and stay at the Miami for a night or two. We'll have to stay until Monday to get our mail before we can drive back here. I'm a hippie. But I've never been a dirty hippie, and you're right, we need a good washing," I said.

Dark storm clouds were gathering in the sky as we pulled the Camper into its parking spot next to the Pension Miami. We heard a clap of thunder over the Mediterranean as rain was about to begin. We hurried inside where a fat Moroccan woman with a scar on her face sat at the desk. This was Latifah, Mina's half-sister, who we knew from our previous stays. She rented us a room.

After putting our bags in the room, I said, "Let's go to a restaurant for a bowl of soup and see what's happening in the cafés."

As we walked out the door, the rain was falling hard. We stayed close to the buildings and occasionally huddled in doorways.

Moroccan men put cutout black plastic bags over their clothes while others were holding newspapers over their heads. When we reached the restaurant, it was crowded with Moroccans and a few Westerners. I saw some hippies I knew and led Steve to their table.

"Greetings, can we join you?" I said as I approached two blond men with long full beards, wearing colorful skullcaps, bead necklaces, and wool djellabas.

"Sure, Fred, good to see you. We heard you left Tangier. What's been happening?"

I introduced Steve to Lars and Eric, two Danish travelers who were well-known for their daring escapades.

I said, "We're living near Larache in a small village. We just came to Tangier for this good food and to get our mail."

"You need any hash?" asked Eric as the waiter brought two bowls of the steaming split pea soup Moroccans called *bessara*.

While living in the Blue Door commune, we would often have *bessara* and a piece of bread from this restaurant at lunchtime. The decor consisted of a large vat of soup and a few wooden tables; it served only *bessara* and bread. It was cheap, delicious, and filling. Steve and I ordered two bowls and bread.

"No, we have a good supply of top quality hash, but we are looking to score some acid," I replied as the men scooped up the soup with pieces of bread they broke off a round, dark loaf that was on the table between them.

"Ha, that's funny. Today is your lucky day. We just got four hundred tabs of pure windowpane acid, and we're actually here celebrating its safe arrival," Lars said with a big smile on his face.

"Get this," said Eric, "we've been waiting for this acid, so we were at the post office every day this week. Nothing. This morning we went again and asked if anything arrived for us. The clerk called over his superior, and they walked us to a desk in the back room. On the desk was a small package wrapped in brown paper. The postal officials had opened it. On the desk were sheets of windowpane acid.

"'What is this?' the supervisor shouted and pointed.

"I almost fainted," Eric continued. "But Lars, cool as a cucumber, says those are special photographic slides that we use to transfer images in order send our photos back to Denmark. He picked up one tab and held it up to the light and said, 'See, they are blank now,' putting the tab in front of the supervisor."

"Yeah," Lars picked up the story, "the supervisor held it up to the light and, shaking his head, pushed the tabs over to us. We put them back in the box they came in. Thanked them and walked out. We're selling them for a dollar a piece. How many would you like?"

"What a story. Lars, how did you stay so cool?" I said.

"I could tell that they didn't know what they were, and doesn't windowpane look like small negatives? So I acted confident without displaying the slightest fear or hesitation. After this long in Morocco, I know how much is determined by the vibrations you project, and I was proved right again," Lars said as he wiped some of the soup off his beard with his sleeve.

"We'll take fifty tabs" were the first words Steve said.

Eric and Lars looked surprised but didn't say anything except, "After we finish eating, walk us back to Pension Victoria. Do you have the money?"

"Fifty dollars cash," Steve said as he lifted his neck pouch up, indicating the money was inside.

Later in our room at the Miami, I said, "Fifty tabs of pure acid. I was thinking about maybe getting twenty. You went whole hog."

"That story and that it just happened today and the price seemed right. I don't see how we can have too much acid. It won't spoil, will it?" Steve replied. "Maybe fifty tabs were too few."

"I'm sure we'll spread a lot of love," I said.

Next morning as we walked in Tangier's Casbah, I said, "That's the hammam," and pointed out a nondescript two-story building without any sign and an old-fashioned arched carriage entryway with big wooden doors and a smaller door painted green off to one side. "Easy to find because it's just around the corner from the Café Royale."

I opened the green door and walked into the courtyard on the other side. Two young muscular men came out to greet us.

"*Salaam alaikum*," I said.

One man replied, "*Buenos dias*, you want a bath?"

"Yes, we want a private room," I said. "I've been here before, and I'd like room number three if it's available."

"Yes, number three is empty. Five dirhams for unlimited time.

I said, "I usually pay less, but five dirhams is okay with extra towels, shampoo, and a bar of soap."

The man went inside an opened doorway; returned with six smallish towels, a packet of shampoo, and a bar of soap; and handed them to me as I handed him five dirhams. He led us down a hallway to the last door.

"*Gracias*," Steve said as he closed the door and pushed the bolt that secured it from the inside.

There was a narrow wooden bench against the wall and some hooks on the wall opposite it. I slipped my djellaba over my head and began taking off my clothes, and Steve followed suit. Both naked, we walked through the swinging door at the end of the changing area into one large room with a blue-and-white tiled floor and walls. Light flooded the room from small high windows on all sides. Three empty buckets sat in front of two spigots coming out of the wall with one plastic chair.

I said, "The water from this tap is boiling hot," as I turned it on, and the room began to fill with steam. "This other tap has cold water, which you use to mix with the hot and pour over yourself."

Steve picked up a bucket and filled it half with hot water and added some cold. It reached a hot but manageable temperature as he poured it over his head. I did the same thing with the other bucket. After Steve poured two buckets over himself, he took the third one and threw it over my chest. I retaliated and threw a bucket of warm water over Steve. A laugh-filled water fight ensued as we enjoyed the steam-filled room and the warm water.

"I haven't had warm water on me since we moved to Khemis," I said as I soaped myself. I took the shampoo and washed my hair. "We used to come here with the commune, five women and five men. Once I fantasized that it would turn into an orgy, but it never happened."

"I thought the Moroccans strictly separated men from women in the baths?" Steve said as he soaped himself from head to toe.

"Yes, traditionally that is true, Muslims separate men and women. The men allowed the ten of us to bathe together because we're hippies and anything goes. The steam and hot water relax you, and you're clean and naked. Too bad I'm with you now that you mention it," I said, laughing. "It is much more fun to bathe with a woman."

We stayed in the bath for a long time, just lying on our towels on the tile, enjoying the hot steam.

As we walked out and returned the towels to the muscular man, he said, "Come again soon."

It was still overcast but not raining as we walked through the streets of Tangier.

"I think I'd like to go back to the Miami," Steve said.

"I'd like to go visit Mustapha and say hello. I want to keep in touch since he's a great connection for hash if anyone we know needs to buy some," I said.

At the next corner, we went in different directions.

I walked the short distance to the Café Royale, and going upstairs, I met Mustapha, who was sitting at the desk in the office room.

Mustapha greeted me and touched his hand to his heart and said "*Salaam*."

I echoed back the same greeting, touching my heart and bowing slightly at the office door.

I explained, "I'm living out of town near Larache. That's why you don't see me here in the evenings. I'll still be coming to town, and if I hear about anyone who needs hash, I'll be sure to bring them by. I'm still smoking the hash I got last time I saw you."

"You're my brother, come by and I'll take special care of you," Mustapha said.

"*Salaam alaikum*," I said with a little bow as I touched my hand to my heart and left the café.

Monday first thing, we walked to the post office, and after showing our passports, we each received a letter addressed to *post restante*, read it, and gave a brief summary to the other.

Gail's letter from New York said, "Visiting my family. Plan to return to Tangier in late April. Will write details of flight. Pick Patsy and me up at airport. Gail."

Jan's letter excited me because of its many sexual references and loving greetings. I didn't show the letter to Steve, especially because this line embarrassed me, "I can't wait to have your cock inside me again," but I did read to Steve the part where Jan said, "I've cleared my calendar and have the girls covered for three weeks until April 30th. Let's make definite plans for you to meet me at the ferry."

The future was going to bring changes and choices. What would they be? Jan's arrival thrilled me but didn't see her as a long-term guest in Khemis for many reasons including the lack of privacy, primitive conditions, and the chaos Gail's return was bound to bring. How would I rendezvous with Jan, and where would we stay, or should we travel? What effect might her coming have on my spiritual journey?

I could see the letter depressed and worried Steve. Gail obviously hadn't hooked up with the man she went to London to see. I hadn't thought they would, but I couldn't see her planning to resume life in Khemis. Gail's wants and desires would definitely change the quiet, calm routine that Steve and I established. I thought about how Milarepa taught that women were a major distraction and obstacle to achieving enlightenment. I recited Milarepa's line, "Women are the major source of trouble."

A week after getting back from Tangier, I said, "I've finished drawing my cards. What about you?" as I looked at the judgement card I just drew.

My version had an angel with upraised arms, signaling to a naked woman standing below also with upraised arms.

"Here's the lovers," Steve said, holding up the card he had just drawn.

It showed a blond naked woman holding hands with a curly haired man, an exploding volcano in the background.

"We've done it! This is special. I'm going to break out some hash even though it's still morning."

I looked at the twenty-two cards spread on the mat, impressed with the artistic merit of some of the cards especially the hermit.

"If we can put ourselves in touch with the wisdom of these cards, we'll be able to make better progress in our quest and make decisions based on our intuition combined with universal forces. Drawing the cards has been so special, and every time I look at them, I'll remember these weeks," I said, holding up the death card, which I thought looked like the original. "Let's prepare a special ritual tonight and do our first reading. We can ruminate on the questions we want answered and see how our cards reply."

After dinner, with the mat cleared and the tarot drawings stacked in the center of the mat, I said, "May this moment be auspicious. May these cards be dedicated to the welfare of all living beings. May we put ourselves in harmony with nature, our deeper selves, and universal forces. May the ancient wisdom come to our assistance as we dedicate ourselves to the Bodhisattva Path. May the readings increase our compassion. I dedicate these cards to growth, understanding, and the harmony of all beings."

Steve nodded his agreement.

"You ask the first question," I said after we'd smoked a pipe of hash. I picked up the drawings and handed them to Steve. "The first card will cover the whole question," I continued. "Now mix the deck, turn half the cards around, mix the deck again, and cut it with your left hand. Keep your question in mind and ask for guidance. Start the reading now."

Steve turned over the temperance card. The drawing showed a winged woman pouring water between two goblets.

I said, "This card seems very calming and serene, and I'm relieved to see it."

Next Steve turned the high priestess, covering the near future.

"Wow, a lot of femininity going on," I exclaimed as the card showed a woman in flowing robes, wearing a cross, sitting between two different-colored columns.

The next card, the emperor upside down, had a negative implication for a male, but neither of us identified with the card.

The last card Steve turned was the sun, which showed a naked child riding on a white horse in front of a large sun. I had drawn it full of bright orange, yellow, and red. I even put sunflowers behind the rider.

"This entire reading is upbeat," Steve said, but it really didn't answer very specifically. "What will happen if and when Gail returns?"

"We will understand more clearly once Gail is here," I said.

Preparing for Jan's visit, I sewed several patches on my sleeping bag. My torn, worn bag is now a work of art with the bright-red fabric.

I said, "I'm up to try that windowpane we got in Tangier. If we want to trip with anyone else, I mean Jan or visiting friends, we need to know how strong and pure it is."

"Great thinking as usual. That first trip had a tremendous impact on me, but I know that LSD has a lot more insights to offer. How about tomorrow?" Steve said without any hesitation.

The next morning, I brought out the envelope that contained the windowpane acid and put two of the thin translucent squares on a plate in front Steve. "I've heard that this is some of the purest, strongest acid that's been made. Some people say that Owsely himself produced twenty-five thousand tabs of this," I said as I sat down opposite Steve.

"May this trip be as enlightening as the last. May we get ever higher and higher until we embody pure compassion for all living things," Steve said as he reached down, took a tab on his fingertip, and put it in his mouth, swallowing it and taking a sip of water.

"I dedicate this trip to the welfare of all sentient beings," I said as I swallowed the remaining acid tab. I reached for our colored pencils and began drawing.

Steve sat on the mat looking through the tarot deck, spending a few minutes on each card as he turned them over.

As the acid hit, we walked up the stairs to the roof and, without saying anything to each other, began to do the series of yoga poses that we used as part of an almost-daily routine. Sweating, we did two complete sessions. Afterward we assumed the lotus posture, and with our back straight and our hands in our laps and eyes closed, we entered a deep meditative state. My mind soared far above the roof into the psychedelic beyond.

I felt surrounded by books of the great teachings. I absorbed the wisdom from the books as I followed the path to enlightenment on my own. I spent the whole day on the roof in silence feeling like a disciple moving rapidly toward the achievement of enlightenment.

The next day, I poured tea for Steve and myself and said, "That acid is truly mind-blowing. I loved being on the roof all day, sitting there, watching the sky, birds, and my own mind. I thought about sex and that it will happen when it happens and that sex is just one part of the flow."

"We spent most of the day on separate trips, but I was thinking of sex too. I realized that sex is just a small part of life," Steve said. "When we started smoking hash, the hallucinations reappeared. I flashed on the idea of taking acid every day. I am so wasted today I don't think that would be a very good idea. I also pictured myself walking through the Himalayas in a white robe among a group following a guru. I sat at the feet of this guru, who sang a song in a magical voice."

"I'm going to walk down to the post office and see if we've gotten any mail," I said after reading a Milarepa story.

I returned carrying a loaf of freshly baked bread, a bag of peanuts in their shells, and two letters, which I dropped in front of Steve. "You've heard from Gerri and Gail," I said.

He picked up the letters and examined them closely. Gail's letter came from the States and had her parents' home as the return address. Gerri's letter had a London return address and a little flower drawn on the envelope.

After smoking kief, Steve said, "I know that these letters are very important. They may determine my fate. Whatever they and the future brings, I am prepared," he said in a way that made me think that perhaps he wasn't really prepared for the upheaval the news contained in the letters might bring. Steve opened Gail's letter first.

I could see it was short, and after Steve skimmed it, he read aloud, "Patsy and I arrive at Tangier airport on April 23rd at 2:30 p.m. on flight 709 British Airways. Be at the airport to pick us up. Gail."

Without comment or hesitation, Steve opened Gerri's longer letter, which covered the front and back of one page. He read it to himself and, turning to me, read aloud, "I'm coming to Morocco for a visit. I arrive from London on British Airways flight 943 at 12:30 p.m. on April 26th. Please come to the airport to pick me up."

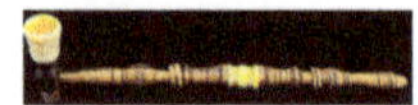

My thinking about the letters interrupted my reliving of my initial time in Khemis. Somehow it shocked me awake to the realization that I couldn't send or receive any letters. My isolation brought me back to the bare yard and concrete wall. The other inmates were drifting toward the area to line up for dinner, and I stood up and drifted with them.

Fred, Gerri, Steve, Summer, 1971, Khemis Sahel, Morocco

CHAPTER 6

Let the Good Times Roll

Don't worry about saving these songs!
And if one of our instruments breaks,
It doesn't matter.
We have fallen into the place
Where everything is music.
—Rumi, *The Essential Rumi*

After taking my pills following the morning tea and bread, I walked around the yard. A man without a brown djellaba walked from the administration building. I moved toward him. As I got closer, I could see that he wore jeans and a plaid shirt. At over six feet tall, his clean-shaven face rose above the other inmates.

Another non-Moroccan I can talk to, I thought. "Hey, brother, what's happening?" I said.

"*No comprendo*," the man replied in Spanish.

"I'm an American. Do you speak English?" I asked.

"*No comprendo. Argentina. Hablo solomente Español*," the man replied, although obviously excited to see another non-Moroccan.

I knew some Spanish but not much. The man's appearance in Beni sparked a rise in my energy, and I said, "*Me llamo Fredrico. Soy de Los Estados Unidos.*"

The man began to cry, tears rolled down his face as he sobbed. "*Dios, por favor, Dios ayudame* (God help me)."

The nearby inmates were looking at the Argentinean and me, gathering around us.

In a hushed tone, I said, "Calm down. Quiet. Calm down." With my palm, I motioned toward the ground, gesturing for him to calm down.

Instead, the man yelled louder, raising his hands over his head and falling on his knees, "*Dios ayudame!*"

Three trustees in white jackets came storming across the yard and lifted the man off the ground. One with a needle pulled down the man's pants and gave him an injection in his butt cheek while the other two held the man's arms. The three trustees then dragged him out of the courtyard and back into the central building.

I stood watching, my mouth agape. I could do nothing to assist the Argentinean. This reinforced my feeling of isolation and hopelessness. I thought about what the man said. I knew "*Dios*" meant God, but stretching my mind, I could not come up with what "*ayudame*" meant. My brain was fuzzy because the morning pills were taking effect. I retreated to an empty spot at the wall and sat down, leaning back. I couldn't focus on helping the new inmate or translate what he said.

Despite my agitation, I drifted off and entered a dreamlike state, taking me back to the time in Khemis when I awaited Jan's arrival from Spain.

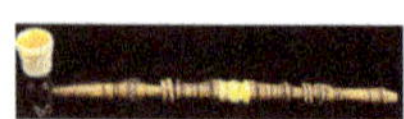

With Jan arriving on the ferry, I worried about the consequences of Gail's arrival three days before Gerri. My spiritual life blossomed, but the arrival of Gail, Gerri, and Jan might spell disaster.

When Steve returned with Gail and Patsy from the airport, I greeted them with a hugs. In our first conversation, Gail told me her marriage was kaput, and she planned to move on.

After a tense two days in Khemis, Gail declared, "Steve, I need to go to Tangier tomorrow. You'll drive me to the Miami. Patsy and I will stay there. I need time. We can straighten out our priorities."

"Fine, I need time to think," Steve replied.

I knew Gerri's plane arrived that day, so at least on the first day, Gail and Gerri would not both be at the Khemis house together. I said, "I'll stay here. I don't need anything and a day alone suits me fine."

Later in private, Steve told me he'd drop Gail and Patsy off at the Miami and go pick up Gerri at the airport.

"I've got some ideas, but everything is too fluid for me to have definite plans. I'll see what happens, but I do plan to return here tomorrow night. Remember, 'No hope and no fear is the accomplishment of enlightenment,'" Steve said, quoting Milarepa.

I waited in a state of anticipation. I jumped up as soon as I heard Steve's knock on the front door.

With a slight bow, I said, "Welcome, welcome, welcome."

I could tell Steve and Gerri fucked by the way they were holding hands and looking at each other.

Gerri's said, "Hello," in her Australian accent and added, "Thanks for introducing Steve to the hammam. It made a perfect start to my time here."

I thought, *Pretty smart, Steve, taking Gerri from the airport to the hammam. I should do the same when Jan arrives.*

After unpacking, I said, "Let me read you a Milarepa story."

Gerri listened intently as the hash pipe circulated.

I read, "Put yourself in the hands of holy beings, don't dissipate your life doing worthless things."

"Marvelous, I heard a lot of wise advice. I'm glad Milarepa doesn't spend too much time on philosophy but emphasizes dedicating oneself to meditation and living a consistent Buddhist life. I'd love to hear all the stories," Gerri said.

"You will. Around here we read a story every day and other spiritual texts too," Steve said.

When Steve took the dishes to the kitchen, I said to him, "Gail is in Tangier for a few days, but her being in Morocco is disruptive. Until yesterday I thought you would follow Gail's bidding because of your feelings about Patsy, but the way you looked at Gerri, now I'm not sure. Jan is coming from Spain the day after tomorrow, so the mix will become even more complicated. I don't want my time with Jan to get ruined. I've thought about picking her up and going south to the beaches along the Atlantic. There's a hippie beach called Taghazout, where people swim naked in the sun and dance stoned under the moon."

Hearing what I said, Gerri replied, "Sounds perfect to me. A honeymoon for us two couples."

On the roof with Steve, I said, "I'll take the van to Tangier and pick up Jan at the ferry. I'll give her a tour of the casbah. Then we'll go to the hammam. To avoid Gail, I'll skip the Miami and rent a room for us at the Pension Amar and have dinner. We'll do some shopping and next morning come back here."

"You're taking Jan to the hammam…I've started a dating fad," Steve said.

I told him, "Gerri's a gem. I can envision her being here with us as a major plus. Focus on what you want. Remember Milarepa's words about the importance of putting yourself first if you are going to stay on the path to enlightenment."

"Okay. Please see where Gail's at. Let's make a list of supplies we need. Gerri suggested Marmite and soup packets," Steve said.

After my reunion with Jan and our loving time at the hammam and our night in bed at the Amar, the next morning, I walked to the Pension Miami. I met Gail in the outer reception room.

Before I said anything, Gail said, "I don't know what I'm going to do. I may stay here or return to Khemis or go back through London to the States."

I just nodded and said, "Do your thing."

Jan and I drove back to Khemis.

Gerri and Steve were lying in bed, smoking kief, when I knocked on the door and called, "Wake up, you love birds, we're here. Gail is staying in Tangier."

I introduced Jan to Gerri, who said, "Welcome, Jan, hope you enjoyed the bath as much as I did when I arrived."

"Just loved the hammam and my reunion with Fred. Tangier is even more exotic than I imagined. It was a great day and look what I bought," she said, showing Gerri the embroidered silk caftan she bought.

"Sit down. We tripped yesterday and needed to rest. Have a pipe of kief," Steve said.

"Jan and I would like to go south to the beaches and warmer weather. We talked with a hippie who just came back from Taghazout, and he couldn't stop singing its praises," I said. "Gail plans to stay a while at the Miami. From what she said, I got the feeling she's not coming back here. I say we pack, leave a note just in case, and head south today or tomorrow."

"Perfect," Gerri said. "There's a tent as well as the Camper van, so we'll both have places to sleep for our honeymoons. We Australians live on the beaches."

Steve looked up from refilling the pipe and said, "Honeymoon, good idea, and I'd like to explore more of Morocco. We won't need much if we're going to be naked."

"Only some of the time, sweetie. We'd better wear clothes as we drive and go shopping," Gerri said in mock seriousness.

After showing Jan the roof, we four sat cross-legged on the straw mat in front of a pot of mint tea and a plate of French pastries we brought from Tangier. Since Jan's arrival, we kept the pipe lit, and everyone was moving in slow motion. When Steve started to get up again to get napkins, he almost fell over and abandoned the effort.

Jan, who was wearing a watch, said, "It's only eleven a.m., and we're too stoned to stand. Is this usual for you?"

"Steve believes in the Moroccan saying, 'A pipe of kief in the morning makes you as strong as a hundred camels,' and he practices diligently," I said.

"I'm a believer now too," Gerri said, reaching for a pain au chocolate, taking a big bite.

"How about a Milarepa story? I'll get the map from the van. I think it's about eight hundred kilometers to Taghazout. We can stop along the way at a campground," Steve said.

Even in the hour or so Jan had been at the Khemis house, the four of us bonded. With very few words exchanged, Gerri and Jan seemed comfortable together and in agreement about our "honeymoon" adventure.

I suggested, "Let's go today. We'll drive as far as we like, finding a place to stay, and be on the beaches by tomorrow afternoon. I'll pack our remaining kief, lots of hash, and a few tabs of acid. What more do we need?"

"A roll of toilet paper, a towel, and sunglasses, and I'm ready," Steve said.

"We women will start putting other supplies together as I see you men would leave a few essentials behind," Jan said.

Within an hour, the van was packed with sleeping bags, pillows, propane camping stove, tea, selected food items, bowls, cups, flatware, sandals, sneakers, clothing, art supplies, and bottles of water. Standing in the doorway as we were about to leave, Steve took a piece of paper and a red colored pen and wrote, "Dear Gail and Patsy, we are headed south for a vacation. We'll be back in about three weeks, when Jan has to return to Spain. Hope you are clear about your plans by the time we return. Be well. Patsy, I love you very much. Daddy."

After camping the night, we continued south, the Atlantic Ocean just west of the highway.

"There it is," I called out, seeing tents, vans, and rude improvised structures on the dunes.

The dunes blocked the view of the water, but I could hear the pounding of waves. Behind the first dune Steve steered right and left to avoid the potholes. A series of small settlements with two or three tents together or a Land Rover with an awning and several chairs or vans parked together spread throughout the dunes. A larger group surrounding a Greyhound-type bus with six tents formed in an outer circle with flags hanging from their poles caught my eye. This area looked like a small village of its own with clothes hanging to dry, guitar cases on benches, and two naked women washing themselves in plain view under an improvised shower. Between the encampments and heading toward the long white sand beach were a series of trails cutting through and across the dunes.

Gerri said, "Down on the next side road and through the gulley, go up to the plateau over there. I see a flat space with a good view of the ocean and enough room for us to pitch our tent and park our van."

Steve followed Gerri's instructions; the VW's engine strained, but the van climbed to the plateau's top, where Steve turned left and stopped at an empty spot.

I opened the back door and jumped out, followed by Jan, who threw her hands into the air and said, "We made it. Taghazout Beach. Smell the sea air."

"It's 2:00 p.m.," Steve said as he looked at the alarm clock Gerri brought. "Let's take out a blanket, set up by the firepit, and have a pipe to celebrate our arrival."

Gerri laid a beach blanket and a straw mat on the ground. Jan carried water bottles, a bottle of wine, and cushions from the van. Within minutes, we created a comfortable smoking/sitting area.

I said, "I can see people on the beach but only a few are in the water. I wonder if the surf is too rough for most people. Those waves look rough."

Almost hypnotized by the rhythmic sound of the waves striking the shore, we smoked two pipes each. I thought about how Jan looked so clean even after a day and half of hard traveling. Her shirt didn't have a wrinkle.

After a period of quiet, Steve stood up and said, "Let's finish establishing camp."

Jan and I made our bed in the tent. Within an hour, we created a homey organized environment and even a shady sitting spot where Gerri was drawing with the art supplies.

"Who would like to walk over to the people who are camped on the other side of this flat to introduce ourselves? They can give us the scoop about this scene. We need to find out about where to get water," I inquired.

No one moved.

I returned about a half hour later followed by a bearded Brit named Jim, who I introduced.

"Glad to meet you," Jim said with a winning smile. "The last folks who camped here were Germans on a two-family holiday. Such pigs. Thought World War II would break out again, but they moved on. Now Yanks, so much better."

"I'm no Yank," Gerri piped up.

"Sorry, three Yanks and a saucy Australian blond," Jim replied.

"I invited Jim over for a pipe of hash. Arrival in Taghazout calls for something special. Sit down. This is Steve and Jan, the other two Yanks, and Gerri, the saucy Aussie," I said, and I handed Jim cigarette papers and hash. "Why don't you roll one?"

Jim's smile got even bigger as he accepted the pouch. Gerri handed him a *Time* magazine with James Taylor on the cover Jan brought from Spain. The headline on the cover was "The New Rock."

Jim took his time with the ritual of heating the hash with the lighter and sprinkling it over the tobacco laid out over three cigarette papers glued together. He folded the papers into a cone and sealed the final edge. Next he took a piece of a matchbook cover and rolled it into a filter. He put it into the narrow end of the cone.

He and handed the finished product to Gerri, saying, "Three cheers for saucy Aussies."

From around the corner of the van, a chunky woman with long black hair appeared with a black dog pulling on the leash she was holding. "Mick wants you to take him for his afternoon run," she said to Jim as the dog began to lick Jim's face.

"This is Liz," Jim said, introducing the group by name and standing up and taking the leash from her. "This beauty is Mick. Named for Jagger of course. We meet on the dune closest to the sea at sunset," Jim continued, pointing to a spot to the west. "Come over." He ran off down a trail toward the long beach with Mick running with him.

Gerri stood up too. "Let's go for a swim before it gets any later. We'll join you at sunset," she said to Liz, who was starting to leave.

"Right on," Liz replied as she walked off.

Steve got a towel and followed Gerri, who was walking toward the water with long purposeful strides. When Steve caught up to her, he patted her butt and said, "Last one in a rotten egg," and began running toward the surf, dropping the towel and his clothes on the way. Naked, he splashed through the low water and dove through a breaking wave.

Gerri was right behind him shedding her clothes and jumping into the water with a graceful dip. Jan and I were watching, laughing as we could see Steve rubbing against Gerri in chest-high water.

I said, "Steve is hot to fuck on the land, sea, and in the air if Gerri's willing, and she seems to be."

"Watch out. Look at them ducking the big waves. I'd hate to see the news report, 'Couple drowns while attempting to couple in rough surf,'" Jan said. "However an afternoon delight in the tent, I'm for it."

As the sun set over the ocean, the few clouds in view turned pink and a red glow held the gaze of people sitting on the dunes staring west. The sun's final disappearance brought a sigh in unison as the last glow of yellow light flashed and faded. We heard the beat of several drums and a scream of delight rose from one encampment.

"It's the Brazilians," Jim said, pointing to where we could see a bonfire, flames shooting up twenty feet. "They play, drink, smoke, and dance the night away. They're open to anyone coming to their party, and if you bring some of your hash, you'll get an even more hospitable welcome." Pointing to the Greyhound bus and the group of vans and tents around it, Jim continued, "Those are Americans, a hippie family who went to high school in Darien, Connecticut. They lived in Ibiza, and now they come here for their winters. Supposedly they get their hash from Achmed Gold Pipe."

"I smoked some of Achmed's hash with my friend Eldon in Tangier, and I smoked kief from the gold pipe with Achmed," I said. That was a slight exaggeration because Sarah smoked the kief and I got the ashes.

"No partying for me tonight. It was a hard day arriving and setting up our camp. Early to bed this evening," Steve said as the temperature dropped noticeably once the sun set.

"We need to eat some dinner and relax and get a good night's sleep," I said. "Let's read Milarepa in the morning, but now let's go to bed and let the honeymoon begin in earnest."

"No objection here," Jan said.

Next morning, the sun rose dramatically above the mountain ridges east of the coastal highway. It bathed the beach with warmth.

When Jan and I emerged from the tent, Gerri was pouring herself a second cup of tea. Steve filled our water containers from a faucet about one hundred yards from the campsite.

"Morning, lovebirds," Steve said.

I said, "The sound of the waves makes me sleep better. Even the drums in the background were soothing. I went outside at three a.m. for a pee. The stars are so bright, no need for a flashlight."

After we ate couscous with fresh milk, butter, and yogurt, I brought out the Milarepa book and read, "There are dangers you should watch for…inflating yourself with pride of priesthood, falling into Yogic madness, indulging in empty speeches."

Jan said, "For all the talk about Milarepa wandering around alone, he actually had quite a large and devoted support system. He had his disciples including this one, Shiwa Aui. He had his special patrons and a general following among the people."

"Yes, but these came after he achieved his enlightenment. I read his biography, and he meditated alone for twelve years in mountain caves after his rigorous trials and study with his guru Marpa," I replied.

"The formula is the Buddha, the dharma, and the sangha—the enlightened being, the teachings, and the community of believers. It seems at times on the path you need all three, although while at other times, perhaps not," Steve said.

"There doesn't seem to be one size fits all for becoming enlightened, except meditation plays a big part moving forward," I said.

"I'd love to see us begin a regular meditation practice. Sitting morning and evening for twenty minutes to start… I'd even set the old alarm clock and time the sessions," Steve said.

"Not on our vacation, but back in Khemis, it would be perfect. We could sit on the roof in the open air," Gerri said.

Bill popped around the corner of the van and said, "We're driving to the market. Any of you like to join us? There's a market near Agadir, and you can stock up on food, buy more ice, and get whatever else you need."

"I'll go, wait a minute while I change into more discreet clothes. If I went dressed like this, this saucy Aussie could cause a riot," Gerri said.

"I'll go too. Any special requests?" Steve said as he reached inside the van and grabbed his djellaba to cover his shorts and T-shirt and transformed himself from a hippie to a visitor respectful of Muslim decorum.

"Here, get me two bottles of dry white wine," Jan said as she took some dirham notes out of her pocket. "I'm enjoying just not going anywhere. I'd enjoy reading my book as I'm at a crucial part."

I said, "Buy two packs of Gauloises. Joints are easier to pass than a pipe, and everyone here smokes European style, hash with tobacco."

Later, after Steve and Gerri returned with some surprises including warm croissants and a richly seasoned cooked fish, we headed for a swim. Dropping our clothes on the sand, we raced toward the ocean's edge and dived through the surf into cooling, revitalizing water. I stood proudly next to Jan, who won the race with her long stride and perhaps by cheating a little by beginning before I said go.

"You're a winner," I said as I hugged Jan and held her arm in the air.

As sunset approached, our group joined the other beach campers sitting on a dune facing west. The scene was like a Renaissance Faire with people in every type of clothing, from German and Dutch tourists in Bermuda shorts and shirts with collars to an attractive blond woman standing on the top of the next dune, wearing a see-through blouse, which didn't quite reach below her waist. She was dancing in a circle holding her arms above her head while a man sat on the sand nearby, beating a drum.

As a green flash of light appeared on the horizon just as the sun went down, and a shout rose up from the appreciative watchers as if everyone exhaled loudly at the same moment. Joining together in appreciation of the beauty of this unexpected show gave the disparate groups of campers a feeling of unity and mutual participation and added to the friendly, cooperative vibration permeating the whole Taghazout scene.

After sunset, we sat in a circle around a sumptuous feast of fresh vegetables.

I reached out, and we joined hands. "We thank Mother Nature for this bounty and wish peace for all beings and may the happiness we feel be spread throughout the world."

"Amen and dig in. Thank you, Gerri, for putting this together," Steve said as he put a big scoop of potatoes on his plate.

"We learned something interesting talking to the Italians camped four dunes over. There's a place called Paradise Canyon about thirty miles inland on the road going east. It's a palm grove where people camp next to a clear freshwater pond, clothing optional. The couple thought it deserves its name, Paradise Canyon," I reported.

"I need fresh water badly. My skin is painfully dry. We don't have the water supply we need under these conditions. I love this beach but look at my thighs," Gerri said, opening her legs and showing red, rough patches from her knee to her crotch.

"Let me rub some oil on those," Steve said.

"Fuck off. This is beginning to itch," Gerri said. "How do you get there?"

"The guy just said drive east, you'll know it when you see it," I answered.

"I'd like to go there tomorrow," Gerri said. "The beach is great. But I'm feeling salt encrusted, and the shade of some palm trees sounds mighty appealing."

"Shouldn't we resupply ourselves before we head off to a place we know has no stores or facilities?" Jan interjected.

"Yeah, let's make a list, and we can do the shopping and preparation. Tomorrow we can take off after breakfast. Next stop Paradise Canyon," Steve said as I knew he was thinking about Gerri's red thighs.

"I'll go to town and do shopping for supplies for a week, including a lot of drinking water," I said as Jan nodded her approval.

Our shopping list included chocolate, ground almonds, and butter, so we could make a *majoun*, the Moroccan hash candy, to share with fellow campers.

After sunset, I pointed out the stars in the constellation Virgo. I said, "We are just an insignificant drop of dust in a vast universe but a drop of dust having lots of fun."

Jan and I had great sex. Morning and night, we were going at it, and if it weren't so hot in the tent, we would have added noon too.

The next day after more than two hours of driving east on a serpentine, paved, but potholed road through rough dry hills, Gerri said, "We must have passed it."

The barren landscape held no large trees and very little vegetation of any kind. Sometimes the road ran above dry gullies filled with rocks but no water and, at other times, through narrow valleys with high walls rising on both sides of the road.

"The guy said we'd know it when we saw it, and we haven't seen anything but rocks. So I conclude we haven't gotten there yet. There were no turnoffs and nothing except 'Hell Valley' along this road," I answered.

"It's hot and dry and lifeless here. We haven't seen one other vehicle and only those two men riding burros crossing the road an hour ago. Are you sure those people weren't putting you on?" Gerri continued.

"Have faith. If you seek paradise, you've got to keep searching and not be discouraged," I said.

Just then, as we crested a hill, the tops of palm trees appeared below along with a blast of cooler air. The green trees contrasted with the brown surroundings. The road descended to the valley floor and followed a stream leading to a few vans parked under palms at a wide spot.

"Far-out, there it is, ye of little faith," I said.

Steve pulled the van into the grove and parked in a previously used empty campsite.

"I'm dry, dusty, and hot so I say first stop is a swim before we make camp," Steve said as he reached into the back of the van and took out two towels.

"Get me to fresh, non-salt water," Gerri said, turning toward the road and beginning to walk in the direction of the stream.

A trail led across the road and a short distance to the other side, where it emerged at a pool below some flat rocks. A couple sat naked on the rocks and called out, "Hello," as Steve dropped his clothes and dove in, followed within seconds by the splash of Gerri hitting the water behind him. Jan and I followed. The cool, clean water sent a chill down my spine and washed away the dust from the drive. The water had a revitalizing effect. As I surfaced, I took Jan in my arms and gave her a kiss as we stood chest deep in the stream.

"You two from Melbourne?" Gerri asked the blonde woman on the rocks.

The muscular man with reddish hair, freckled, deeply tanned skin, and high cheekbones wearing nothing but a smile responded, "How ga know?"

"Ga jus' cand hear it," Gerri replied, imitating his Melbourne cadence and pronunciation.

We three remained in the water while the three Aussies caught up.

I heard Gerri say, "When you were at the festival, did you get any of the bad acid?"

"This is Max and Joan. This is Steve, my bloke, and Fred and Jan," Gerri said.

"Pleased to meet you," Joan said. "Actually, Gerri has been talking highly of you. On your honeymoon I hear."

"What a place to honeymoon. Look around, a totally unspoiled swimming hole. Is this an oasis?" Steve asked.

"Technically no," Max began and launched into a long explanation about oases and palm groves and how they weren't the same, and it had to do with size and water source.

Max worked as an engineer on big projects around the world for long time spans but then had enough money to travel for years when the project ended. He and Joan had been traveling for two years in a specially equipped van Max customized. Max was working on their van's motor, so they were camped here for three weeks.

I jumped into the pool again, appreciating the surroundings. I looked in the four directions. From the east, the creek came down and hit a bend and bent again to create this pool and swimming area.

After going around a large rock, it spread out and became shallow again.

After a while, Joan said, "Look, we have cocktail hour at our campsite most nights at five p.m. The sun goes down early in this narrow canyon, and the moon is getting fuller. But five is our cocktail hour. Most of the people camped here come over, and we share the shit. Please, make sure to come. You'll know it's time because I ring a Chinese gong five times." She then stood up, brushed herself off, said, "See ya," and dove into the pool, swam directly to the other side, got up on the bank where she put on a pair of sandals and a robe, and walked off.

Max looked at his complicated waterproof watch, and said, "It's two thirty p.m. now. I'd better head back. Drinkers or smokers, mates?"

"We're both and we can bring both," I said.

Back at our campsite, my nap came to an end when a loud bong resonated through the palm grove, a short pause, and another bong. Our campsite pleased me because our tent was far enough away so Jan's screaming orgasms wouldn't be heard, and we could continue our uninhibited lovemaking.

An hour ago, the sun disappeared behind the steep cliffs to the west, and as Max warned, the temperature dropped.

Jan came over carrying a bottle of tequila and taking an empty water bottle poured it about half full. "This should help get people get loose," she said.

Gerri just completed rolling four large cone-shaped European hash and tobacco joints. Putting one into the small purse she was carrying, she held the other three out and said, "Bombs away."

"Remember to bring warm clothes," Steve said.

Max and Joan had a premiere site with benches on three sides of a large firepit. Indian fabric covered their shade area and a private area next to their van with an awning covering it. Max was standing at a table wearing a flowered shirt and khaki shorts with a bottle of Tanqueray gin in his hand and a cutting board full of sliced limes in front of him. On the other half of the table was an array of bottles, two French red wines, cognac, Irish whiskey, vodka, and a pitcher containing what looked like a fresh fruit punch.

"Welcome, newcomers. Quiet, everyone," Joan said as we entered the encampment.

Surprisingly, the people stopped talking and turned toward her.

She said, "This is Gerri, she's Australian."

And two couples standing at the edge shouted "Hurrah!"

"This is Jan, she's from California."

And the same four shouted, "Hurrah!" again.

"This is Steve and Fred is over there. We welcome them to Paradise Canyon. Now let's drink and smoke up."

Everyone resumed his or her previous conversations, and I took a joint over to Max and, holding it out, said, "Want to smoke?

"No thanks, mate, I'm an alcohol man. My lungs can't take smoking anything," Max replied as I lit the joint and took a hit.

Steve appeared at my side with his hand out for the next toke.

"Do you eat hash?" I inquired as Steve passed the joint to a woman standing on his left.

"Definitely. But the next day can be as bad as a hangover. Once I couldn't even get out of bed," Max replied as he handed a gin and tonic to the women, who in return handed him the joint, which he passed back to me.

Another man joined the circle and took the joint after Steve's second hit.

"I'm Pascal, one of the crazy Brazilians," he said as he passed the joint back and nodded toward three men and two women dressed in bright green, red, and yellow, kicking a soccer ball in a small circular clearing.

"Guess you heard I'm Fred," I said as I accepted the joint back.

"I say they are crazy because they would rather kick a ball than smoke this fine hash," Pascal continued. "Also, they are embarrassed because they have so little English."

"I agree they are crazy," I said, sitting down as I thought, *I'm always sitting when I smoke this hash. Standing is so difficult.*

Six groups occupied the palm grove, and as the evening went on, they came to Max and Joan's cocktail hour, which lasted past midnight.

Besides the six Brazilians who slept in one large tent, there was a couple from Ireland who were so fair skinned they couldn't go to the swimming hole until the sun went behind the hills about 4:00 p.m. The woman was attractive in a full-bodied way, and the man was big and beefy with a loud laugh and always held a drink in his hand. Two couples from France were parked a bit far from the others. The French group looked gaunt and extremely thin, and Joan told Gerri they were heroin addicts and to keep them away from their campsite. Two athletic English college students got roaring drunk, made some sort of fuss by trying to climb a palm tree, and left the party early.

Max and Joan, the unofficial camp monitors and grove historians, developed a technique of sitting back-to-back comfortably leaning on each other. Max told stories of recent excitement like when the Dutch guy tried to run off with the Italian's girlfriend.

Max intervened and stopped their budding knife fight. Max said, "Let the girl decide."

And the girl said, "Why not both of you as my lovers?"

The men agreed. They stayed three more days in a ménage à trois until they left together for further adventures.

The flames from the fire made shadows jump through the trees around us. Later, only Jan, Gerri, Steve, and I sat with Joan and Max, absorbing the fire's warmth. None of us spoke as we stared into the flames and red-hot coals, listening to the crackle of the burning dried palm fronds.

"I'm going to get the Milarepa book and I'll read a story. How about it?" I said.

Steve hoarsely said, "Good idea. Water, please, bring water."

When I returned, Jan reached out to take the bottle of water. As the water passed around, the group revived, and Gerri stood up and stretched.

Max said, "I'm going to sleep but make yourselves at home and stay as long as you like."

Steve walked away to pee, and Gerri did the same and squatted down next to him.

"Great having a long skirt. I can pee just about anywhere a man can," Gerri said.

"It's cold away from the fire. I didn't realize how cold the night would be," Steve said as they returned to where Joan was seated across from me while I shined my flashlight on the open book.

Jan was drinking what looked like a tequila drink with a blanket spread across her lap and another draped around her shoulders. Our faces were glowing red from heat of the fire.

I read to the stoned group with Joan sitting close, paying rapt attention, "Before you fully master the awakeness within, engage not in blind and foolish acts."

After the reading finished, Steve, Gerri, and Jan went back to the campsite, but Joan started asking me questions about Milarepa and Buddhism.

Joan said, "We've been smoking your hash, try some of ours." She took out a small ceramic pipe. Joan pressed the question of whether a person has to submit to a guru because so much of the story recounted Milarepa reflecting on his guru Marpa.

I said, "Milarepa taught ultimately your self-mind is your guru, so having a guru isn't necessary if you are in touch with your mind."

Joan questioned, "If your self-mind is your guru, perhaps you need a guru to get there."

I contemplated her question as I crawled into the tent next to Jan.

Waking up groggy the next day, I picked up Jan's wristwatch; it said 12:30 p.m.

At the Camper, a note read, "Gone swimming," in rainbow-colored letters. I took out the hidden key, got inside, and poured myself a glass of freshly squeezed orange juice. I looked at the golden sandstone cliffs with streaks of orange sparkling in the bright sun. As I sat preparing to join the swimmers, I heard a cheer from the pool and a cry of, "Well done."

A half hour later at the pool, the two English students—Rod and Claude—were sitting with Jan, Steve, and Gerri while Joan and Max swam in the pool. My first dive into the refreshing stream cleared my head and revived my body. When I surfaced, Joan was standing in chest deep in the water as Max climbed back onto the rock ledge with the others.

"I appreciated your talking to me last night. It meant a lot to me," Joan said in a low voice. Her tan body didn't have any lines from bras or blouses.

The fully browned, blond beauty queen was seeking wisdom from me, and I happily obliged. The question of the need for a guru to reach enlightenment resonated as Steve also a seeker needed a guru.

"We read a Milarepa story every night after dinner. Come by our campsite, I'll be reading one tonight," I said.

"We cancelled cocktail hour tonight, so I'll come over for sure," Joan replied as she ducked under the water and swam to the rock ledge and climbed out.

On the ledge, I sat down next to Jan. "You know what time you crept in last night, 5:30 a.m.," she said.

"It's hard to believe, but we got into a discussion about Milarepa. I gave Joan a lot of background. She's really interested and I invited her to hear a story tonight and she said she would," I said.

"I believe you because I rubbed your dick when you fell asleep and smelled my hand, and you were clean," Jan said. "The bad news is I got my period, and I feel like shit. Sometimes it really is a curse, and this one is starting like a super curse. I'm going back to lie down in the Camper."

"I've got some pills if you need them," Joan said as everyone on the ledge could hear what she said.

"What was the cheer about?" I said, changing the subject as Jan lowered herself into the water and breast stroked across the stream.

"See the rock up there?" Rod said, pointing to a ledge sticking out over the pool about forty feet up. "Well, Claude said I couldn't climb up there and jump into the pool, so I showed him I could."

"I said dive into the pool and you jumped, so you'll have to do it again," Claude said in a whiny, nasal voice.

The next three days passed with combination of writing, reading, eating, drinking, swimming, and some fucking as Jan's period subsided. Seeing just a narrow patch of stars above the valley made the sky more mysterious. The light of the moon reflected in odd patterns, creating illusions of giants standing among the cliffs.

One night, the Brazilians got out their musical instruments, including some improvised scratchers and shakers, and got a rhythm going. Soon, everyone was dancing madly around the flames. We joined this gathering of tribes celebrating in the firelight with intoxicants and dance. The women and men ended up topless, moving alone and in various combinations with each other. The whole gyrating group exuded love and friendliness with not even a hint of hostility, competition, or jealously.

Joan continued to show interest in Milarepa and talked to me about the Buddhist teachings. One afternoon, she came over while I was looking over the tarot cards Steve and I drew. I told her Gail took the printed tarot deck with her, so one of our projects in Khemis was drawing our own deck from memory.

"Can a reading from the cards predict the future?" Joan asked. "Because I have a question I'd like to ask."

"The cards help put a person in touch with the universe," I replied.

"We have a big opportunity and I'm wondering if Max and I should take advantage of it."

"Let's see what the cards say," I replied. "Keeping your question in mind, mix the cards and turn half around. Then mix the cards again," I said while relighting a roach. "Now cut the cards with your left hand and turn over the top card."

With some hesitation, Joan slowly turned over the top card. The tower turned upside down appeared, depicting a building struck by lightning with two figures crashing toward the ground.

"This looks awful," said Joan. "It seems to say my question is heading toward a disaster."

"Not necessarily," I said. "An upside-down card symbolizes the reverse of the card's usual meaning. This could mean something being built rather than destroyed.

"Place the next card above the tower. Your aim or ideal in the matter questioned."

Joan turned the hermit also upside down.

"The hermit card refers to me. This connects me to you and Max in regard to your question.

"The next card indicates the foundation of the matter," I said.

Joan turned over justice. She said, "I like the way the woman in the picture looks with the scales and the sword."

Next Joan turned the lovers and the hanged man. Looking at the four cards in front of her, Joan said, "This looks like a positive reading to me. Positive energy. I'm going to tell Max about our reading, although he's cynical about this sort of thing." Joan got up, gave me a hug, and walked toward her campsite.

In the evening, Max cooked a delicious fish over the open flames, and Joan baked a lemon pound cake for dessert. We gave them directions to Khemis telling them to stop on the way north when they left Morocco.

After dinner, I said to Steve, "Tomorrow's our last day here. Let's expand the cocktail hour tomorrow night by making a *majoun* for everyone in the campground. We'll be back in Khemis in four days, so we don't need the extra hash we have with us."

"Great idea. We've got the ingredients—peanuts, chocolate, butter, sesame seeds, and dates. We can mix them together and melt them in a pot adding hash," Gerri chimed in.

"When people come to the cocktail hour tomorrow, we'll spoon them some candy and away we'll go. Total peace and love and a grand farewell to Paradise Canyon," Steve said, making a sad face.

The next day, the mood shifted from shear bliss to anticipation of the end of sheer bliss. No one outwardly acted any differently, and the meals, reading, drawing, and swimming went on as usual but questions like, "Where should we pack this?" signaled the end of our stay.

Making the *majoun* took my mind off the future, of which I was unsure. Jan would leave. The success of our honeymoon did not blot out our irreconcilable paths. I was staying in Morocco, and Jan would never consider moving her girls here. I knew the ferry back to Malaga would end our connection. I couldn't leave because I wanted to keep my long hair and might not be readmitted. Steve and Gerri seemed committed to life in Khemis, but what the reunion with Gail and Patsy would bring remained a mystery.

"Add more butter," Gerri said as I stirred the ingredients in our largest pot.

"Nifty," I said as I dropped another large spoonful into the mixture.

"Everything seems in order. After breakfast tomorrow, we can take down the tent and pack away our remaining gear. If we leave early enough, we might make it home in one day," Steve said, sitting down, watching us prepare the hash candy mixture.

"Be in the present," Gerri said, but I sensed her anticipation for what might lie ahead.

With the first sound of the gong, we four walked to Max and Joan's camp carrying the pot of *majoun* and our warmer clothes.

"Here, I want you to try our candy. Since you didn't smoke our hash, I don't want you to miss this sweet *majoun*," I said to Max as soon as we arrived.

"Sure, mate. How much should I take?" Max answered as he looked into the dark mixture taking up half the pot.

"Start with a big lovin' spoonful," I said, handing Max a clean spoon, which he took and dipped into the pot. "Can you dig it?"

"Here, let's take a spoonful," Steve said as he distributed spoons to Gerri, Jan, Joan and took one for himself. When we filled our spoons, Steve held up his in the gesture of a toast and said, "To peace and love. Did you know *majoun* means love potion in Arabic.

"I heard it is hash candy tonight," Pascal said, and he and the other five Brazilians lined up for their spoonfuls.

The four French junkies came over and each got a spoonful but left for their campsite after eating it. The Irish couple came over, and when I explained what was in the *majoun*, both took a spoonful. Everyone in the grove participated.

About a half hour later, a booming voice started to sing, "Oh, they're hanging them in Ireland for the wearing of the green." Sean, the big Irish guy, sang the whole song at the top of his voice and fell on his knees and started to bawl like a baby.

Lynn, his girlfriend, dropped beside him but, instead of comforting him, started to bawl as well; the two lay on the ground holding each other and crying. The others stepped around Lynn and Sean, who weren't crying any longer but were whispering as they continued to lie on the ground.

Bang! the noise of something breaking came from the French people's camp. *Bang!* something else being smashed. Max led me and several others over to the French camp, where one woman was standing naked with a hammer in her hand, hitting the side of the Citroën and screaming in French. If any of the others approached her, she threatened them with the hammer.

One of the men came over to Max and said in broken English, "Bummer. She thought we had more stash in the secret compartment, but now it's gone. She's mistaken, she doesn't remember we used it. It's nothing to worry about…we can handle this."

As we walked back to the campsite, I noticed Joan sitting off by herself, staring into the brush; she said, "Plants take sunlight and water and air and produce beautiful blooms. It's magic. Look, a perfect red flower."

I didn't see any red flower where Joan was looking or anywhere nearby. I did see a red wrapper from a popular Moroccan candy bar stuck on a plant where someone carelessly threw it away.

Steve and Gerri excused themselves. I could tell the *majoun* made them both horny.

I walked over to Jan, who said, "Let's get back to our tent, but I'd like to walk down to the stream first to sit there quietly for a bit."

She put her arm around my waist, and we walked together to a place on a log, where we looked out over the water. Jan turned and kissed me softly. Just as the embrace got passionate, a rustling in the dry leaves caught our attention. A large black scorpion was crawling toward us with its stinger raised, ready to strike.

Jan gasped and jumped backward and said, "Kill it. It looks deadly."

I replied, "We Buddhists don't kill," and calmly picked up a palm frond.

When the scorpion got on the palm frond, I carried it to the edge of the clearing and dropped it into the brush. Jan sat down again, and I reached to kiss her when we again heard the rustling. This time, the scorpion came out in a rush and looked angry.

I stepped aside, held the frond like a golf club, and yelling, "Fore!" swung and hit the scorpion across the stream. "I always was a good shot with a four iron."

Jan screamed again, "If that scorpion comes back, I won't kill the scorpion! I'll kill you!"

I replied with an incantation, "Mother Nature, please keep your realm in harmony and do not send the scorpion toward us again."

The incantation and the golf stroke didn't allay Jan's fears, and she said, "Let's get out of here."

Meanwhile, Claude and Ron arranged a game of *fútbol* (soccer) with Max and the Brazilians and shouted as they kicked the ball. One of the Brazilian women took the ball and dribbled the length of the court, causing Max to fall over when he tried to intercept her. Crossing in front of the goal, she kicked it into the net in a flash. In a typical gesture of success, she lifted her shirt and ran around the field in celebration as the other players fell down spent from the physical exertion.

The Irish couple was gone, and no banging came from the French camp. The Brazilians began to play music with more guitars and low percussion. One woman was singing in a mournful voice. Max and Joan went to their Camper with sex in their minds.

I opened the door of our tent and ushered Jan inside as a cloud crossed the moon and the canyon fell into darkness. A chill went down my spine. The honeymoon was ending. As we stripped off our clothes, we touched each other with an urgency and energy tinged with desperation and sadness.

During our lovemaking, Jan cried out, "Oh, Fred! Oh, Fred! Oh, Fred, oh, God."

I was thrilled to know I was only one step from God.

We rose early, but even after preparing breakfast, we couldn't say goodbye to Max and Joan because they were gone. We left a note saying we expected a visit from them in Khemis.

After driving back to the coast, we decided to head north and so we could reach Khemis the next day by noon. Jan especially liked the idea because she wanted more time in Tangier to buy more gifts for her daughters.

We spoke little during the trip north. Each person looking out a window, but it was plain everyone's mind focused on the future rather than the pleasures of where we just were. Steve pulled the van into a scenic view spot overlooking the mouth of a river with large gray storks wading along the riverbanks. I took over the driving.

"The way the hash affected everyone at the palm grove surprised me," Steve said. "I always thought marijuana and hash brought out peace and love, but yesterday I saw they just bring out hidden areas in a person's mind. The way those French people reacted scared me."

"We find peace and love but not everyone will react the same way. I believe ultimately hash will bring out the good, but a person may have to work through some dark experiences to finally reach a peaceful place," I answered as we passed a caravan of camels walking along the roadside, carrying heavy loads.

"I'm not sure about using hash to work through dark places. Hash often confuses my thinking, and some of the images seem as real as this van. But later I realize they were projections of my mind," Steve said.

"Milarepa says exploring your own mind can be dangerous if you don't do it in the right way. I'm sure meditation, spiritual study, and self-awareness are enhanced when combined with kief, hash, and acid," I replied.

"I wonder. Last night troubles me because we don't know what might come forth. If a person is on hash, they might not be able to cope with what's revealed as they themselves might not even expect or be aware it's there," Steve said.

"I guess you'll stop smoking now," Gerri called out from the back seat.

"No danger of that I'll wager," I said.

"I'm serious. The Moroccans say, 'Hash will make you crazy,' and we saw a little of how it can bring out craziness last night. But

I'm still going to smoke hash. Don't worry, I'm not crazy yet," Steve said.

"I think the opposite, hash can be a shortcut to enlightenment," I chimed in.

When I turned the Camper into the alley leading to our house, four neighborhood dogs ran toward us, barking as they always did as the van passed.

After I unlocked the door, I saw most of Gail's personal property no longer inside. A note dated a week earlier in the center of the mat read, "Dear ones, I am returning to Spain with Patsy. This life is not for us. I plan to go to London and probably go back to California. Gail."

"Frankly, I'm glad she wasn't here," Gerri said. "Her leaving frees us to continue our life in Morocco."

"It's like the Zen story. Her leaving is neither good nor bad. It just is," Steve said. "Let's unpack the van, I need a pipe."

Two days later, Jan and I were in the van on the way to Tangier. Jan would be taking the ferry to Malaga and our time together coming to an end. My eyes welled up as I held back tears. I didn't want to lose a smart, sexy, wonderful girlfriend. Months earlier, while exploring a used bookstore in Tangier, I found a first edition of *Alice in Wonderland.* I gave it to Jan as a parting gift because she loved books, and I knew she would treasure it.

I wondered would this be the last time I might see her. I did not want our romance to end. However, she needed to return to her daughters. I needed to return to the path of enlightenment. She had real responsibilities I had none. Maybe I could visit her in Spain, but from this fork in the road, our paths diverged.

We stood on the pier holding each other while a line of passengers boarded the ferry. I kissed her as long as I could, but while I waved goodbye, she sailed out of sight.

In the van on the way home, I cried when I heard The Rolling Stones singing the Smokey Robison song, "My Girl."

"I've got sunshine on a cloudy day / When it's cold outside / I've got the month of May / I guess you'd say / What can make me feel this way? / My girl, my girl, talkin' 'bout my girl..."

A siren woke me out of my sad memory. I looked across the yard and saw an ambulance waiting for the guards to open the gate. I could see through the back window the Argentinean strapped to a gurney in the back. *Adios, amigo.*

CHAPTER 7

Do You Believe in Magic?

Joining the Sangha and renouncing worldly life is necessary in order to devote your whole life and all your energies toward the dharma.
—Tenzin Palmo

Day drifted into day. After breakfast, I still felt the numbing effect of my morning pills. I looked around at the other men wearing dirty, brown wool djellabas and leather slippers with tire treads for soles. Walking with heads down, little interaction between them. Some inmates looked like they might be under thirty, most looked older with some over seventy; nearly all skinny, fragile, and physically weak. I guessed the facility held about sixty to eighty men.

The night following the removal of the Argentinean, as I lay on my bed with two smelly feet inches away from my face, I reflected on the afternoon's scene. Maybe I should cause a disturbance and be taken away from the depressing routine of my present captivity. I'd be transported to another facility where I would have an opportunity to demonstrate I had recovered my connection to reality. I'd explain I knew my imagined appointment to see King Hassan II resulted from smoking too much hash. I rejected this course of action as I might end up subjected to a lobotomy or electric shock or confined to a padded cell. I couldn't take the risk of putting myself in a worse situation; besides, I was sure any day now, the American Embassy would intervene on my behalf.

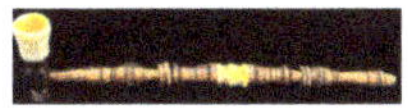

I thought about Jan's departure for Spain. Steve and Gerri took a three-week trip away from Khemis. When they returned, I told them I'd been meditating for an hour each morning after doing a hatha yoga session and my days were blissful.

I placed the round clay tagine cooker on top of three tiles in front of us and said, "I mark this day as auspicious because we are prepared to seek enlightenment as a serious endeavor. I know we'll need to overcome many obstacles, but what other endeavor except the Bodhisattva's path to Buddhahood is even worthy of consideration. May this food give us strength as we move ahead on the path. May all beings be happy."

Gerri said, "I am so happy to be part of this quest. Now let's dig in, I'm starved and the veggies look so good."

"We have some parts of our practice in place, but we need more of a routine, more form to our days. We should do a complete hatha yoga session. We need to have structured times to meditate. We want to study spiritual books and, of course, read Milarepa. I need a pipe of hash just to contemplate how much we'll need to do," Steve said.

From his tone, both Gerri and I grasped his seriousness.

"I want time for crafts every day, an unstructured time when I can embroider, draw, write letters, and do things with my hands. After dinner is a perfect time to read serious teachings and smoke hash of course," Gerri said.

"I suggest *Tibetan Yoga and Secret Doctrines* as our evening reading. I'm sure there's a wealth of knowledge that will enhance our understanding of some of the philosophical parts of Milarepa's stories," Steve said.

"Morning hatha yoga is essential before it gets too hot. While you were gone, I developed a series of postures from the yoga book. The three of us can go up on the roof, and I'll show you the routine. I start with ten salutes to the sun. You can add and suggest if you want," I said, reaching down and picking up the yellow yoga self-taught book with a Buddha seated calmly in the lotus posture on the cover.

The effects of the hash and the flickering light turned the room into a magical cave. From our dress, we looked like journeying pilgrims in biblical times.

I starting reading, "This book of seven books of wisdom of the yoga path I dedicate to them that shall succeed me in the quest on earth."

"That's us, Evans-Wentz dedicated this book to us. We are on the quest," Steve said.

I continued, "The foundation of all is uncreated, uncompounded, independent, beyond mental concept and verbal definition… To realize it is to attain Buddhahood…"

Steve was staring with an agitated, wild look in his eyes and said, "It's all right here. This book has the wisdom and also the methods used by Tibetans to attain it, experience it. This is the formula for enlightenment that obviously can't be reached overnight, but with super effort, to use Gurdjieff's term, we can do it. Did you feel the impact of what you just read?"

"Yes, I accept the challenge to reach enlightenment, but I know I'm infected with the 'five poisons' of lust, anger, selfishness, delusion, and jealously. I'm not naive about how difficult it will be to overcome them and get them out of my life completely," I said. "It's a good thing hash goes so well with Buddhism."

Each day, we fell into a gentle rhythmical pattern with slight variations. Sometimes there would be almonds and honey with the morning couscous and some days yogurt and dates. Some days, we would draw with rapidograph pens or work with watercolors and lead pencils. The vegetables in the tagines varied, depending on what the local farmers brought to the market. Lunch was full of surprises like sardines, cheeses, or peanut butter or just nibbling on almonds, dates, and oranges. Each week on the day following the souk, Sunday, we took the straw mats and cardboard tables out to the courtyard. Steve and I mopped the floors with a scented mixture Mina had advised us to use. We initiated weekly trips to Larache for hot showers, where I washed my long hair with a ten-cent packet of shampoo. We worked together on an ongoing embroidery project, each of us embroidering in bright silk colors on a drawing of a mountain lake Gerri sketched on cloth. We each had our own notebooks for drawings, poems, thoughts, and the occasional tarot reading and played a daily Parcheesi game. Steve and I also played chess, Steve usually winning. On our roof, I built a shade structure of bamboo poles I cut from the banks of a nearby stream. I wove bamboo leaves on the poles, creating shade for the hot summer days.

At night, we stared at the sky, watching the moon wax and wane. On full moon nights, the landscape was beautifully lit, and on moonless nights, I marveled at the billion stars.

One morning, I said, "It looks like the landlord's family is opening the two closed buildings on the other side of the courtyard and moving in for the summer."

The family moved into the buildings, which added a festive atmosphere and additional security to our living arrangement. Fatima, his wife, had given birth to thirteen children and was very pregnant with the fourteenth. Her eldest daughter, Jasmina, who had been "divorced" by her husband and sent back to her family in disgrace, always accompanied her.

I missed having a girlfriend but knew other women would come along. Milarepa's songs and tantric yoga taught the positive aspects of celibacy. I was transmuting sexual energy to make up for the absence of a sexual partner. I made a point of showing no interest in the Moroccan women, knowing that could only lead to trouble.

One night after dinner, Steve said, "Did you hear in this morning's story how Milarepa attended a feast and a celebration? Even he had parties to attend and enjoy."

"You know I was thinking the same thing. No special days or holidays. My birthday is August fifteenth and should be a holiday anyway. What's the date? Do we know?" Gerri asked.

"Gerri and I arrived in Khemis on July fourteenth, a Friday. And yesterday was our third souk, so today is Sunday, August fourth," Steve said.

"Feasts, celebrations, special events, let's make the whole month of August special. We'll work up from now to Gerri's birthday August fifteenth, and we'll end our celebrations with my birthday September first. Most Moroccan holidays are at least a week, so why shouldn't we have a month? Let's take acid tomorrow to start it off," I said.

In the evening as the hash pipe came out, Steve took the *Secret Doctrine* book and read, "The supreme path of discipleship, the precepts of the gurus, the ten things that must be practiced… By quitting one's own country and dwelling in foreign lands, one should acquire practical knowledge of nonattachment."

Exactly, I thought, *we are practicing so many foundation precepts for reaching the higher meditative states and enlightenment. I live in a foreign land, nonattached, ready to go anywhere with only a backpack. This stone house served as my cave where I studied the most important topic, "The road to enlightenment," with a sangha of two other dedicated seekers.*

I watched my mind shift to another line from Milarepa. I was experiencing "the mother-like essence of mind." Hash helped me achieve the crucial control of my own thoughts, a key to the teachings of Buddhism. When we smoked hash, little talk followed because words couldn't capture the experience or adequately describe it. I saw this as the state "beyond all play words" Milarepa sang about.

In the background, I heard Steve read, "The ten grievous mistakes, for a religious devotee to be idle and indifferent, instead of persevering when all the circumstances favorable for spiritual advancement are present, is a grievous mistake."

Gerri opened her eyes and said, "I remember Milarepa saying, 'There is no idleness in the life of a devotee.' We better sleep now as tomorrow's acid trip will start our holiday of August. I see our special activities as adding to, not subtracting from, our quest."

The next day, as we relaxed still recovering from the acid trip, I jumped up with a start in response to sharp rapping on the front door. "*Momentito, momentito!*" I shouted and pulled on my pants.

Michelle, a Belgian woman in her midthirties, and Todd, an Englishman ten years her junior, a veteran of the London music scene who I met on the beach at Taghazout stood outside. Michelle's long, dark hair flowed over her shoulders. She looked beautiful, and I would have made a pass, but she was with Todd. He also had long, dark hair, a wiry body, and sharp facial features.

"Hello, welcome! Good to see you." Turning inside, I said, "Michelle and Todd are here."

I saw Michelle's daughter, a twelve-year-old girl, standing to the side, and I said, "Sorry I forgot your name. I'm Fred."

The girl looked up and replied, "Lola."

Usually the household would have been awake at this hour, perhaps 10:00 a.m., but as a result of yesterday's acid trip, we were lying in bed. The tripping had us on the roof in our sleeping bags looking at the stars in the clear sky until practically sunrise.

Gerri asked Lola, who had her mother's dark good looks, if she wanted to do an art project and set her up with pens and paper on the roof. Todd, Steve, and Michelle sat down on the straw mat in the front room.

I said, "I'll make some tea and bring in some water. Do you need anything special?"

"Sorry to wake you. We're coming north from the southern Moroccan beaches. What a life. We only broke away because we ran out of hash and kief. We're on our way back to El Majaz on the Mediterranean, east of Tangier. A friend is staying in our house and taking care of our dog," Todd said as he watched Steve take out a big piece of hash and heat the edge in a candle flame.

Michelle reached down and picked up the hash and rubbed it with her finger and smelled it. "Good shit," she said.

Lola, who came down from the roof, asked, "Where is your watchdog?"

"We don't have a dog. Our neighbor's dogs protect the compound," Steve replied. "We have each other."

"I miss our dog, Ute, more than anything else when I'm on the beach," Michelle interjected.

I was listening as I put down the metal tray holding the pot of brewed tea. "We're in a special month of celebration, and yesterday we took acid. It was beautiful but exhausting," I said as I thought back to how colors swirled, merged, and broke apart again as I looked at Shiva seated calmly with the Ganges River flowing out of the top of his head.

"Why a month of celebration? What's the occasion?" Todd asked as he slumped back against the wall.

Gerri told them, "My birthday and two years away from Australia. We practice a loving, healthy, spiritual lifestyle, so we need some spice and fun."

"Day after tomorrow is my birthday. Can we horn in on your celebration and have some type of party on my birthday?" Michelle said, showing a mouth of white teeth.

The guests added to the celebratory atmosphere. Lola organized a special art project where each person drew on an area surrounding a large lake and garden she and Michelle were drawing on a big piece of cardboard. Michelle insisted on cooking dinner and turned our regular vegetables into a gourmet treat with cumin and thyme she had with her. Todd smoked hash continuously and talked about the London music scene. In his British accent, he talked about The Rolling Stones who I saw in concert in Amsterdam a year ago. Steve and I spent our time on the mat with him while Gerri, Michelle, and Lola had activities on the roof and in the kitchen together. Even with guests, the next day, we three still did our morning yoga and read a Milarepa story.

On Michelle's birthday, we got up early and sat around the morning teapot. Each person produced beautifully wrapped items Michelle opened with shock and joy. I gave her a Tibetan prayer flag. Gerri gave her a drawing she made of Michelle, capturing her dark, sparkling eyes. Steve gave her a blue Goulimine bead, a glass bead historically used by the Berbers for trade. Lola bought a bracelet she gave wrapped in a woven scarf. Todd gave her a beautiful straw basket, which Michelle stood up to open. Inside was a handwoven Berber tribal dress. It even had the authentic desert smell.

Michelle started to cry but laughed instead and said, "Where's the acid?"

Steve opened a small envelope and dropped five tabs of windowpane on a white plate, wet his finger, and picked up a tab and put it on his tongue, saying, "Happy birthday, Michelle. Let this celebration be auspicious and lead to connections as only tripping together can."

Looking at those tabs of windowpane, I thought back to the scene when we scored them and remembered saying, "I'm sure we'll spread a lot of love," and now we were.

After swallowing my tab, I passed the plate to Todd and Michelle, saying, "I agree, I read the tarot cards yesterday and I see this trip as just the beginning of our being connected."

Michelle and Todd each took a tab on their fingers and put it in their mouths then turned and kissed.

Michelle said, "I see us connected in a powerful way. Thank you and may our enlightenment be furthered."

I left the main room and went to do a series of yoga asanas, waiting for the acid to kick in. Michelle and Todd sat together saying nothing, just looking into each other's eyes.

As night fell, I brought out the hash pipe and said, "Let me read a short Sufi story, and we can have some dinner."

"Read on but people can eat when they want. There's stew on the stove and dishes in the kitchen. I feel like I don't want to eat now, but I do want to hear some wisdom. Read on, Fred, and refill the pipe, Steve," Gerri said as her eyes closed and opened again as if she had seen a flash of light.

I read, "The superior experience and knowledge will be made available to a man or woman in exact accordance with his or her worth, capacity, and earning of it." I drifted into thoughts of being a Sufi dressed in a ragged cloak accepting other people's trash as treasure.

After the story, we gathered sleeping bags and pillows so we could enjoy the night sky. Lola seemed used to her mother tripping and made herself practically invisible throughout the day. She joined us on the roof and lay under a sleeping bag as we gasped at the shooting stars in the dark star-filled night sky.

After we settled down, I said, "There's Sirius, the dog star," pointing to a group of stars midway above the horizon.

"My constellation is our sixty-pound girl, Ute," Michelle said. "We have the greatest dog in the world, and we'll reunite with her in a few days."

I said, "I grew up with dogs, and sometimes I really miss their companionship and love."

"Look, a shooting star! There's another one. Tonight is magical," Lola said.

The next day as Todd and Michelle reloaded their Citroën, Michelle said, "Thanks so much for your wonderful hospitality. I'll never forget my thirty-sixth birthday."

"She looks real good for an old lady, don't she?" Todd said. "Thanks for the piece of hash. I like what you smoke. Any chance of buying more?"

"I sometimes make introductions if you want to buy a quantity. We'd have to arrange to meet in Tangier," I replied. "Remember, I'm a hash guru, the source, like the hermit in the tarot."

"Right now we're broke, so it's just a dream but who knows. I bet on the right deal you can make a good commission," Todd said as he closed the rear compartment door and locked it.

We hugged and Lola turned to me and said she liked our home and hoped to visit again.

Gerri said, "Good on you. We intend to stay here for a long time, so you'll be safe dropping by if you come south again."

As the Citroën pulled away, Steve turned to Gerri and me and said, "I'm exhausted. Let's make today recovery from acid trip day. Easy on any schedule."

Sitting in a circle in the late afternoon, we began what we called *"The Little Hippie Handbook"* of phrases and sayings to keep in mind. The first one suggested was, "Waiting is full," from *Stranger in a Strange Land.* I suggested something a woman named Kat said on the beach at Taghazout, "You always come down higher than when you started off."

As we were suggesting and rejecting phrases, I stood up and said, "Remember the Russian expression, 'To call a man a friend you must eat a barrel of salt with him,' or was it one thousand loaves of bread? I'm off to the store to get our loaf."

"Bring back something interesting. A surprise," Steve said.

"You know the limited choices at the store. Your surprise might be a can of mackerel in tomato sauce," I said as I closed the door behind me.

Later when I returned, I said, "I bargained for the surprise," pulling out a bag of fresh roasted peanuts.

"They're still warm and delicious," Gerri said as she cracked one open and put it in her mouth.

"They could not be fresher. They're grown in the fields near here and roasted with the bread in the shopkeeper's oven," I said.

As we were sitting around eating peanuts, Steve said, "We've heard about your days playing poker in Chicago, Fred. You played in some big stakes games, but I suggest tonight we could be playing for even more beneficial stakes, peanuts. Let's each grab a pile of peanuts, and we'll use them as chips for betting, dealer's choice. We can do something we haven't done before. A night of poker."

"Right on. I used to play poker with my aunt Louise back in Sydney. I see myself with the all peanuts if Lady Luck is with me," Gerri said.

Later I had a huge pile of peanuts, Gerri had a medium-sized pile, and Steve had just a few peanuts in his pile.

"Okay, let's divide the peanuts and eat them!" Steve said after losing a big hand.

Returning to our routine for a few days revived us. I noticed my meditation progressed after a bit of a break.

Sitting on the mats, Gerri said, "We need to go to Tangier for an overnight to buy supplies for my three-day birthday celebration. I have an idea for a surprise to start my birthday on next Wednesday eve. I'll have to go to a housewares store to buy a plastic shower curtain. On my birthday, I say two tabs of acid each. The following day, we can have special events where I'm open to suggestions."

"Sounds great to me. We need to go to Tangier for more kief. We should buy pastries, some regular supplies like peanut butter, canned cheese, and sardines. We'll get two rooms at the Miami, go to restaurants, and do some café sitting," Steve said.

I knew he already arranged for Mina to buy a blue silk embroidered caftan for Gerri.

"Tomorrow we can drive to Tangier. I'd like to check the hippie scene and perhaps visit Mustapha just to keep in touch. I'll get thirty more *rabitas* of kief from Baba's as well. Who knows whom I'll run into? I could even get lucky," I said, thinking about perhaps meeting a hippie chick.

Next day, Steve parked the Camper outside the Pension Miami.

At the desk, Mina greeted us with her big smile and hugs. "You look so tan and healthy. You're liking your life in Khemis, although I can't understand why," Mina said in Spanish.

"We're here to do some shopping so two rooms for one night. We'll drive back to Khemis tomorrow afternoon. It's my birthday, and we're buying supplies for a special celebration," Gerri said as Steve translated for Mina.

"*Feliz cumpleaños.* Happy birthday. Welcome," Mina said, pretending she didn't already know.

After dropping our gear and paying a ragged boy to watch the Camper, we threw ourselves in the energy and bustle of Tangier. We sat at a sidewalk café and ordered espresso drinks instead of mint tea. We absorbed the scene around us. A circus of belly dancers, handicapped beggars, haggling carpet dealers, one-eyed fishmongers, camel drivers, and a seemingly endless supply of pesky street peddlers inhabited the labyrinth of streets and alleys. Except for hot shower trips to Larache, we hadn't been away from Khemis since early June.

I didn't want my commitment to the ideals of Milarepa to be corrupted by Tangier life. In this atmosphere, I had to be careful to stay on the spiritual path. With my eye out for "hippie chicks," I surrendered to fate, an essential tenant of tarot and Buddhist wisdom. Ready to accept whatever would happen and "go with the flow."

Because Gerri dressed very conservatively with her hair under a scarf and an outer garment covering her purse, even as a tall Western woman, she moved with minimal hassle through the casbah. She gave off the vibration of "I'm a married woman," which gained her respect and ease of movement.

I said, "Let's meet back at the Miami around sunset, and we'll go out to a special dinner."

"Right on. Steve, let's go to the housewares store around the corner and buy the plastic shower curtain and rope. I'll take care of pastries and cakes. I'll order a special one to take back with us," Gerri said as we got up and paid the bill.

"I'm going to cruise the bookstalls and maybe stop by Mustapha's. May all beings be happy," I said as I turned toward the Café Royale. I wanted to see Mustapha as I thought perhaps I could get some especially trippy hash for the celebration weekend.

At a store across the street, my eyes fell on wooden boxes with carved covers. I could use one for art supplies. I asked the man, "*Cuanto?*" and the bargaining began. After a longer bargaining session than usual, I walked out, paying the equivalent of two dollars—a good deal given the intricate geometric patterns on the box.

Walking to the Royale, I saw Mustapha talking to a man in an army uniform and waited for the man to leave before I entered.

Mustapha placed his hand on his heart, saying, "*Salaam alaikum.*"

I returned the greeting and said, "I didn't want to walk in while you talking to a soldier."

"He was placing an order for the base. I supply them weekly, but now they want more as for some reason more soldiers are moving in and around Tangier," Mustapha said before changing the subject and asked, "You need more hash?"

"Not a big order but something special for a celebration. Do you have an ounce or two of the high, get-us-real-high, groovy quality," I asked as Mustapha led me into the hippie sales room.

Seeing the psychedelic posters from Haight/Ashbury gave me a jolt, as did hearing Cat Stevens singing, "Oh, baby, baby, it's a wild world / it's hard to get by just upon a smile…"

Mustapha went out the back door. When he returned, he handed me what looked like one hundred grams of hash in a slab as thick as book and said, "Forty dollars. This is a special shipment I shared with Achmed. You'll be smoking the same hash as The Rolling Stones. Now you will have a good celebration."

Without any hesitation, I reached through the slit in my djellaba and took two twenty-dollar bills and handed them to Mustapha.

"Thank you," he said in Arabic and Spanish.

I picked up the hash and put it into the wooden box I just bought. It fit perfectly.

At dinner at our favorite backstreet Moroccan restaurant, we talked about our day. Steve lied about everything to cover his birthday presents for Gerri and his celebration surprises.

Gerri said, "I've bought everything I need."

I couldn't wait to see Gerri's face when she saw the fine drawing pens I brought her. The special foods including cheeses from France, Holland, and Denmark; canned oysters and smoked clams; and the sweet rolls from the French bakery excited Steve.

Next day arriving back in Khemis, Gerri said, "I'll carry the cake. I don't want it dropped after I had a special inscription written on it."

After dinner, Gerri outlined her plans, "Tomorrow evening, I want to start the festivities. We will have a psychedelic experience, tying a plastic shower curtain from the ceiling and lighting the bottom on fire. The colored drips will fall into a bucketful of water making a whooshing sound. After we smoke, a celebration bowl of 'Rolling Stone' hash and read a prayer, the shower curtain will provide a mind-blowing light show," Gerri said.

Reading at random from Milarepa's songs, I read, "A good Buddhist is one who conquers all bad dispositions."

Gerri interrupted me by asking, "Does this mean a truly spiritual person must always be in a good mood?"

"Yes, radiating friendliness over the entire world," Steve said. "Remember the precept, 'Seek a delightful solitude endowed with psychic influences as a hermitage.' That's where we are right now."

I experienced us as a sangha, striving toward enlightenment together under the Buddha's teaching.

I slept fitfully, dreaming I followed a large, gray shorthaired dog through alleys and backstreets of a white-walled Moroccan neighborhood. The dog was definitely leading me. At an open archway, the dog stepped aside, and I entered. When I got inside, a bright light blinded me while a deep voice asked, "Are you a holy man who can reach enlightenment?" The light faded, and the surroundings began to weave together like being on acid. I reflected on my status as a holy man.

We completed our preparation by afternoon the next day. Wall hangings and vases of fresh flowers we brought from the Tangier market transformed my sleeping room. We spread pillows in a circle, focused on the shower curtain hanging down in the center of the room.

After an afternoon yoga session followed by twenty minutes of meditation, I said, "Let's have a pipe of Rolling Stones' hash now."

Gerri was glowing especially brightly in the light of the ten candles illuminating the room. As the pipe passed from hand to hand, we appreciated the extra impact of the special hash. By the second hit, we were slumped backward, entering relaxed dreams as we drifted into our own worlds.

"This pipe won't seem to go out," Steve said as he took his fifth hit. "Let's not even think of moving for a while."

I struck a match, walked to the center of the room, and lit the bottom of the shower curtain in several places. Flames shot up and shocked us as we sat wide-eyed with excitement. The flames died down, leaving burning plastic, giving off green, blue, yellow, and orange hues as it liquefied and melted downward, and the windowless room filled with an acrid chemical smell. As a piece of the burning curtain dripped off and sailed down to hit the water, it gave off a sizzling sound and a shot of steam. This was a psychedelic light show. *Plop*, *sizzle*, colors flashing, *plop*, *sizzle*, everything was melting together in a swirl of love, love, and love.

Repeated pounding on our front door broke the mood. No one ever knocked on our door at night. I thought I might be dreaming.

Steve stumbled to his feet, and I could hear the landlord's voice calling in Spanish as he knocked, "*Por favor*, open the door. My wife needs help."

Steve shook his head and rubbed his hands across his face. "*Momentito*." When Steve returned to us, he said, "It's the landlord. He needs something. I'll get rid of him."

I could see and hear Steve as he said, "*Buenas noches, senior*," as he opened the door.

In front of him stood the landlord, his very pregnant wife, and their twenty-year-old daughter.

"*Mi espousa*…my wife is having the baby. You must drive us to the hospital in Larache," the landlord said.

"*No es possible*. We can't drive now. There must be another way," Steve tried to communicate in Spanish.

The thought of driving the fifteen kilometers from Khemis to Larache over a curving, narrow two-lane road terrified both of us.

The landlord said, "You must drive," as his wife moaned in pain.

"*Bueno. Un momento*," said Steve and, coming back inside, said, "I have to drive them to the hospital. Fred, please ride shotgun. Gerri, you'll have to stay here because they will take up the whole back of the Camper. Where are my glasses? Is this insane?"

"You guys can make it. Cheerio. Remember Milarepa's fortitude," said Gerri as she handed Steve his djellaba.

I already put on my djellaba, and as we walked across the courtyard, I said, "Remember, we need to be able to do everything when we're stoned. The more stoned we are, the better we can do it."

Once in the Camper, Steve stopped at the intersection of the alley and the two-lane highway south to Larache. I looked back at the landlord's wife's pained face and thought briefly about the impending birth of her fourteenth child.

"Snap out of it! Focus! This is the highway. Make a left," I said.

He replied, "I'm opening my window wide. The cool air will help."

"Hash can make you more competent. Slow down a bit. Not only is your mind expanded but also your physical senses are heightened. Take these curves slow," I said in a calm voice as the Camper met an overloaded truck coming from the other direction at a sharp curve.

A loud moan from the back seat made me turn around while the landlord said in Spanish, "*No problemo. Niño pronto.*"

I encouraged Steve to pay full attention to the road. "Watch the centerline. Don't look at the thousand-foot drop on the right. 'Never hurry' is one of our sayings," I said. "We're almost halfway there."

"Birth and death, we reflect on them so much when we're reading the teachings," said Steve with a fixed stare on the centerline.

"Remember, this trip is building good Karma," I said.

As we drove up to the well-lit entrance to the Larache hospital, I let out sigh of relief. Steve stopped the Camper, but as he got out, he almost fell over and grabbed hold of the door handle to steady himself.

"Easy, big fella," I said, helping the landlord and his family out.

The landlord came over to us and said, "*Shukraan. Gracias, muchas gracias.*"

Steve asked if we should stay, but the landlord explained after the baby's birth, they would stay at their house in Larache.

The landlord bowed and said in Spanish, "Thank you so much. God be with you."

We looked at each other, smiled, and gave each other a hug.

Steve said, "What are we going to do with so much good Karma?"

When we got home, Gerri had the birthday cake on a tray in the center main room surrounded by candles.

I said, "We made it through the curves, and all is well." I stared at the inscription on the cake, "May All Beings Be at Their Ease."

Not wanting to stop the celebration, the next morning, we took two tabs acid each. Emotionally drained, we spent the entire day on the roof while I read aloud *Journey to the East* by Herman Hesse. He wrote, "As travelers on the journey, our goal was the home and the youth of the soul."

After Gerri's birthday, our daily routine became more focused. We discussed aspects of the teachings and talked about how they applied our way of life. "Was it valid to eat fish, or should we be total vegetarians?" We learned Tibetan Buddhists often ate meat, but Muslims did the butchering, which further confused the issue.

The Bodhisattva's highest goal after attaining enlightenment was aiding others. Living our peaceful and fulfilling life, we questioned our selfishness in retiring into our own Moroccan Nirvana.

About a week after the birthday celebration, as we three sat in the front room drawing, the landlord knocked on the door. His wife stood behind him, holding their newborn baby.

The landlord proudly announced in Spanish, "Mira. Look, this is my fifth son."

Gerri rushed forward and embraced the landlord's wife, shouting, "Let me see the little bugger! We heard you had a boy."

The landlord's wife smiled and pulled back the blanket covering his face.

I nodded, saying, "*Niño guapo.*"

As I looked forward to my twenty-fifth birthday on September first, I compared myself to Buddha and Jesus. With continued effort, I'd blossom before they did.

Steve and Gerri acted conspiratorial on my birthday eve. I thought they were arranging my gift. The new sleeping bag along with drawing supplies and a long-sleeved sweatshirt they gave me was just what I needed. Every aspect of my life was excellent except a not having a Shakti, a female partner. However, the symbols of the tarot and the teachings of Milarepa supported me in my celibate life. Observing Steve and Gerri, I noticed the many hassles and conflicts a relationship with a woman brought.

I started my twenty-sixth year with a tab of windowpane in my mouth. I vowed to spend the day fasting in silence. Going up to the roof, I did a double morning yoga session. Then I sat in the lotus position under the shade structure, meditating and listening to Crosby, Stills, Nash, and Young. I played the cassette over again and again. I embodied their words when they sang, "You who are on the road / Must have a code that you can live by / And so become yourself because the past is just a goodbye." In the late afternoon, I did a second full yoga session.

Steve and Gerri got involved in looking at some of the travel books among our collection, and seeing pictures of the Taj Mahal, Steve told me about his fantasy of standing outside the amazing tomb in the moonlight. I knew thoughts of travel and the exciting world outside our isolated life swirled in Steve's mind.

The day ended with the three of us sharing tea, and as we often did after a day of tripping, when night came, we lay under sleeping bags on the roof looking at the stars. I maintained my silence, not intending to talk until the following morning. Gerri cuddled close to Steve as a chill was in the night air. I could feel the change of season in my bones but was confident our happy band of seekers would continue on the path.

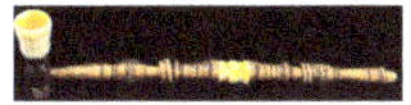

The next morning, I woke up confused as one of my bedmates accidently kicked me in the face. In Khemis, I had celebrated my twenty-fifth birthday, but what had happened to my twenty-sixth? I pondered the thought and realized it had passed during my confinement in Beni. I knew it was August when I rode to meet the king, and I'd been inside at least a month. As I got out of bed and walked with the others to line up for our morning meal, I felt a pain in my heart and became agitated. However, the morning pills calmed me down, although they didn't completely relieve my sadness.

Fred's birthday, September, 1971, Khemis Sahel, Morocco

CHAPTER 8

Fire and Rain

If you reflect on death and impermanence, you will begin to make your life meaningful.

—The Dalai Lama

My days began to blur one into another. Most of the time, I sat alone leaning against the wall, looking out at the same group of drugged isolated men.

One day, I looked down at my denim jeans and noticed a white stripe. Figuring I was hallucinating again, I didn't give it much thought. So what if my clothes changed color? I touched the white line and pulled my hand back as if I just touched a hot stove. The line was made up of tiny white clothes lice living in my pant seams. My clothes and body like every other inmate was infested with lice.

I couldn't control my black blood-sucking head lice, and I only rarely even picked one out of my hair to crush for fun. I learned about head lice in Khemis, where they appeared in our hair at about this time last year. In Beni, head lice and clothes lice, I just had to accept them.

I remembered the day after breakfast in Khemis as I lit my pipe when I moved my long hair aside and reached behind my ear. After a moment's struggle, I picked out a small crab-like bug.

"Ouch," I said as I tried to crush the bug between my thumb and index finger.

"Let me see it," Gerri said as she took the bug off my finger, dropping it on the back of her thumbnail and crushing it between the nails of her two thumbs. "Head lice. Nasty buggers."

I looked down on the spot of blood left by the crunched bug and cringed, knowing it was my blood. "I'm going to meditate and send the lice cosmic vibrations, telling them they are not welcome." Just then I reached behind my ear again and brought out another louse, which I dropped on my thumbnail and crushed, hearing a pleasing crunching sound. "We're charged with bringing enlightenment to all living things. We need to consider the lice," I continued.

"Head lice. We can't even bring along the Liberals," Steve said as he felt or imagined something crawling in his hair.

"Head lice are sentient beings," I said.

"Fuck off. We're getting the ZZZ killer DDT shampoo. We'll go to Larache tomorrow. We need to scrub this house and wash our clothes and bedding. You hypocrites, what about sardines? We're doing this today, or there will be two dead sentient beings in this house," Gerri said as she stood over Steve and me.

After complying with Gerri's nonnegotiable demands, we showered and sat with ZZZ on our scalps and towels on our heads, eradicating the lice.

Two days later after dinner, Gerri said, "This tagine smells of too much of garlic," as she put down her unfinished plate and put her head on a pillow.

"You haven't eaten anything lately, and you're laying down a lot," Steve said.

"Anything else weird?" I inquired, concerned.

"My piss seems bright orange, almost psychedelic. I'm just beat. Sometimes it feels hard to lift my head. And my head's strange inside too. I'm having bizarre thoughts," Gerri said without raising her head from the pillow.

"Bummer. It could just be the hash. We did smoke a lot lately. Hash can knock you out and play with your head," I said as I studied Gerri.

After Gerri fell asleep, Steve walked to the kitchen and said, "Remember those Moroccans told us hash makes you crazy. Maybe it's happening to Gerri."

"I don't think it's the hash. She has the classic symptoms of hepatitis. I thought her yellow skin was not just from sunbathing and orange piss means hepatitis," I replied.

"How do you treat hepatitis?" Steve asked.

"You rest, take plenty of vitamin A, rest some more," I replied.

"We should go to Tangier for supplies. We'll get some vitamins and interesting food. Besides, we've only got a four-day supply of kief left," Steve said.

The following morning after making Gerri comfortable, Steve and I drove in silence to Tangier.

"At the Blue Door, Eldon told us we should go to the British hospital first for any health problems," I said. "Let's go there."

Steve drove up to the white stone pillars marking the entrance to the hospital compound.

At the hospital entrance, a nurse asked us in a clipped British accent, "How can we be of service?"

I said, "Our friend's urine has turned orange, the whites of her eyes are yellow."

Before I could say any more, the nurse said, "She's got hepatitis," and walked away into another room. Five minutes passed before she returned with a large dark-brown glass jar filled with football-shaped black pills. "Have your friend take one pill in the morning and one a night, drink plenty of liquids, and rest," she said, handing me the jar.

Steve thanked the nurse and handed her twenty dirhams for the pills.

I stopped when I saw two attractive hippie chicks standing in front of the building next to hospital. "Wait a minute while I go over and say hello to those women," I said.

I thought maybe I would get lucky, and the women with their long hair and colorful clothes would join us for a smoke and perhaps for something more.

I met with disappointment and returned to the van, telling Steve, "Those women are hippies, but they are in love with Jesus. They don't smoke dope. The nurses and doctors here are Christian missionaries. There's a group of young Jesus freaks doing missionary work with hippies. They invited us to join them for dinner."

Steve replied, "Forget about it."

Returning home, when we entered the dark room, Gerri did not move or awaken from under her sleeping bag.

"Jesus, I'm worried. Hardly seems as if she moved since we left early this morning," Steve said in a whisper.

"You're already affected by our trip to the missionaries. I think it's the first time I ever heard you say Jesus. The nurse said rest, liquids, vitamin A, and these pills to strengthen her liver, and she'd recover. This is the rest part," I whispered.

Gerri turned on her side and looked up. "Hi, what time is it? I haven't moved all day. I feel like hell. Did you get some medicine?" she asked as she struggled to raise her head and sit up.

Steve said, "We got some pills from the missionary hospital and vitamins from the pharmacy. They said you'd be okay, but you need to rest," as he bent down, assisting her to sit up and lean back against a wall.

"I don't have the strength to move. I'd like you to help me stand up and go outside to use our toilet area," Gerri said in a low, pleading voice.

"Sure, lean on me and I'll hold you and we can walk outside," Steve said as Gerri got to her feet with difficulty, showing pain and strain on her face.

I opened the door as Steve, holding Gerri, walked in small slow steps outside and around the corner to the place behind our house to the area we used for elimination.

I straightened the bed and made a comfortable place for Gerri to lie down.

"Gerri's asleep," I said after Steve returned from washing his hands. Her labored breathing worried me, but I took the opposite tact and said, "The nurse said despite hepatitis' nasty symptoms, she should suffer no permanent damage."

"This too will pass," Steve said.

"I'll read a Milarepa story and even if Gerri can't physically hear it, just the words being in the air will assist her recovery." I read, "In the monastery of your heart, you have a temple where all Buddhas unite."

While I was reading, Gerri moaned in pain several times. Once she woke up and drank water from a glass Steve held to her lips. She gasped, "I feel like shit. I have the shits. This is shit."

As it got dark outside, I said, "We knew there would be trials and hardships on the path. Gerri is hurting. We'll do everything to return her to good health, but we need to continue our practices."

Steve answered, "Once we see Gerri's comfortable, we can go onto the roof and meditate for half an hour. Maybe tonight skip dinner, so we'll be in harmony with her. We'll meditate, smoke, and study."

"Amen, brother. Our encounter with those missionaries has affected both of us," I said.

During our meditation, my mind jumped from subject to subject. I couldn't stem the flow of thoughts and bring my mind back to my breathing. After a short time, I just sat there fantasizing without any attempt to watch or control my thoughts. What if the three of us got hepatitis at the same time and became helpless like Gerri? I finished the session with an uneasy feeling.

When Steve and I came downstairs, Gerri was laying in the exact position as a half hour before. She appeared to be asleep but stirred when we lit the candles and lamps.

She said, "Please help me go again. I need to get up and out."

Steve threw a blanket over her shoulders and, holding a kerosene lantern in one hand and Gerri with his other arm, guided her outside.

Next morning, I said, "Let's continue our fast today to honor and assist Gerri. Milarepa's meeting with Gampopa is a long story. Let's read it in sections today."

Steve nodded his approval.

We did our yoga session in the morning without Gerri and later drew get-well cards and wrote her a poem, but there was a pall over our home. Gerri hardly moved, occasionally turning to her other side or lay with her knees drawn up to her chest. She took her morning pill, but when awake, she just lay staring blankly. She never reacted to the stories being read. At the end of the day, she only said one word as she pushed herself up on one arm and called out, "Water." I thought Steve seemed both overly concerned yet at the same time not concerned enough. I pressed Steve to follow our routine and added an extra meditation session since we weren't eating.

The chill of September weather and Gerri's illness was replacing the sunny warmth of our August celebrations. The siege of the head lice ended just before Gerri announced her orange pee.

A cloud hung over the house as I picked up the story of Gampopa, "At times you may think of your native land. Whenever such yearning arises, realize that your true home is in dharma essence…"

I thought I could live with no hope and no fear, accepting the present, taking whatever comes with equanimity, but looking at Gerri's obvious suffering made the philosophy seem insufficient.

Three days passed with Gerri hardly moving, although she gained the strength to go outside to the toilet area when necessary. The next day, I brought her some hot broth, which she was able to spoon into her mouth.

She struggled to sit up, and after eating her soup, she said, "I can tell I'm getting my strength back. I feel a little better." Five minutes later, she lay prone again.

"She's still yellow and she hasn't eaten solid food in days. I sure hope she's right that she's starting to recover," Steve said.

"Maybe we should cut back on our hash smoking in case we might be in line to turn yellow next. We couldn't function if we all got sick at the same time," I said as I lit the hash pipe.

"I don't see any reason to restrain ourselves. I feel healthy and strong as a thousand camels," Steve said as he took a long hit of hash.

As the days passed, Gerri recovered more of her strength and rejoined the household routine with an abbreviated hatha yoga session and sitting with us for our evening meditation. A Parcheesi game celebrated the beginning of Gerri's recovery. She lost about thirty pounds and now looked like a tall, lean fashion model. Her face was a gaunt, but her eyes glowed brightly.

The first night Gerri smoked hash, we celebrated. Just as I began to breathe a sigh of relief, Steve began to act strangely. Without saying anything to Gerri, or me, he packed items into a straw basket, took his passport and extra money, and walked the short distance to the highway.

Three hours later, he returned and announced, "I'm peeing bright orange, and you know what that means."

"Bummer," I said.

"That's why you've been acting so strange the last few days" Gerri said, "It's a relief. Your liver is affecting your brain. I thought you might have gone bonkers."

"We know the drill—rest, liquids. We still have the pills we got at the hospital. We've been taking vitamin A. Milarepa says, 'Think not that all suffering is ill,'" I said, looking into Steve's dazed eyes.

"I'm too weak to have a pipe of kief," Steve said, unable to reach the pouch and pipe sitting a foot and half away from his hand.

"Want me to light a pipe for you?" I asked, not sure if I was joking or serious.

"No thanks. It looks dark outside. Did I sleep all day?" Steve said without moving any part of his body.

"Record sleep. You were up about eight a.m. to pee in the pee jar and went back to sleep. It now after eight p.m. Want anything?" I responded.

"A new body. I ache all over but especially in the nodes in my groin. I just feel like I have to move and don't have the strength to make my arms and legs respond. If this is a test of keeping a positive attitude under any circumstances, it's a hard one. It's certainly an effective diet," Steve said as he grimaced but pulled himself up on his arms, raising his chest and head.

I came over and assisted Steve to get to his feet, gently pulling him up. He stood unsteadily with his hand against the wall for support.

"Shall I walk you out to the loo?" Gerri asked.

"No, no. Thanks for your support in my hours of need. If I haven't already told you, thanks," Steve said.

"'You wiped my ass. I'll wipe your ass.' It's an old Australian expression, and now I see how it originated," Gerri said.

Steve smiled slightly as he said, "Can you hand me the pee can?" Using his hand on the wall to steady himself, Steve turned away. Using one hand to hold the can and the other to get his cock, he peed into the can. When he finished, he gave a sigh of relief and handed the can to Gerri, who took it outside.

Steve lay on the mat the entire day, sleeping most of the time but obviously experiencing hours of mental drifting.

Gerri and I continued the daily routine with Gerri able to participate almost fully in our activities, although her bout with the illness shook her. With Steve incapacitated, I attended the weekly souk on my own.

In the evening, I lit the hash pipe and looked over at my yellow-eyed friend, who looked pitiful and said, "None for you. I wish I could do more. Can you still hear and understand my reading?"

"Yes and no. I drift in and out, and sometimes my stomach, side, and back hurt so much I can't concentrate. Other times I feel tuned in and almost feel the wisdom seeping in, not only through my mind but actually entering my body. Don't stop the reading, I'm with you," Steve said.

Gerri said to Steve, "I know what you're going through. This too will pass."

"You were really shivering last night. Now look where I am in the *Secret Doctrines* book, 'The Doctrine of Psychic Heat.' This may be very helpful," I said and read, "In the first of the preliminary exercises, visualizing the physical body as being vacuous…" I looked over, but Steve was snoring.

Because of the earlier sunsets, we started our meditation in midafternoon. Gerri and I adopted our eating, reading, and other activities to Steve lying on the mat, where he remained unless he went outside to relieve himself.

After a week, one early morning, Steve lit his sebsi and said, "I finally feel like smoking again. Hallelujah! I ate a little couscous yesterday, and today I have a bit of an appetite."

I sat down, looking at Steve in disbelief. Yesterday Steve began eating solid food and today already smoking again. Steve's demeanor meant he was feeling a lot better.

I said, "You've been down about the same amount of time as Gerri. I'm glad you've returned to the world of the smoking."

Gerri turned over in the sleeping bag and said, "The no-smoking sign is off. Praised be to God."

At breakfast, Steve ate couscous with yogurt and almonds and drank several cups of mint tea. "I'm twenty-five percent better," Steve said as he took one of the missionaries' pills.

Gerri said, "What timing, two pills left and then I don't think he'll need anymore. This morning, Steve will be able to pay attention to the reading. Why don't you read some Sufi stories?"

"Gladly," I said as I reached for the Idries Shah book.

The first story I read contained the line, "You never know how strong you are until being strong is the only choice you have." Shah also said, "Enlightenment must come little by little. Otherwise, it would overwhelm."

After I finished the tale, Steve said, "We're almost out of cleaned kief. We better clean some more today."

"Sorry. I cleaned the last *rabita* while you were in dreamland. There is no more kief to clean. We should go to Tangier for the day and restock our kief and other supplies," I responded.

Gerri said, "I don't feel like a trip to the city. I feel too vulnerable. You guys can go, but I'll spend the day here, drawing and sewing and having a day to myself. Remember to buy more sardines, peanut butter, toilet paper, and cheese and bring some treats back as well."

"I can't go today, but if I continue to recover, I can make a quick trip tomorrow," Steve said.

"I want to check my mail at *poste restante* Tangier. Some people are still writing to me there," I said.

For the rest of the day, Steve slowly resumed his activities, embroidering a few sections of the tarot card cover. I could already see a brightly shining rendering of a mountain above a lake.

The next morning while Steve smoked a sebsi, I said, "I guess you're ready for Tangier."

Steve replied, "Actually, yesterday tired me out. I know we need to go to Tangier, but instead of making it a round trip, let's stay overnight. We need to get the kief, some more pills, and we have shopping to do. We can share a room at the Miami and eat dinner at our favorite restaurant."

Gerri interjected, "Spend the night? I thought you'd exhaust yourselves if you tried to do everything in one day, knowing how long it takes when you have to bargain for everything."

As we drove north along the highway, I took out a fat hash and tobacco joint rolled with a filter European style. "Are you ready?" I asked, holding up the joint.

"Ready or not, here it comes," Steve said. On the first hit, Steve started coughing and almost drove off the road as he said, "Just what the doctor did not order."

We found our way to the Miami, where Steve lay down on the bed and said, "I'm bushed from the drive and joint. Why don't you figure out what you can do now and come back later this afternoon?"

"Groovy," I said, although I felt slightly nauseous.

I browsed the bookstalls and bought another book by Idries Shah, *Wisdom of the Idiots*, for thirty cents. The smell of cumin, mint, and cooking vegetable stews filled the air and reminded me of life at the Blue Door commune. I wondered where I'd be now if Eldon hadn't approached me in this same café ten months earlier. Later at the missionary hospital, I picked up more hepatitis pills.

At the *poste restante* window, I asked in Spanish if there were any letters for "Fred Zola," showing the clerk my passport. After shuffling through three packets of envelopes, the clerk brought out one letter. I recognized my grandmother's writing, and I stuffed it in my pocket without opening it.

When I returned to the Miami, Steve lay asleep in a fetal position with an extra sleeping bag draped over him. The paint in our room was peeling and cracks crossed the ceiling. I pulled up the window shade that covered a half broken window through which chilly air streamed into the room. A single bare light bulb hung down from the ceiling.

Steve slowly pulled himself up and said, "I've got to go down the hall to take a leak."

When he returned, I was opening the letter I received. My grandmother in Chicago sent an article cut out of a recent *Time* magazine. The headline read, "Hippies living in squalor," and showed a photo of a room with sleeping bags on the floor and five long-haired men in ragged clothes, cooking on a one-burner stove.

"Help needed to get hippies out of the dilapidated houses where they live without realizing how they are wasting their lives living without modern conveniences…" I read from the article, which concluded that hippies did not realize the barrenness of their lifestyle.

"Look at this room. Look at us. I just reached my junior high school weight of a hundred and twenty pounds. My eyes are yellow, and a cold draft is blowing in through a broken window. Yet we're perfectly happy," Steve said as he filled his sebsi.

"If my grandmother saw us now, she just wouldn't understand how our minds allow us to transcend the material plane and in fact enjoy the sparseness of our material existence," I said. "Talk about sparseness, I'm on my last few pipes of kief."

"I feel joyful, but I don't think the people who wrote the *Time* article understand. Material things aren't the basis of happiness. Friendship, love, service, study, and plenty of drugs can be the pillars of real happiness. Now I'm ready to have a beautiful vegetarian meal," Steve said, disturbed by *Time's* negative report.

The next morning, we completed our food purchases and walked to Café Baba to get *rabita*s before returning to Khemis. As we entered the café, the patrons paused briefly, but everyone continued playing board games or drinking tea or coffee. The smell of black tobacco smoke with just a hint of kief filled the air.

Rocky, from whom we bought kief for the past ten months, greeted us. "Come sit down. What would you like to drink?" Rocky asked.

"Good to see you. *Salaam alaikum*," I said as Steve sat down next to me.

"*Mualaikum salaam*. I haven't seen you in nearly a month. Not even on the streets. I hope all's been well with you. What will you drink?" Rocky said.

We both opted for mint tea.

Rocky signaled to the waiter and said something to him in Arabic. He turned and said, "Bad crop this year in Katama."

"I'm not around Tangier as much. I'm studying Buddhist teachings and practicing yoga. I aspire as a righteous man to take just action in any situation," I said.

Rocky responded approvingly, "It is the teaching of Muhammad, blessed be his name, always be just and honest in any transaction. The farmers have raised their prices, meaning each *rabita* now cost ten dirhams. I can't help that there's bad weather in the mountains."

Steve turned to me and said in a low voice, "That's nearly double what we paid last time."

I said, "Strange, I haven't heard anything about a reduced kief crop."

The tea arrived, served on a beautiful brass tray, and Rocky poured it in the traditional way.

Rocky said, "You are right, my friend Fred. I could give you a volume discount if you took thirty *rabitas*."

"Yes. We want thirty *rabitas* but not at double the price. We could pay a little more per *rabita*," I responded.

"Final price, eight dirhams per *rabita*," Rocky said.

"I can't accept that price, but I will wait here until you sell us the *rabitas* for six per *rabita*, which is higher than we paid last time," I said as I sipped my tea.

Rocky stood up and said, "Do as you like. Final price, eight per *rabita*." He walked away and joined a group of men in the middle of the café.

Steve said, "What now?"

I looked at him as if he was a child and said, "I will sit here until he sells us the *rabitas* for six dirhams."

We sat silently, finishing the tea, watching the scene, and reflecting.

I thought, *In America, time is money. In Morocco, time is time and money is money.*

After about a half hour, Rocky came over and sat down again. "This is ridiculous. You just can't sit here. I have the thirty *rabitas*. I'll give them to you for seven dirhams."

I said, "Six is a fair price. I will not leave until you accept it and give me the thirty *rabitas*. After I've looked at them to see they're right, I will give you the money."

"Never will I sell the *rabitas* for six. You can leave here now," Rocky said in a somewhat threatening manner as he stood up and walked away again.

"I've got to pee and I can finish the last shopping. Let's pay the seven dirhams. A thirty-day supply of kief, we've got the money," Steve said.

I stretched and made myself more comfortable. "We can't let Rocky keep raising the price. It's not really about the money, it's the principle. We're regular no-hassle customers, and we don't deserve to be treated this way. The man of principle will not be moved. I'll sit here until he sells them for six. You go around town and pick up the things we need and come back here. If he sells them for six, I'll meet you in front of the Miami at about four p.m.," I said.

I thought about what Milarepa would do, although I knew Milarepa would not buy drugs. Buddhist teachings prohibited the use of intoxicants, but I thought of kief and hash and acid as aids on the path. What better way to study your own mind than to view it on hash? Milarepa would stick to principle and not deviate from proper action, so I remained seated, periodically adjusting my legs as I sat in the lotus position in a semi trance.

About three hours later, Steve returned to the café and saw me exactly where he left me. My mind drifted, and I didn't notice Steve until he was standing over me.

Steve asked, "What's happened?"

I could see his shock at my complete calm.

I replied, "The just man can sit and wait. One of Siddhartha's great qualities was he could wait. I can wait also. Waiting is full."

Rocky approached us and said, "You must leave."

"I will leave with my thirty, and I will pay you six. When friends bargain, neither one should feel happy with the resulting price," I said.

"Okay, six." Rocky signaled for a boy to come over, whispered something to him, and the boy turned and walked out of the café.

I got up slowly and stretched each leg and reached my hands over my head to revive and get my blood circulating. The boy returned, carrying three plastic shopping bags, which Rocky handed to me.

"*Shukraan*," I said and counted ten *rabitas* in each bags, looked at a few, and opened one.

There were three strips of black tobacco and about fifteen separate seeded flowered marijuana buds.

I reached into my pocket and took out 180 dirhams and handed them to Rocky, saying, "*Shukraan*."

Rocky took the money with a respectful grin and said, "Come back soon. Enjoy yourselves and go in peace."

The sun was setting when we returned to Khemis, and Gerri greeted us, saying, "I was worried. I expected you back before this."

Steve said, "Small price dispute over the kief. Fred's a bargaining genius, but it took longer than we expected. Now we have thirty *rabitas*," as he gave Gerri a hug.

"I'm a little dizzy. I think I'll lie down. You two have the food we brought back, and if I feel less queasy, I'll eat something later," I said and went into my room.

Steve unwrapped the goodies and spread them with a flourish. "I hope your appetite is back. Mine seems to be just about fine, but Fred didn't eat yesterday. I sensed his discomfort on the ride back to Khemis," I heard Steve say.

Then Gerri said to Steve, "I was having odd and crazy thoughts just before I came down with the hepatitis. Then you were acting odd and crazy just before it got you. Looks like Fred's odd behavior in Tangier might be a prelude to the onset of hepatitis."

I went out to pee, and when I came back, I said, "Orange pee, my turn." I walked slowly into my bedroom hurting in every part of my body. I couldn't help letting out a moan.

Steve lowered himself next to me, saying, "We're here to help you. I'll bring you some pills, and I can help you outside when you need."

I said, "Yes, pills, a little water. I feel like I need to sleep. Somehow, I thought I wouldn't get sick, but I feel awful."

Steve filled a glass that he handed to me, saying, "Just rest, sleep. I'll be in the next room if you need anything. Here, take two pills now."

Gerri said, "Shit. I thought Fred was going to stay healthy. He seemed so strong when I was down, and he continued to support you. We know the drill, and we can now give Fred the attention he deserves and needs. But we need to stick to our routines, so you read the Milarepa story after breakfast."

As I slept, sometimes fever made me throw off the covers, and other times because of chills, I covered myself with a sleeping bag and extra blankets.

I heard Steve reading, "Full of mud is craving meadow, full of thorns is jealous swamp, savage and malignant is the furious dog of hate—"

He stopped abruptly when I moaned as I stood in the doorway, balanced against the wall, and said in a low voice, "Furious dog," and pointed to the door.

Steve came over to me, but I held my hand in front of me in a stop sign position and said, "Just let me stand. Get me a walking stick to lean on."

Gerri said, "I'll make some tea. Hot tea will make you feel better."

"Thanks, maybe later. I'm going to hobble outside. What would be nice is some hot water and a washcloth for me to clean up when I get back," I said, stroking my thick black beard.

I used the basin and hot water to clean up and said in a low voice, "Thanks. I need to lay down," and went back to bed.

I remained in a dreamlike state and heard Gerri say, "He's bloody sicker than either of us were."

Just to punctuate her point, I groaned, which reverberated off the stones walls.

"We were thin but not like him. I don't remember either of us moaning in pain," Steve said. "Let's watch his fever because he's hallucinating too."

I could hear every word Steve and Gerri were saying. The illness made some of my senses much stronger, especially smell and hearing. In contrast, any physical activity took total concentration and all the coordination and strength I could muster. I hadn't eaten in days, and I had to force myself to drink water.

I dreamt of a hermit following the simplest of lives, but a sharp pain coming directly from my liver would jolt me out my dreams. I thought it must be night because I smelled the kerosene lamps and candles burning in the next room. Every part of my body ached, especially the inside of my groin.

Steve came in, holding the evening hash pipe. He sat down near my head. "You've lain here since morning without moving. Want anything? I'm not suggesting the pipe unless you feel it would make you feel better. Might ease the pain," Steve said.

"Can you hold a glass of water to my mouth?" I said.

Steve put down the pipe, poured the glass half full, and held it to my mouth, tipping it up so I could take in a small amount at a time.

I said, "Many seekers have died on the path, and I would accept being one of them."

"What is death anyway?" Steve replied.

"Reincarnation, the bardo is after death, the illusorily nature of life and death…there's so much to study. I ask for Buddha's blessing and protection for me to complete my studies and walk the dharma path," I said as I thought of my peril.

"When you survive, I will join you in the vow. We will study the question of death, the *Tibetan Book of the Dead*," Steve said with seriousness that surprised me.

I wanted to turn from my back to my side. I concentrated my attention on the movement. I needed to lift my left arm from my side onto my hip, shifting toward the right to give me the momentum to turn to my right side. I lay on my back, building up every bit of my energy to attempt the move. I knew I must focus, but my mind drifted to scenes from my childhood, sunbathing at the lake. I remembered the sun draining my energy as I developed my summer tan. Now just turning over might be beyond my power.

Hours later, I remained on my back, unable to even begin to turn, when Gerri came in with a glass of water in her hand. "It's late afternoon and you haven't moved since this morning. Can I do anything to help you? Need a piss? I'll get Steve or bring you a pee can."

"I can't move. No strength," I said. "Perhaps you can move my arm and leg and push me, so I'm lying on my right side."

Gerri got on her knees and said, "When I say go, you relax, and I'll push you up to your side."

"Wait a minute, I ache. My left side is killing me. Let's take this slow," I said as I prepared to shift my weight. "Okay, please be gentle."

Gerri put one hand on my shoulder, and she turned me slowly. She needed to stabilize me so I didn't turn completely and end up on my stomach. My breath came in short rapid bursts as if I just finished a sprint. Beads of sweat formed on my forehead. Gerri raised a glass of water, and I took a small sip, coughed, and took another sip as water ran down my chin. I drank about a quarter of the glass.

"I'll get a cloth to wipe off the drippings and also just clean you up with a little face wash," Gerri said as my head hit the pillow.

I fell asleep.

Later, Steve, seeing my condition, said, "It's after dark and he hasn't moved all day. I'm worried. Maybe we should wake him to give him the pills and some vitamins."

"I agree. Also, he might need a pee can or, if he can stand, a walk to the toilet area," Gerri said.

I opened my eyes and said, "I hurt everywhere. I don't have the strength to move."

"You need medication," Steve said and called, "Gerri, please bring the pills, more water, and the vitamins.

"I can help you stand up to pee or go outside. You can make it with my assistance," Steve said.

Gerri came into the room, carrying a glass of water and some pills. Together Steve and Gerri raised me so my back rested against the wall. Gerri gave me the pills, putting each in my mouth individually. She went out and returned with a basin of warm water and a washcloth and gently washed my face, neck, and hands.

"Thank you," I said as I tried to reassure Gerri, even though my whole body felt as if I'd been run over by a steamroller.

"How about a hit from this pipe?" Steve asked as he lifted up the hash pipe.

"Yes, please," I responded from the depth of my distress.

Steve lit the pipe and took a deep hit. He then placed the pipe to my lips.

I managed to take a hit. "You're a true friend," I whispered.

"Remember the basic premise of the ancient wisdom, 'This too shall pass.' You'll get better just as Gerri, and I have. Meanwhile, I'll smoke for the two of us," Steve said.

"Please, help me stretch out. I can't sit up anymore," I said, wanting not to think about illness, wisdom, or hash. I didn't want the process of my dying to be drawn out much longer as the discomfort and inability to function were unbearable.

As I lay alone, I thought about Steve's remark and other aspects of the wisdom teachings we were studying. Milarepa's body was covered in calluses and bruises from long hours of meditating. He became a green-tinted skeleton from eating just wild nettles, but he did not veer from his practice. The hanged man in the tarot deck was accepting and relaxed even while suspended upside down.

"Go with the flow" was a hippie motto I lived by. Now "the flow" brought weakness and pain on the floor of a stone house in Morocco. I accepted this as part of my journey. The precepts of the gurus taught, "To look on mud and gold with an equal eye is the sign of a superior man."

A sharp pain shot up from my lower left side, and I cried out in response to it. I needed to reach the open air on the roof. I wanted to see one more sunrise before I died. Mustering my strength, I turned and pulled myself up to all fours. After I rested for several minutes, putting my right hand in front, and dragging my right leg forward, I started to crawl toward the stairs. Each time I moved, I rested. I wasn't sure I could get to the roof, but I struggled inch by inch until I did. I crawled to the old lawn chair we kept for sunbathing. I shifted the chair so it faced east, so I could see the sun coming up. After further rest, I pulled myself onto the chair. I waited for the first rays of the sun to appear on the horizon. As I saw the light and the sun's rays, a surge of healing energy pulsed through my body. My nightlong struggle achieved its goal; my recovery was beginning.

When Steve and Gerri came onto the roof to do their morning yoga routine, they couldn't believe their eyes to see me in the lawn chair.

"How'd you get up here? I thought you were in the sleeping bag downstairs," Gerri said.

"I crawled here because I needed to see the sunrise, the rebirth of light in the world. Water please?" I said.

Water? Thirsty, I needed water. Lice were biting me behind my left ear, and I grabbed one. Instead of crushing it, I watched it crawl across my palm and jump onto the ground. I got up and walked slowly to quench my thirst.

CHAPTER 9

Dealer and Disciple

He who lacketh discrimination, whose mind is unsteady, and whose heart is impure never reaches the goal but is born again and again.
—Katha Upanishad

The faucet in the toilet area provided the only water for inmates in Beni. I reached down with my right hand, cupped water in my palm, and splashed it on my face. We used the right hand because the left hand was used as our toilet paper.

After I quenched my thirst, I walked three times around the yard until my legs hurt, and I sat down. I drifted back to a year ago when I recovered from the attack of hepatitis. From my current sparse diet I lost almost as much weight as I lost during hepatitis.

After I dragged myself to see the sunrise, my recovery progressed slowly. I regained my strength, and we resumed our studies and routines. When my appetite returned, I ate the entire daily loaf of bread myself. Although we peed yellow again and gained a bit of weight, the bout of hepatitis cast a shadow over the three of us. Gerri said she did not want to ever experience anything like her illness again. She feared a reoccurrence if she stayed in Morocco too long.

The days were growing shorter, and a chill was in the air mornings and evenings. The vegetables in the weekly souk changed, less chard and greens and the last of the squash and melons as the summer crops faded. Fall arrived.

One afternoon, Gerri was drawing a card to send to a friend in Australia including a few tabs of the windowpane acid. She drew a balloon floating above the head of a bearded character who looked a bit like me, containing the words, "expand your mind," written in it. Steve was embroidering, and I was drawing a tropical-looking flower with my colored pencil set. A knock on the door interrupted our artistic endeavors.

Steve went to the door, saying, "*Quien?*"

Then an Australian-accented female voice responded, "It's Max and Joan."

After a series of hugs, Max and Joan sat down in the main room with us.

"Welcome, we're so glad to see you. What's been happening since we left you in Paradise Canyon?" I asked.

"We stayed south longer than we intended as there were delays getting the parts I needed to repair the van," Max said. "We're heading to Spain and where we will rent a house near Malaga to relax after the intensity of our time in Morocco."

"Can you spend a few days here? We'll make it special," Steve said, extending his usual hospitality.

"Sorry but we just wanted to see you and give you these," Joan said, handing a box to Steve. "We're giving you these cassette tapes since you told us about your limited selection. We needed to get an extension on our visas because of the broken-down van, but we must be out of Morocco by day after tomorrow. We want to stop in Tangier for the night."

"Too bad, it's hell being always outnumbered by these Yanks," Gerri said as I took out James Taylor, Santana, and Creedence tapes among others in the bag.

"Let's have a pipe of hash. Can we offer you food or something to drink?" Steve asked with disappointment in his voice as he wanted them to stay.

"You know I'm not much of a hash smoker, but I'll try a pipe. You seem to have access to the best hash," Max replied.

I went to bring out the hash, and Gerri went to get tea and oranges.

Joan looked at the embroidery and said, "Nice work. We're thinking of making a cover for our spare tire with an embroidered design on it."

When I returned, I prepared a pipe and passed it to Max, who took a hit and started coughing wildly. Gerri motioned to Joan in a conspiratorial way, and they went up to the roof as Steve took a hit on the pipe and passed it back to Max, who took a much smaller hit that he managed to keep down without coughing.

Handing the pipe back to me, Max said, "This is very powerful. Can I get a little from you?"

"Sure. We can give you some. I have a contact in Tangier for more," I said as I blew the residue out of the pipe.

"No, no. I just want a small amount to smoke on rare occasions with friends. You know I'm not a big smoker. Give me some gin any time but hash rarely," Max replied as he began to slump down with a far-off look in his eyes.

As often happened, after smoking the hash, conversation stopped, and we three sat staring at the center of the mat. Steve dubbed this state, "A social evening with hash," but it applied equally during the daytime hours.

When the women returned, Gerri said, "Told you they'd be sitting here staring," to Joan, who seemed a little upset seeing Max leaning sideways with only the wall behind him keeping him upright. "Let's make some food. They'll be hungry when the stupor ends," Gerri said as she led Joan to the kitchen.

They returned after a time with a platter of cheese, tomatoes, bread, olives, and a bottle of wine Joan got from their van. We looked up as the women returned, each of us trying to rise from our stupor. Steve moved clumsily to clear the mat so the food could be put down.

"What a knockout," Max said as he straightened up and seemed to be checking his body parts.

"You're a lightweight," Gerri said. "Those two Yanks can smoke twice as much without any visible impact."

"I've been fantasizing about Paradise Canyon and the good times there. I remember the sound of the palm fronds clicking in the breeze. I'd love to revisit," Steve said.

As we ate and drank the wine, the talk turned to future adventures. Max and Joan were heading to Nepal. Their slogan was, "Kathmandu in '72." After spending the rest of the winter in Spain, they would drive across Asia. Gerri said she was thinking of going to England to work as a nurse.

I adamantly insisted I wanted stay longer in Morocco, saying, "I've been here about a year now, only a beginning in a country like this."

"Doesn't 'Katmandu in '72' sound good? We could be among Milarepa's people. Tibetan Buddhists who are practicing what we've been studying. I'm not sure about the future. I need a teacher to progress beyond a certain point on the path. Listen to what Milarepa says about the need for a guru. There's only so far seekers can go on their own," Steve contributed.

I responded, "It's the practice that counts and a seeker can practice on his own." I pointed to the books piled against the walls and continued, "All the wisdom a person needs to reach enlightenment is at our fingertips. Remember the greatest pith instruction in Buddhism is 'practice.' Practicing in solitude on his own is what Milarepa did."

"Yes, but only after years of teachings from his guru Marpa," Steve countered.

"You can be your own guru," I responded.

"This is as close to an argument I've seen you two get into," Gerri said. "I believe both paths can lead to the same place if properly pursued. There's no one size fits all for spiritual seekers."

"Well said," Max exclaimed as he refilled every wine glass, finishing the bottle.

"I'd like to do a tarot reading before you leave," I said, unwrapping the new Waite-designed tarot deck Steve and Gerri bought.

Joan said, "I feel so close to you now, but are we going to be connected in the future?"

I removed the green tie-dyed cloth Steve made. With everyone sitting in a circle, I asked Joan to cut the deck with her left hand.

I laid the cards out in a circle of twelve cards like the face of a clock and said, "We need to take a moment and, with the utmost respect, focus on these cards as they will tell us what's going on right now." The first card I turned was death, inverted on the north tip of the circle. I explained, "An inverted card means the opposite." Next I turned the knight of swords charging directly in a warlike manner from the south edge of the circle. "This card symbolizes life racing forward with full force, moving forward toward inevitable death."

When the eight of pentacles appeared, I said, "This indicates some financial transaction will occur between us." I thought this could indicate some dealing with hash.

I explained the last three cards would be related specifically to me, and the reading ended on an ominous note. It was the three of swords showing a heart with three swords running through it.

After sitting for about five minutes reflecting on the cards and my interpretation of them, Joan said, "The cards spoke to me, and I'll be thinking about this reading as we travel. It sure seems as if we'll be connected again. Max, let's get going as we need to arrive in Tangier before dark."

Our daily practice of yoga and meditation times increased. Our recovery from the hepatitis seemed complete, but we occasionally reported the color of our pee to each other. The dense teachings in the *Tibetan Yoga and Secret Doctrines* book confused me, and I couldn't grasp the "yoga of the simultaneously born great symbol" and other esoteric subjects.

About three weeks after Max and Joan visited, three men and a woman appeared at our door one early afternoon, saying Max and Joan told them to come by on their way to southern Morocco.

"I'm Carol and this is my husband, Jake," said an athletic woman with large brown eyes and long dark hair.

I gave my usual salutation, "Greetings, greetings, greetings."

"Come in and sit down. How are Max and Joan? Would you like some tea or water?" Gerri said, glad to have company.

I could tell Gerri was beginning to feel isolated, and she was thinking about leaving Khemis before the cold winter rains hit.

"Max and Joan have rented a big house near Malaga. They have a lot of art projects going. We couldn't find your place from the directions, but we stopped at the post office. And the man there directed us here. Max and Joan spoke so highly of you, and since we were coming here, they asked us to bring you these," Jake said, handing Gerri a box of cassette tapes, including the new releases by The Rolling Stones, Neil Young, and The Who.

Since I mentioned I liked the blues, Joan included a Muddy Waters tape. I slipped a Rolling Stones cassette into the player and heard Mick Jagger singing, "Just another mad, mad day on the road."

"How about a smoke, hash or kief?" Steve asked.

Soon, we seven sat staring at the ashtray in the center of the room. No one said anything, and it appeared one of the men nodded out. Even though no one communicated, I thought the guests were experiencing hash's very beneficial effects. I counted this as a service I gladly provided.

Carol said, "We didn't mean to impose on you… We better move on. It's starting to get dark."

"Please, stay for dinner and spend the night," Gerri said. "You shouldn't leave this late and drive through Larache in the fading light. You can sleep here, and we can make a large dinner. We've got plenty of food."

I agreed as extending hospitality, united hippies with a scared Muslim custom.

"I accept because driving might be difficult right now," Jake replied.

Everyone pitched in as I lit the charcoal for an extra-large vegetable tagine. Carol and Gerri cut vegetables. Steve and Jake cleared the area where the dinner would be served.

Once the clay tagine pot was on the coals, I said, "It will take about half an hour for the vegetables to be ready. I can read a Milarepa story if you'd like."

“Please do,” replied Carol. “Joan told me how you read these Buddhist poems and how powerfully they affected her.”

I read from a song called, “A Woman’s Role in the Dharma,” a story giving instructions on meditation practice, “Resembling the unchanging solid mountain before you, you should meditate with steadiness and solidity.”

When I closed the book, I brought in the clay pot, removed the cover revealing a mound of steaming potatoes, cabbage, turnips, and beets. I said, “May our meeting be auspicious. May this food give us strength to aid all living things. May all beings be happy.”

As the group departed the next morning, we hugged, and I said, “Stop by on your way north. Thanks for the cassettes.”

“We’ll be sure to see you again,” Carol replied.

At the Saturday souk three weeks later, large trucks carrying booths, tents, colored lights, and decorative awnings arrived. We learned their arrival signaled the annual Festival in Khemis in celebration of a local saint, the biggest event of the year. Our neighbor, Karim, told me we would be welcome to participate in the activities.

Two evenings later, we heard what sounded like gunshots and saw fireworks exploding above the souk area. The sky was lit with red, green, and white stars as the rockets announced the festival’s start.

“Let’s go,” said I.

“You better cover up well,” Steve said to Gerri as he put on his djellaba and took out a small change purse into which he put some dirham bills and coins.

Gerri tied a scarf to cover her head and wore a loose-fitting caftan flowing down to her ankles. We walked out of our compound and along the highway then turned onto the side road leading to the souk area. Women with their covered heads and men wearing brown wool djellabas crowded the area. Carnival rides were set up along with a small Ferris wheel decorated with colored lights. There were booths where we could buy silver jewelry, beads, scarves, knives, and assorted children’s toys and dolls. Vendors sold bright-pink cotton candy and fried *sfenj*, the Moroccan churro-like donuts, as well as several other types of pastries. Moroccan music blasted from speakers.

Gerri stopped in front of a young woman seated next to an assortment of embroidery threads and picked out some especially bright-red and greens ones, asking, "*Cuanto cuesta?*"

The woman responded in Arabic because she apparently did not speak Spanish.

Another older woman standing nearby came over and translated, "*Cincuenta* (fifty) dirhams."

Gerri, already an experienced bargainer, said, "No, too much," in Spanish and offered twenty dirhams.

The woman translated for the seller, who said, "*Bien*," and Gerri bought five packets of thread.

As we walked among the booths, I pointed out three large men in suits standing at the edge of the crowd. "Police," I said. "One has a shoulder holster, and just looking at them, I sense they are police, probably from Larache, keeping an eye on the fiesta."

As we looked at them, the three men stared back.

After buying an order of *sfenj*, Steve said, "Let's go back home. Eat these, smoke, and read."

"Good idea, I've seen enough," Gerri said, and we walked back home.

Two days after the festival, frantic pounding at the door interrupted a Milarepa reading.

I dropped the book and jumped up and said, "*Quien?*" as Steve swung the door open.

Carol rushed into the house, crying hysterically.

Gerri took her in her arms. "What happened?"

After Carol calmed down, she sobbed, "My husband's in jail in Larache. A Moroccan man jumped in front of our van. The man was badly injured and taken to the hospital. Jake was driving slowly north on the highway at dusk. So many people were walking on both sides of the road. After the accident, these militaristic national police officers surrounded us. They took Jake to jail and won't release him."

Steve asked, "Did you buy a Moroccan car insurance policy?"

Carol responded, "Yes, we have a policy, but the police would not accept it as valid. We're going to drive to Tangier right now to get help. I'll return with the car insurance information. I'll be come back to Larache in the next day or two to get Jake freed."

Gerri, ever empathetic, told them to go to the Pension Miami and talk to Mina. I thought about how crowds thronged along the highway. Even driving five miles an hour always made me tense.

Later that day, the storeowner told me a foreigner driving a van killed a father of eight children while he was crossing the road in Larache. When I returned with our daily loaf of bread, I related the sad news; the person Carol's husband hit died. Carol did not return, and we heard nothing more about the accident.

Three days later on Friday, while I prepared to read a Milarepa story, hard knocks on the front door interrupted me. Steve walked over and asked "*Quien?*" before opening it.

"*Policia*," a loud voice answered, "*abre la puerta* (open the door)," sent a chill through the three of us.

I whispered to Gerri, "Go to the roof and hide behind the low wall. They won't be able to see you from below." To Steve, I whispered, "Don't let the police inside. We don't want them to see the hash."

Three large husky men in suits stood on our doorstep, their guns clearly visible.

Opening the door, Steve greeted them in Spanish, asking, "What do you want?"

After some back and forth, Steve said he and I would get our passports and follow the police in our van to the station in Larache. We wanted to get them away from the house and our hash.

With our passports and wearing our djellabas, we drove behind the unmarked sedan along the highway to the Larache police station. We followed the officers inside to a small office, where one of the men sat down behind a wooden desk and asked to see our passports.

Steve took them out, asking, "Why are we here?"

He got no reply.

The higher-ranking officer thumbed through my passport until he found the stamp indicating the date I entered Morocco. I recalled Gail saying, "March fourth," as we passed the entry booth from Ceuta. It was now November; my three-month visa was long expired.

After doing the same with Steve's passport, the officer looked up and raised his fingers one at a time until he was holding five fingers from one hand and three from his other in the air across from us. We looked at the officers' upraised fingers but said nothing.

The officer called in a uniformed policeman and instructed him in Arabic. Turning to us, he said, "*Vaya con el,*" and pointed.

With one officer in front and one behind, we walked down a hallway and around a corner to a place where another uniformed policeman sat at a desk. A door to his right with bars across a tiny peephole led to a short hall leading to similar doors. The officer at the desk gestured to us to remove our belts and shoelaces. We emptied our pockets, and the officer put the van keys, Steve's money pouch, and our other items in two large manila envelopes, placing them on open shelves behind the desk.

He got out of his chair, unlocked a heavy door, and pointing, said, "*Entre.*"

We went through a doorway ahead of the officer and to the two narrow doors with small, barred openings at eye level. The officer opened one of the doors and ordered the three raggedy-looking Moroccan men who were in the cell out. He opened another door and put the men in the cell next door. I could see the cell already held three men. After locking the six Moroccans in one cell, he pointed to the now-empty cell.

Steve tried to say something, but the officer responded harshly, "*Entre.*"

We stepped inside the cell as the door closed behind us, and we heard the key turn in the lock. The officer walked away through the first door, slamming it shut. For several minutes, we said nothing. We were in the Larache jail for overstaying our visas. We didn't know what would happen next.

The narrow cell was about eight feet long and five feet wide. A gray metal slab with no mattress hung down on chains from the wall, which left about two feet of space from the opposite wall. Otherwise, the cell was empty. There was no toilet. One bare light bulb was attached in the ceiling, protected by a metal cage. The one window was so high there was no way to see out of it; however, it allowed in a small amount of light. The walls were stone and the floor concrete.

Steve sat down on the slab and said, "They took our belts and shoelaces. What do they think, we're going to commit suicide because they put us in jail for overstaying our visas?"

I replied, "I see this as an opportunity for us to apply the wisdom we've been studying. The flow has taken us here and presented us with this," sweeping my arms toward the inside of the cell in all its barrenness. I continued, "Now as disciples, we have to stay on the path in spite of obstacles," sweeping my arms again.

"Think not that all suffering is ill," Steve answered, "and we're not even suffering. Gerri is out there, and she'll take steps to see we get out of here. I'm sure she'll contact Mina and maybe the landlord. They'll know what to do to help us."

"Let's meditate, which will help to center us and begin this part of our journey with calm, clear minds," I said.

"Good idea. Jail seems like a perfect setting for a meditation retreat," Steve replied.

I sat cross-legged on the metal slab while Steve sat in the same posture on the concrete floor.

I said, "I dedicate this meditation to the happiness and welfare of all living beings, especially the Larache police for providing us this opportunity to advance on the path."

After what seemed a longer time than our usual sessions in Khemis, I opened my eyes and stretched my legs. "Good deep meditation. Maybe we should have asked to be arrested as a tool to improve our practice," I said as Steve stretched his cramped legs too.

"I've been thinking a lot about our meditation, and I worry we can only go so far just from books for instruction. I need more personal instructions from a teacher if I'm going to deepen my practice," Steve said very seriously in response to my lighthearted comment.

"We have the wisdom. We have an ideal place to study and practice, and we've got the hash, kief, and acid to support our quest. There's nothing a person can tell you that isn't in our books," I responded.

"I'm really wondering if the hash and kief are positive when it comes to meditation. I'm finding hash makes my mind drift, thoughts continually coming, and not much of an ability to focus. I'm thinking hash makes it more difficult to achieve the 'one pointedness of mind' the texts describe as a key initial ingredient in meditation practice," Steve stated.

"I know the first thing you'll do when we're released is smoke some kief or hash or both, so your actions won't conform to that philosophy," I answered.

"Yes, you're right. I'd love a pipe of kief right now, but that's the point, isn't it? In Morocco, we'll always smoke hash, but maybe leaving Morocco would be good for that reason too. I've thought of going to Nepal where I could find teachers and gurus as well as less opportunity to stay continually attached to hash smoking," Steve said.

We heard noise in the hallway outside the cell, and the door swung open. A short scruffy-looking man in a torn djellaba placed a metal tray with two cheese sandwiches on white bread and a bottle of water on the floor inside the door and shut it behind him.

Looking at the food, Steve said, "This proves we're really in jail. I hope it's not for too long because those sandwiches are mighty thin."

I poured the water into one of the plastic glasses on the tray, and holding it up to see its clarity, I drank two glasses. Steve also drank the water and ate a cheese sandwich in three big bites.

After we ate, we sat in silence, absorbed in our own thoughts.

Finally Steve said, "I think we should make a mark on the wall for day one, like the prisoner did in *The Count of Monte Cristo.* This is day one, and the time does go slowly in an empty concrete cell."

"Let's tell each other a movie we've seen to help fill the time," I suggested.

Steve said, "*Goodbye Columbus* was a good book and movie I know well. I'll tell it to you. You've come up with a good idea to pass time."

"Go ahead. I'll lie on the bed and we can switch spots. Later I'll tell you a film or story," I replied.

"The opening scene shows Neil, a boy in New Jersey, meeting Brenda at a swimming pool." Steve gave the action in detail, including describing the girl's mother finding Brenda's diaphragm. When he finally said, "The end," I applauded.

"Very good. I visualized the movie. Very entertaining," I said. "Your turn on the slab."

"There isn't enough room for us both to do our yoga at the same time, but I thought we should each do a session. If you're up for it, I'll lie down now, and you do the yoga. And I'll do a session after you're finished," Steve said as he got up from the floor.

"Perfect," I said as we changed places. I removed my djellaba and centered myself, starting a series of movements, coordinating my breathing to the rhythm of the pose. I did ten "Salutes to the Sun" for a start.

After Steve completed his turn doing the yoga, we realized we were going to spend at least this night in the cell. Our conversation turned to our situation and what alternatives faced us.

"I heard of people in Tangier sentenced to three months in prison for just being a month over the expiration of their visas," I said. "We've been eight months over. We could get a year in a Moroccan prison."

"I doubt it," Steve replied. "I expect us to be released tomorrow. Gerri, Mina, and the landlord will work to get us released."

"What if they returned to Khemis arrested Gerri and found our hash?" I replied, more worried as the discussion continued.

"The wisdom says, 'surrender.' We can't do anything about what will happen. We have no control from in here. If we're thrown in a Moroccan prison, at least you know some of the ropes from what you learned from Eldon," Steve said, sounding a positive note. "Besides, from what you said, there's good hash in prison."

Again, the door to our cell opened, and the same scruffy man took our empty meal trays and plastic glasses and replaced them with two more cheese sandwiches and a glass of tea. Steve said something to him in Spanish, trying to ask about any information he might have about our status, but the man did not reply and simply relocked the door.

Soon, we both needed to pee, so I called out for a jailer to allow us to go to the bathroom.

Steve called in Spanish, "Please, help us, we need to use the *baño*."

The cell door and another thick wooden door separated the cells from the main hallway, and Steve's calling brought no response.

After waiting about fifteen minutes, Steve said, "I'm in pain. I've got to pee. I don't want to pee on the floor in here, but if I don't get to the bathroom, I will."

I began shouting in English though the small peephole, "Help us! We need help!" as loud as I could. I also slammed the peephole bars with my fists and continued screaming until the hallway door finally opened and a jailer came to our cell.

Steve said in Spanish, "I need to pee. Please, take me to the bathroom," but the jailer didn't respond. Steve again said, "I have to pee. Please, take me to the bathroom."

The jailer took a large skeleton key and unlocked the cell door. He led Steve down the hall to a small door. When Steve returned to the cell, the jailer led me to the same door opening into a concrete room with a hole in the center of the floor. In Spanish, we both thanked the jailer profusely.

"What a blessing just peeing can be," Steve said.

"It's been an exciting day, but it's night now. And I'm tired, so let's see about sleeping," I said. "I'll sleep on the floor, and you can have the slab, although there isn't much difference."

"Okay, and if we don't get released tomorrow, I'll take the floor tomorrow night," Steve answered.

I heard Steve softly snoring just before I also drifted off to sleep.

The opening of our cell door roused me, and I jumped up, hoping someone was coming to free us, but it was only the same scruffy man bringing two cheese sandwiches and two glasses of mint tea.

I said, "It's the weekend. I don't expect we will be released until Monday when the officials are back in their offices. If I'm right, we have at least two more days here, so let's figure out how to make the most them."

"Getting to like cheese on white bread would be a good start as that seems to be the jail menu," Steve said as he handed me a sandwich.

"Let's just keep to our routine. After this, let's meditate, do our yoga, and see what we can create to pass the time. I'll tell you a movie today," I replied.

Now when we called to go to the bathroom, the jailer came. We knew there were Moroccans in the next cell, but those prisoners remained very quiet. We spent a lot of time speculating on what was happening outside, about if Gerri was finding assistance, how the landlord was pulling strings on our behalf, and how on Monday morning we would be freed. As evening was approaching, we were discussing the law of Karma and how sometimes a person could clearly see the cause and effect of their actions and at others it was impossible to understand the connection. I wondered what part of our personal Karma might have led to our arrest.

The smell of cumin and other spices coming from a nearby restaurant filled our cells, and my stomach growled. The scruffy man who brought our cheese sandwiches came through the hallway door carrying a tray with a plate of couscous, lamb, and vegetables. He walked to next cell, opened the door, and gave the tray to someone inside. He locked the cell door and started to walk out of the cellblock.

Steve jumped up and ran to the small window and said in Spanish, "Please, is it possible for us to get some of that food also?"

The man said, "*Floos, floos, floos,*" the Arabic word for money. He rubbed his fingers together in the universal sign for cash.

Steve responded in Spanish, saying, "We have *floos*, *floos* with our property. Use our *floos* and please bring us food."

The man replied in Spanish, asking what we wanted to order.

Steve said, "Fish, couscous, tea, vegetables for two."

The man nodded and walked out of the cellblock, closing the door behind him.

A little later, the door to the outer room opened, and I could see the scruffy man in front the uniformed jailer who pulled out the brown manila envelope, which contained our money. The officer counted out a few dirhams and gave it to the scruffy man.

I watched the transaction and said, "If that's for those dishes of food, we are getting them at the Moroccan price, not the tourist price we usually pay."

The scruffy man approached the cell door. He opened it and handed the dishes one at a time to us. We both thanked him profusely in Arabic and Spanish before we calmly began to eat. The food was delicious and the portions so large we couldn't finish.

Later when the man came back to get the nearly empty plates, we again thanked him, and Steve asked if they could get some eggs for breakfast the next morning.

The man said, "*Si, porque no*. (Yes, why not.) You have money. I will bring you the food you desire."

Feeling full and satisfied after the excellent dinner and with jailers responding when we needed to use the toilet, we started our second night in the Larache jail in an upbeat mood. Steve lay on the floor, and I slept on the slab when the guards turned off the light. Not ready to fall asleep, our conversation went on a tangent from our usual spiritual topics.

"Let's tell each other our sexual histories," I suggested. "We need to pass the time. And that's something that's interesting, personal, and we've never talked about."

"I wish I could contribute more, four women I fell in love with including Gail and Gerri and my girlfriends in college and law school. I might have to exaggerate a bit," Steve answered, but he agreed.

I began by recounting tales of girls I knew in the summers at the lake. Junior year in high school, it was Francine; senior year, Jackie and Teri; freshman year of college, Carol; sophomore year, Cheri. Wonderful memories. I talked about going to a hotel bar in Chicago where rich people gathered and an orchestra played dance tunes. I met a woman and took her to another nearby less-expensive hotel. It turned out she, like me, had chosen the fancy hotel to connect with a rich person. Although we both enjoyed the hot sex, neither accomplished our goal of finding a "sugar daddy/mama." Traveling in Europe, I met women in Sweden, France, Ibiza, and Holland, but these were stories of short-lived hot sex. I reminisced about the love of my life, Sarah. We enjoyed a passionate relationship throughout my later college days, but her seriousness did not mesh with my carefree ways.

Steve's stories were more about extended relationships.

"You're a serial monogamist—Susan to Barbara to Gail to Gerri," I said.

Steve didn't provide any details about his and Gail's sex life, finding it easier to talk about women I didn't know and feeling disloyal to say much about the ones I did.

"The whole question of sex and the spiritual life confuses me. Milarepa obviously had nothing to do with women, and there's a lot in Buddhist teaching about transmuting sexual energy into spiritual energy. But the symbol of the deities with their female consorts, sometimes even depicted in sexual intercourse, is also basic. It seems an enlightened being could have a partner of the opposite sex," Steve said, bringing our discussion back to the spiritual plane.

"Sex is always complicated, whether a person's a seeker or a playboy, but we'll have to deal with it when the opportunity arises, which won't be in here," I responded.

Sunday morning after we meditated and I completed my yoga routine, the cell door opened, and the scruffy man entered carrying a tray with two plates of fried eggs, a roasted tomato, toasted white bread, and couscous. He also brought a pot of mint tea.

"Breakfast in bed, I could get used to the luxury," Steve said as he took one plate and poured a cup of tea.

After breakfast, the talk returned to the prospects of our release. Not having any communication from the outside world left us guessing. We wondered what steps Gerri and others might have taken to free us. I worried the police returned to Khemis and searched our house and found the hash. I thought we might be facing more serious charges than overstaying our visas.

The time moved slowly. I narrated the movie *Hell's Angels '69*, starring Sonny Barger, the founder of the Oakland Hell's Angels. Sonny led the angels at the concert at Altamont providing security for The Rolling Stones. That concert was the opposite of Woodstock.

Instead of "peace and love," it was "darkness and death." Steve remembered working in San Francisco the day of the concert and being glad an important case affected the rights of welfare recipients prevented him from attending.

Later we talked about our families. We contrasted my growing up with deaf parents in Milwaukee to Steve's childhood in Brooklyn and Long Island with a mother who knew no bounds in her interference in anyone's personal affairs.

The scruffy man did not return with food during the day, but in the late afternoon, he came by to ask what we wanted for dinner. Later he brought us an especially tasty vegetable couscous platter with flan for dessert.

After dinner we did a third meditation session that calmed us, and we fell asleep easily. We both thought some progress would be made on Monday, the next day. We badly wanted and needed some information about our situation. However, nothing happened, our situation remained the same. Steve repeatedly questioned the jailers, who replied, "*No se* (I don't know)" or "*Inshallah* (what God wills)." No police officer or other official ever came into the cellblock.

For me, who tended to worry the isolation and lack of information, it became the worst part of our jail situation. We were running out of topics of conversation, movies or books to recount, or spiritual topics to discuss. We recited poems from memory. We recounted events from our past. Steve told me the details of his 1963 summer as a civil rights worker in Mississippi. I told Steve some of my golf highlights. At nineteen, I was the youngest player to win the Nippersink Country Club Championship. Then I played on the Northwestern golf team for two years. When the coach told me I had to cut my hair, I quit the team. The hippie life was calling to me and saving the world became more important than golf.

Going to sleep on Monday night proved difficult.

Out of the darkness, from my position lying on the floor, I said, "I think we were arrested because we went to the fiesta where the Larache police noticed us. That's why they came to our house. We should have kept a lower profile and stayed in our house."

From the slab, Steve replied, "No way. Our reputation in Khemis is good. They came because Jake ran down that man. When they questioned him, he told them the group stopped at our house. I'm sure that's why, the timing fits."

Tuesday we woke up early, and as we completed our meditation, the cell door opened. Instead of the scruffy man with breakfast, a police officer in a suit said, "Follow me." We walked to the outer office where the officer took out the manila envelope holding the possessions we surrendered at the time of our arrest. He gave us back our shoelaces, belts, and car keys, also the remainder of our money along with a written bill explaining the deductions to pay for our restaurant meals. He held up our passports and said he was keeping them. He told us we needed to appear on Friday, 10:00 a.m. at the Larache courthouse for a hearing. He asked Steve if he understood and pointed to the door and told us we were free to leave.

I walked outside amazed and happy. I appreciated breathing fresh air as we walked rapidly to the van, got inside, and drove away.

"Did he say we have a trial on Friday?" I said, making sure I had properly understood the police officer's Spanish. "Let's check with Gerri in Khemis."

"Yes, court Friday but now we're free. I can't wait to wash up, smoke a pipe, and hug Gerri. We should go to Tangier and talk to Mina too," Steve said as he drove north toward Khemis.

When we arrived at our house, Gerri was not there, and our stash of hash was also missing. We found some kief and sat down, prepared pipes, and smoked, savoring every puff. We washed, changed clothes, packed overnight bags, and drove to the Pension Miami.

The desk clerk told us Gerri checked in but went shopping. Mina wasn't there either, so we took a room and lay down on the beds, which were soft and comfy after the metal slab and stone floor of our cell.

About an hour later, Gerri burst in, giving us both hugs and kisses. "I was so upset and worried. I came here Friday right after you were arrested and brought the hash with me. I told Mina what happened. I couldn't tell if she did anything specific, but she did tell me not to worry. But I've been so upset anyway."

"We have to go to court on Friday, they kept our passports. Jail wasn't too bad once we replaced cheese sandwiches with excellent restaurant food. It's the uncertainty that was the worst part, not knowing how long we'd be there or what was happening outside," I said.

"We did well keeping our yoga and meditation sessions going. We meditated more than usual so jail had its spiritual benefits," Steve interjected. "Where's the hash? We didn't have anything to smoke, and I want a pipe."

"I've got the hash, but I didn't bring any pipes. I hitchhiked from Khemis, so I traveled light. I got a ride with a very nice man who brought me right to the Miami. He was polite and solicitous but disappointed when I told him I had a boyfriend," Gerri said. "If you weren't released in a few more days, I was thinking of contacting him."

"I'm going to buy a sebsi and clay bowls," I said and went out the door.

Mina did not return until the following evening, and we sat down with her in the Miami's vestibule.

She said, "Overstaying visas isn't a serious crime."

Steve accepted what Mina said because in Khemis, our neighbors knew we respected Muslim customs and sensibilities, never drinking alcohol or causing disturbances.

Thursday, we returned to Khemis and cleaned the house and mopped the floors. We arranged everything for Gerri in case we ended up jailed. I took special care to create a hiding place for our hash and acid in the event the police returned.

Thursday night, every word of our evening reading was impactful. I read, "Sentient beings are Buddhas in themselves, yet they are veiled by temporal defilements. Once these defilements are cleansed, then they will be Buddhas."

A discussion of how every person could become a Buddha ensued. I vowed if I were spared going to jail, I would increase my effort to reach Buddhahood.

Friday morning, wearing respectable clothes, we hugged and kissed Gerri goodbye and drove to our court appearance. I tucked my long ponytail into the back of my sweatshirt. Steve was shaved with his hair neatly in place.

Just outside the courthouse, I said, "I'm wearing another pair of pants under my outer pants. Eldon said warm clothes really help in prison, and cold, damp weather is coming."

The ornate court building, a relic from the Spanish rule of northern Morocco, had an arched portico entrance with wide steps. Entering the courtroom, we faced a raised bench where three judges sat in black robes, looking down. The rows of seats were crowded with Moroccans. As soon as we entered, an armed officer directed us to the front row of seats. He ordered the Moroccans sitting there to get up and give us their seats. Before we could sit down, the lead judge motioned us forward. He asked in Spanish if we were willing to proceed or if we wanted to obtain a lawyer. Steve responded in Spanish he was ready to go forward with the case, and he could participate with the proceedings.

The judge asked in Spanish, "*¿Puedes pagar una multa?* (Can you pay a fine?)"

To which Steve replied, "*Si, si, no es muy alto* (Yes, if it's not too high)."

Hearing this, the courtroom burst out laughing. The judges smiled too, and hitting his gavel, the lead judge said, "One hundred dirhams ($25)." The judges also ordered us go the next day to the national police office and obtain residency papers.

After paying the fine with our passports in our pockets, we shook hands in victory.

"We got fined $12.50 each and told not to do it again," Steve said as he hugged Gerri on our return from the Larache court.

"Yes, and the judge told us to apply to the Gendarmerie Nationale and get residency permits," I added as I hugged Gerri too.

"Incredible. I bet Mina and the landlord wired the case. Everything is done behind the scenes in Morocco," Gerri responded.

"Maybe so, but I credit it a little to my courtroom behavior. I've still got some lawyer left in me," Steve said.

I went to change out of my two pairs of pants.

The next morning, the three of us drove to the gendarmerie headquarters in Larache to make the application for resident permits as ordered by the court. The national police force represented the king and wasn't comprised of local residents like the Larache cops. The national officers had a reputation for violence and acting arrogant and surly. Just entering the headquarters scared me, especially when seeing the large photograph of the king, Hassan II, hanging above the entry desk. We stood in front of a dark short-haired officer with a mean face for nearly ten minutes before he looked up and asked us in Arabic what we wanted. Steve replied in Spanish that we were in court yesterday and the judge ordered us to apply for residency permits. The officer said we were wasting our time to apply as no residency permits could be obtained. Steve replied we didn't want to get into more trouble. He insisted we needed to apply because the court ordered us to. Angrily, the man directed us to a bench in the hallway and told us to sit down and wait. We politely thanked him and sat on the bench. The man continued to look at papers on his desk, paying no attention to us. The clock on the wall said 10:15 a.m. At 11:45 a.m., Steve got up and went over to the officer again, asking what we needed to do as we were sitting for over an hour and half. The officer said again that no permits were being issued, but Steve told him the court ordered us to apply. Obviously frustrated and angry, the officer said we needed to go to a photographer and come back with four passport-type photos each.

As most businesses were closed from 1:00 to 4:00 p.m., we raced outside and down the street to a studio offering, "*Fotos para pasaportes*." The photographer took our pictures with a Polaroid camera and gave us the four copies. When we returned to the gendarmerie, the door was locked as apparently the officer and staff went to lunch. We went to a small café on the square.

"That police guy scared me. His whole vibe was frightening. There was hate in his eyes, and he definitely doesn't want to issue us residency permits," Gerri said as she drank lemonade.

"He scared me too, but what can we do? The court ordered us to get the permit. If we don't get one and something happens, we'll be in deep shit. I doubt it will be a small fine for a second and continuing offense," Steve replied.

"This is just the Moroccan way of doing things. It's never easy getting anything from any official. It's almost required that a person, especially Westerners and hippies, be given the runaround. I'm sure he'll process the permit after a little more persistence," I said, acting as the knowing Morocco hand.

"Okay, siesta is over, let's go back with the photos," Steve said and paid the restaurant check.

The same officer sat at the same desk with the same hostile expression on his face. When we entered, he stood up and said, "Put the photos here," pointing to his desktop, "and take a seat on the bench."

We could see the officer did not even touch the photos but continued to look at other papers, occasionally standing up and putting things in a file cabinet behind him.

After two more hours of sitting, Steve got up with me and Gerri standing behind him. "*Que passa?*" (What's happening?) Steve asked in a demanding tone.

At this point, the officer picked up the phone and, staring at us with added hostility, dialed a three-digit number and began speaking to the person on the other end in Arabic. It became apparent he called the court to find out if what we told him was true. His face changed, and we heard the word, "*Athnan*" (Arabic for two). He said something that seemed to mean that three were now applying in his office.

He put down the phone and said in a gentle way with a particularly evil expression, "Come back tomorrow morning, and I'll take care of you."

We rushed into the street with Gerri saying, "I'll not be back there tomorrow. The court said there were only two, and now there are three and I'm the third. Who knows what that sadistic-looking cop would do to me."

"We can't just ignore what the judge said and not go back for the permits," I said as Steve drove out of town as if the police were already after us.

At the house, Gerri shouted, "I'm leaving tonight even if I have to hitchhike by myself!"

"I'll go with you. We wanted to go to Spain for Christmas anyway, so now we'll get there a few weeks earlier. We'll celebrate in Malaga with Max and Joan," Steve said as he also began to pack.

"I'm staying here," I said. "I don't think anyone will come here from Larache. I don't want to run away. I'm going to stay here now and then come to Spain just before Christmas."

"Fine with me. I want to get to the border," Gerri said as she began putting together her possessions. "Since the hepatitis, I've been thinking of going to England and working there for a while, and that guy just sealed the deal."

"Let's calm down. I don't want us to break up just because some cop throws a scare into us. We can go to Spain, and when we return, we'll have new three-month visas, be legal, and can continue our lives," Steve said.

"I don't want to break up either, but Morocco doesn't feel good to me now. We'll have to be together somewhere else. I hope you'll meet me in England in the spring, but if not, I'm sorry. I won't live in fear, which I'd do if I stayed or came back here," Gerri said.

Steve and Gerri evolved a plan where she would go from Spain to England now and he would meet her there after returning to Khemis with me in January for another three months.

In the dark, Steve and Gerri packed the van, fleeing like refugees.

I remained tranquil, saying, "I'm more determined than ever to devote myself to the dharma path. I'll use these weeks before I come to Spain to meditate and practice with more diligence."

"We'll see you in Malaga. I'll come back here to resume our study and practice together, although I'm feeling more and more like I need a teacher if I want to advance my meditation," Steve said as he hugged me goodbye.

"Let's get out of here. I want to be on the ferry to Spain before that jerk in Larache realizes we're not coming back," Gerri said, giving me a hug and a kiss.

We joined hands and said, "May all beings be happy and peaceful." Then they drove off into the night.

After Steve and Gerri departed, I sat cross-legged on the floor of the living area and prepared a large bowl of hash. As I took my first hit, I began to relax from the excitement caused by our arrest, time in jail, trial, and today's encounter with the Gendarmerie Nationale. Confident there would be no visit by the police officers to Khemis, I did not fear any further police action. The gendarmerie officer did not want to process the application for residency, so why would he pursue us?

Being alone in Khemis, where I lived for the past nine months, gave me a chance to increase my dedication to the spiritual life. Without companions, nothing in my surroundings would distract me from my quest. I'd continue a routine similar to what I did in the jail cell. I would do two yoga sessions and two longer meditation periods every day with the added plus of having the holy texts at my fingertips.

Gerri not coming back made me sad. She added an artistic spark to our activities, and she became a true devotee of the dharma. Together the three of us comprised a band of seekers, a Buddhist sangha. On the other hand, at times, her presence served as an irritant and a distraction. Steve and I, both without a woman, both focused on the path and both ready to work hard to advance our practice could make rapid strides.

As I smoked more hash, I reflected on the impossibility of deeming whether an occurrence was "good" or "bad" as the Zen story taught. Being arrested seemed "bad," but now the results seemed to be "good." Now I'd taste the hermit's life as the tarot predicted. Looking forward to the future with enthusiasm, I passed out.

A few days later, a knock on the door surprised me. I put down the Sufi book. Max and Joan were standing on the doorstep with big smiles on their faces and a box of French pastries in their hands.

"Greetings, greetings, greetings," I said and hugged them.

"Steve and Gerri are in Malaga staying at our house. They send their love and said we should bring you a treat from them," Joan said as she handed me the box.

I said, "Want to smoke some hash or kief?"

They declined, so we dived into the rich treats they brought.

"You look healthy and fit… Being on your own seems to agree with you," Max said. "Gerri in particular was worried about you."

"I'm more than fine. I'm planning to come to Spain before Christmas. What brings you to Morocco now?" I asked.

Max looked around sheepishly; his handsome, tan face made him look like a movie star as he said, "I've come on business. I'm not a retired engineer. I'm a hash smuggler. Our van has a secret compartment. I fill it with hash and sell in bulk through connections in the States. I want you to help me buy hash in Tangier." He continued, "All I ask is for you to introduce me to your connection in Tangier. I'll make the purchase and pay you for your help. I'll get the hash to Spain and into the States. From our conversations, I thought that was something you could do. You have the best hash, and after the introduction, you won't have to do anything else."

Surprised, I contemplated Max's offer. I could introduce Max to Mustapha. I did small deals like this before without any problems. I could use the money, whatever the amount. It would go a long way in Khemis. Having money of my own would give me independence, and if Steve did pursue his idea of seeking a teacher and leaving Morocco, I would be in a position to continue without Steve's financial support. I believed I was doing a public service by supplying hash.

I didn't see any downside to Max's proposal, so I said, "Sure, I'll happily help you."

"Can you read a Milarepa story before you get it together to go to Tangier to make the deal?" Joan asked. "I love listening to you read and appreciate the wisdom. We're going to Milarepa country next year. 'Kathmandu in '72.'"

I reached for the Milarepa book, opened it at random, and saying, "Obeisance to all Gurus," I began to read. "Be humble and practice diligently, never hope quickly to attain enlightenment but meditate until you die."

After reading the story, I put The Rolling Stones cassette, "*Sticky Fingers*," in the player. The song "Sister Morphine" filled the air. Mick sang, "Can't you see, Sister Morphine, I'm trying to score?"

I changed into my hippie outfit—a fringed shirt, leather vest, blue jeans, and desert boots. As I put on the shoes, I noticed how different it was to wear them after having spent most of my time wearing Moroccan slippers.

When I reentered the outer room, Joan said, "Very handsome, I don't think the women of Tangier will be able to resist you."

"We'll see, but now my first priority is getting you the good hash you want to buy," I said as I locked the front door and put the key in its hiding place.

Max showed me two thousand dollars in hundred-dollar bills. He told me he wanted to buy as much hash as he could get. The usual price of hash was two hundred dollars a kilo, so Max could buy ten kilos (about twenty-two pounds) with his money. I'd never dealt in this quantity before.

In Tangier, we rendezvoused with a friend of Max, who was driving an expensive new rental car. Joan got out of the van, gave me a hug, kissed Max, and wished us good luck. Max already arranged to meet the man and Joan on a hill outside Tangier after we completed the deal.

When Max and I arrived at the Café Royale, Max parked the van and, picking up a large straw basket, followed me inside. Mustapha greeted me warmly and guided us to the upstairs psychedelic room.

Mustapha brought out some oranges as he asked me, "How is your life in the country?"

I responded, "*Mumtaz*," the word for very well.

After about fifteen minutes of small talk, I said, "My friend here would like to buy ten kilos of your fine hash."

Mustapha replied, "Excellent."

I continued, "At our usual price," to which Mustapha nodded his head.

Max and I sat, silently listening to a Jimi Hendrix tape playing "And the Gods Made Love" as Mustapha left the room. When he returned, he held ten slabs, each about the size and thickness of a book, and placed them on the table. Max looked at the pile and took a slab from the middle and, reaching into his pocket, withdrew and unfolded a pocketknife. He drove the knife into the middle of the hash and cut out a piece he smelled and examined carefully. Usually people tested hash by cutting off a corner, but Max, cutting into the middle of a slab, surprised me. Max knew that street hustlers would put good hash at the corners and camel shit in the middle.

After examining the hash, Max said, "Fine," but he added, "With this volume, I should get a better price."

Mustapha said, "You're with Fred, you are getting my good-friend price."

They haggled back and forth as with every purchase for every product in Morocco. Finally, Mustapha took another half slab from under his desk and added it to the pile. Max took the twenty hundred-dollar bills from his pocket and laid them on the table one at a time. Mustapha scooped up the bills quickly as Max opened the straw basket and put the hash into a green nylon sports bag inside.

When we got up to walk out, Mustapha handed me a chunk of hash, saying, "*Shukraan.*" Downstairs Mustapha picked up a leather wallet for sale in the gift shop and handed it to me, saying, "I'm always glad to see you. Please, come by when you are in town."

On the way to the prearranged meeting place, Max reached into his shirt pocket, took out five one hundred-dollar bills, and handed them to me. We never discussed my fee, but five hundred dollars exceeded my expectations. I never touched the hash and so I wasn't a "dealer." Just by making introductions, I created a source of income. Besides, based on my expenses in Khemis, I could live like a king for six months with this fee. I also got a nice piece of hash and a wallet.

We met Joan and the other man at a dusty parking area on a hill overlooking the ocean. When Max drove up and parked next to them, Joan got out of the car and started to freak because of how long it took us to return. Max held her in his arms until she calmed down. Max put the straw basket it in the other man's car, and he and Joan drove me back to the center of Tangier, where they dropped me off.

I walked slowly around the courtyard. *When would the American Embassy arrive to free me? Maybe no one knew my situation. Maybe I'd never be released.*

The dinner gong brought welcome relief; I needed my evening downer pills to calm my agitation.

CHAPTER 10

Book of the Dead

Buddha cannot be found through searching
So, contemplate your own mind.

—Milarepa, *The Gray Rock Vajra Enclosure*

Soon after breakfast, as I walked around the yard one morning, I noticed the armed soldiers opening the metal gate to admit a newer model auto. I caught a glimpse of the driver, who did not appear Moroccan and wore a suit jacket and tie.

Could this finally be a representative of the American Embassy coming to free me?

I couldn't see the area where the car parked, but the appearance of car gave me renewed hope. I decided to remain in a position to see any further activity at the gate and sat down against the wall. However, as my morning dose of downers hit, I got drowsy and drifted into thoughts of how I began my second year in Morocco when Steve and I returned from Spain.

After the deal, ten days later, I got off the ferry in Malaga expecting to see my friends. However, only Steve greeted me.

I asked, "Where's everyone?"

"They've gone north. Gerri rode to London with Max and Joan," Steve said. "From London, Max and Joan will ship their van, with the hash hidden inside, to Boston.

"Right now I'm committed to reaching enlightenment," Steve continued.

The following day, we bought supplies for our return to Khemis. Walking on the main street in Malaga, we passed a fine leather goods store. In the window, a pair of boots caught my eye.

I said, "Those boots remind of the Dylan song 'Boots of Spanish Leather.'"

Steve said, "I've been wanting to buy you a special gift. This is it. They sure would complete your hippie look."

The boots fit me perfectly, and we left the store with them and tin of shoe polish.

On January 6, 1972, my ferry trip from Malaga to Morocco differed from my March fourth crossing almost a year before. Gail and Patsy were long gone, and Gerri left too. Steve remained, but he intended to reunite with Gerri after his three-month Moroccan visa expired in April.

Seeing the white towers of the casbah rising above Tangier signaled my return home. My heart swelled as the sounds and smells of the city enveloped the boat. I relished the opportunity ahead for concentrated study and practice.

We intended to return to Khemis without spending a night in Tangier. We needed one vital item, our stash of kief. Remembering our last bargaining session with Rocky, I didn't relish making the purchase. We parked near Barbara Hutton's mansion, where men on the street watched vehicles for a small fee, and walked up to Baba's

Rocky greeted us with the traditional slight bow and, touching his hand to his heart, said "*Salaam alaikum.*"

I responded with a bow and said, "*Mualaikum salaam.*" I looked Rocky in the eye and said, "We've just come back from Spain, and we want to replenish our kief supply. But we're also anxious to get home. We want thirty *rabitas*, and we'll pay the same price as last time." I paused dramatically, catching my breath, and before Rocky could say anything, I continued, "And we'll pay you a little extra for prompt, no-hassle delivery."

Rocky bowed and called over a man, who he instructed in Arabic. "Of course, my friend Fred, I just sent Saleem for thirty-one as you are such good customers."

I counted out two hundred dirhams as Saleem returned with a straw basket filled with white-wrapped conical packages. I looked into the basket and counted the packages without taking them out. Thirty-one.

I handed the money to Rocky, saying, "*Shukraan.*"

Rocky didn't count the bills but just slipped them in his pocket.

I transferred the packages into my backpack and said, "*Vaya con dios.*"

To which Rocky replied "God be with you."

Our Khemis house, unoccupied for three weeks, felt like an icebox.

"Since we don't have any gloves, we'll have to wear socks on our hands," I said. "Let's put on the wool sweaters we brought in anticipation of this winter weather."

"Let's get our blankets, sleeping bags, and warm gear. How about some hot tea after we smoke a bowl of hash," Steve said, putting the sleeping bag behind his back as insulation from the cold wall.

I retrieved the can of hash plus a shopping bag filled with pipes, ashtrays, pouches, a cutting board, boxes of wooden matches, and our kief knife.

When I handed a filled pipe to Steve, I said, "Hash will lead us on our quest. May we find the enlightenment we seek through study and practice. May all beings be happy and peaceful."

As Steve took a drag, he said, "May our thoughts and deeds be a credit to the dharma. May all our actions be motivated by love." As he finished, he broke into a coughing fit, blowing out the smoke with a heaving chest. On his second hit, he coughed just as much. With his eyes bulging, gulping down some water, he said, "Good shit."

After the fourth go-round, I braced my leg muscles to prevent falling over onto my side. When Steve offered me another hit, I raised my palm outward in the stop motion and said, "*Kafia*," Arabic for "enough."

I hadn't smoked hash in three weeks. My head was swimming as I focused on the flickering candlelight reflecting and bouncing off the sides of the metal cheese can candleholders.

Steve put on a tape, and I heard James Taylor singing "Country Road." We sat silently listening to the cassette, but when Taylor sang, "I guess my feet know where they want me to go / walking on a country road," I imagined walking on the spiritual path in the Moroccan countryside. We cherished our battery-powered cassette player, our only modern appliance. We moved to Khemis with two tapes, The Rolling Stones *Flowers* and Hendrix *Electric Ladyland*. Now we had close to thirty. We'd stocked up on *D* batteries and, at times, removed the battery from the van and carried it to the house to power the player.

Although I wasn't sure I'd be able to stand up, pulling myself first to my knees and to my feet, I stretched my arms above my head and said, "I'll make us a pot of tea. Want anything else?"

After I poured chamomile tea, I picked up a paperback book with a black cover and large red letters reading, *The Tibetan Book of the Dead*. When hepatitis brought me to the edge of death, I remember thinking I should have studied this book as preparation.

I said, "This book contains the central embodiment of Buddhist teaching in the Tibetan tradition. We've been scattered in the way we've been studying, but this book can give us a focus for our study and practice."

Steve responded in a slurred voice, "*The Tibetan Book of the Dead*."

I interpreted this as Steve's agreement, and pulling three candles and placing them in a semicircle in front of me, I examined the photograph showing the translator and the editor in Gangtok, Sikkim. "Look at this picture, tell me they aren't stoned."

I handed the book to Steve, who looked at Evens-Wentz wearing an embroidered silk vest, holding a rose with his head tilted back and his eyes closed, standing next to a Tibetan man wearing a robe and holding a *dorje*—the thunderbolt of enlightenment—looking directly into the camera.

"No more reading tonight," Steve said just before he passed out, using his down jacket for a pillow.

Next morning, still wearing the djellaba I slept in, I stumbled out the front door as the cold air refreshed my senses.

In the courtyard, a sense of peace surrounded me. The sun was shining, and although I could see my breath, I knew soon the day would warm up. I heated water on the propane stove to wash my hands and face, and after I finished, I threw the water at the base of the rosebushes.

Returning to the main room, I reached for the small amount of kief I left behind when I went to Spain. One toke and my heart started to beat noticeably faster as my muscles relaxed and my mind drifted to the poster of Shiva hanging on the opposite wall.

When Steve woke up, he said, "First order of business is cleaning a *rabita*. I left a pipeful for you, but now we'll be out of cleaned kief."

"My kief-cutting callus has faded a bit," I said, rubbing the area on my right hand where I had developed a callus from the pressure of the knife I used to cut the marijuana flowers and black tobacco. Without saying anything, I began reading a story, "Like a mountain standing firm, meditate with steadfastness. Like a river flowing on and on, meditate without interruption. Like sun and moon in all their glory, meditate clearly without darkness. To make yourself a vessel of the dharma, meditate beyond all words."

After the story, Steve said, "Meditate, meditate, meditate—that's Milarepa's message. He gives his disciples instructions and guides them. We'll be meditating plenty, I foresee, but who is going to give us assistance as we delve deeper?"

"The guidance comes from *Secret Doctrines*, our other readings, and beginning now from *The Tibetan Book of the Dead*. The instructions in these books are the modern substitutes for going to a human teacher. Besides, we're getting the instructions from Milarepa by our repeated readings of his wisdom," I replied.

"Yes, we have the generalized wisdom and instructions, but we aren't getting any individual, specific attention," Steve responded.

"We sound like scholars debating a philosophical point instead of yogis practicing, practicing, practicing. Let's get warm clothes on, take our sleeping bags to sit on, and go up to the roof in the sunlight and meditate," I said.

Steve followed suit, picking up the plastic travel alarm clock we used to time our meditation sessions. When we arranged ourselves with our legs crossed in the half-lotus posture, Steve set the alarm for twenty minutes and said, "I dedicate the merit from this practice to the welfare of all living beings. May all beings be happy," and closed his eyes.

I started by closing my eyes and concentrating on my breathing, thinking to myself, *Rising*, as I inhaled, and *Falling*, as I exhaled. *Rising, falling, rising, falling*, but after only a few breaths, my mind went to the statements Steve made. Was a teacher really necessary? Could a seeker achieve enlightenment without one? Once I noticed my mind drifting, I returned my attention to my breath, *Rising, falling, rising, falling*, but again, thoughts about studying with a teacher entered my mind. *Where would we find a teacher of Buddhist wisdom in Morocco?* I didn't want to leave Morocco, so seeking a teacher elsewhere wasn't even a possibility. When I became aware of losing my concentration, I returned to *Rising, falling*, but when the alarm, rang most of my time was not spent focused on my breath.

As we both stood up, Steve said, "I had real difficulty keeping my mind focused. I kept drifting to thoughts and fantasies about looking for and finding a teacher. Every time I brought my mind back to my breathing, I drifted off again."

Not wanting to rekindle our disagreement, I merely responded, "Let's make breakfast and clean some kief. I'd love to smoke a pipe right now."

After breakfast, I brought out the paraphernalia for cleaning the kief—the knife, cutting board, shoebox top, our pouches along with two of the *rabita*s we bought yesterday. Steve unrolled one of the *rabitas* and took out the three pieces of black tobacco and put it aside as I examined the marijuana flowers approvingly.

I said, "Very good dope, look at the size and number of flowers on each stalk," and held up a flower top.

After removing the marijuana seeds and all but the smallest green leaves surrounding the flowers, a white mound remained on the cutting board between us. I pushed it to one side as I picked up a piece of black tobacco and began chopping it after removing the hard veins.

"I'm going to use the flowers without the tobacco, so I'll take half of what we prepared now before you mix in what you're cutting," Steve said as he scooped part of the pile into his pouch. "I feel this is a new phase for us, and we should take the healthy approach of not smoking tobacco and not smoking hash. We'll save our lungs. My idea is after dinner, we make a *majoun* and eat our nightly hash starting this evening."

"Eating the hash sounds like a good idea to me, but I'll stick to the tobacco with the kief. I honor the Moroccan way of smoking," I said as I chopped some tobacco and mixed it with the flowers remaining on the cutting board. I studied the mixture and sprinkled in more tobacco and said, "This is plenty white and is a bit more than two parts marijuana and one part tobacco. I'd be proud to share it with a Moroccan."

At the same time, Steve filled his pipe with just the flowers, lit it, and inhaled. With one draw, he sucked in the entire small bowl. He sat for a few minutes reflecting on the experience and said, "Now it's hitting. I like the taste, but it feels a bit different without the tobacco." He refilled his pipe and smoked another bowl, again finishing it in one toke.

After I smoked a traditional bowl, we sat silently for quite a while.

Finally, I stood up and stretched and said, "The sun is shining, and our roof is now as warm as it's going to get. Let's take advantage and go up for a yoga session."

Steve nodded his agreement and followed me to the roof, where we arranged ourselves side by side, facing the sun. We began by doing a series of ten salutes to the sun. By the time we finished ten salutes, we were sweating. We continued one asana after another for close to an hour. We ended with "the corpse pose," which the book described as, "Become like a dead body lying peacefully with no plans and without any worries."

Steve said, "Leary and Alpert wrote a guide for acid trips called *The Psychedelic Experience* based on *The Tibetan Book of the Dead.* We'll work with the original text. It contains a psychological commentary by Jung."

I commented, "If we are diligent, it will provide the necessary guidance we've been seeking."

In the evening, as we returned our dinner bowls to the kitchen, Steve took our small frying pan and heated some olive oil. He took out a can of peanuts, a bar of chocolate, and some sesame seeds.

Steve was preparing to make a *majoun* and said, "Let's add some raisins and chopped dates." As Steve stirred the ingredients over a low heat, he broke off the corner of a chunk of hash into a mortar and pestle, ground it into powder, and added it the mixture.

Bringing the frying pan into the living area, I took out *The Book of the Dead.* I waved my hands over the frying pan and said, "May this hash bring health and enlightenment to our heads, hearts, and bodies." I handed a spoon to Steve, who dipped into the gooey mass.

He tasted the mixture and gave thumbs-up and said, "A gritty but delicious hash candy."

I opened the book to where I stopped yesterday and read the forepiece, the dedication, and some quotations preceding the preface. At first Steve was listening closely, but soon he drifted away.

I thought about the life of a seeker and how good it was to be immersed in studying the holy Buddhist dharma. The everyday world's illusory nature became clear as the walls shifted and the poster of Shiva came alive. I recognized the dreamlike quality of life and how everyday experiences were just one rather limited form of consciousness. I was reading the words of ancient wisdom, but I was also floating above the room, looking down on it.

When I read a quote from Milarepa contained in the Introduction, "Combine in a single whole, the goal of aspiration, the meditation, and the practice, and so attain understanding by experimentation," I knew exactly what he was talking about.

After a period of silence, we looked at each other, and I said, "This is it. We can do it. Eating hash is brilliant. I feel great and my mind is opened."

Steve mumbled a response and lay over on his side, passing out.

The next morning, we both slept later than usual, but when I got up, I felt energized and full of enthusiasm as we resumed our regular practices. We even took a short walk in the surrounding countryside where the barren fields were waiting to be planted. We both expressed how successful we felt the shift from smoking to eating hash had been. Steve enthused with a long monologue about the healthiness of the switch we made.

However, Steve said, "I don't think smoking kief without the tobacco is as satisfying as adding tobacco to the mixture." He took out some pieces of black tobacco and chopped them and added them to his pouch. "I can see what benefit the tobacco has in making the kief burn slower, so it lasts longer. Plus, the tobacco makes my heart beat faster and gives me an extra rush. A small amount of tobacco isn't going to hurt my health, and I want the kief to help my head."

"The Moroccans know what they are doing. This is a centuries old custom. There's a good reason for it. I respect the Moroccan traditions. I think when they say, 'Hash makes you crazy,' it's just a superstition. They fear the transition to the truly enlightened state and call it crazy, but it's really finding the god within each of us," I said.

"Eating the hash worked well, and I can't wait until we do it again this evening," Steve replied.

For our evening meal, Steve cut some cabbage and turnips and added two packets of Knorr instant vegetable soup for additional flavoring to the already half-full pot of last night's carrot, potatoes, and onions. Depending on the amount of water, we called our dishes either a soup or a stew.

I took out the frying pan and, using the last bit of butter, stirred a mix of the same *majoun* ingredients as we used the night before. "I think I'll up the quantity of chocolate tonight to finish this bar," I said while holding a Toblerone bar. I thickened the candy goo by adding ground hash I carefully sprinkled in. After heating the mixture for a short time, I put it aside, saying, "Maybe we should have measured the ingredients we used last night. The result was so perfect."

"I have faith in you," Steve said. "Hash, chocolate, and other healthy stuff…how can we go wrong?"

In the sitting room, I waved my hands over the *majoun* and said, "May this aid us on our path to enlightenment. May all beings be happy." I dipped two spoons into the mixture, handing one to Steve, who put it in his mouth.

"I like the flavor better, but this seems grittier than last night's confection," Steve said as he took another spoonful.

I ate three spoonfuls, savoring each one. Finally licking my spoon, I picked up the book and read a poem attributed to the Buddha, "Throw off the chain of birth and death—thou knowest what they mean… So free from craving, in life on earth. Thou shalt go in the way calm and serene." I stopped reading and took several sips from the glass of water I kept nearby. Instead of resuming reading, I said, "Calm and serene."

Steve replied, "Calm and serene, calm and serene. The Buddha said, 'Get away from distraction's craze.' We've certainly done that."

I stared at the now nearly empty frying pan. The difficulty of the path weighed like a physical pressure on my chest. Overcoming death presented a rather lofty goal.

Sunlight coming through the closed shutters woke me up. I lay a few feet from the spot where I read the Buddha's poem. The frying pan remained where we left it. I tried to get up, but I slumped down again. I hadn't felt this weak since the most debilitating phase of my hepatitis. Using both my arms, I pulled myself to a seated position, leaning against the wall, and rested there for several minutes before marshaling my strength, and using the wall for support, I pulled myself to my feet. After resting against the wall, I slowly walked outside. From the sun's position, I could tell it was late afternoon.

Back inside, Steve was still sleeping. I fell asleep again.

Steve's saying, "It's afternoon, can you get up? I'm worried. Are you okay?" awakened me. Then he said, "We slept late. The hash hit harder than the night before."

"If it's afternoon, you missed an entire day because I got up and went outside yesterday afternoon. It's been a day and a half and two nights since we ate that *majoun*," I said.

I realized we lost a day after eating the hash. It hit me that we had no way to control the dosage or the effects if we ate the hash instead of smoking it. When I smoked too much hash, I passed out, a regular occurrence, but Steve's idea of eating instead of smoking hash wasn't practical.

My stomach growled, and I took out some peanut butter, jam, and crackers and made a pot of chamomile tea. I brought these together with two plates and mugs back to the main room.

As I entered, Steve said, "Knocked out by hash. Blown away by hash. Psychedelicized by hash. We OD'd. Sometimes I forget the power of hash. We just experienced an object lesson in how powerful it can be."

"Don't freak out. The formula was just out of proportion. Don't start getting down on hash. We'll return to our routine of smoking hash in the evenings and reading *The Book of the Dead*. Now have some food and tea. I see you're already smoking kief," I said as I poured two steaming cups from the teapot.

After finishing every cracker piled high with peanut butter and jam, we relaxed. I turned on the cassette player to the sound of the Jefferson Airplane singing, "If you go chasing rabbits and you know you're going to fall / Tell 'em a hookah-smoking caterpillar has given you the call / Remember what dormouse said / Feed your head, feed your head."

"We don't know if it's two a.m. or four p.m.," Steve said.

"Time and space are just illusions anyhow. This was our dinner. I'm sure you're not tired, so how about a pipe of hash and some reading?" I countered, filling a large clay pipe bowl.

Steve told me he found his mind constantly drifting. Was hash help or hindrance to meditation? Why did the wisdom teachings warn against the use of intoxicants? Could just reading the books in our library provide the answers? I thought the hash freed my mind from its habitual anchors. Just as *The Book of the Dead* directed the deceased to be fearless in the soul's journey from death to rebirth, hash provided the opening to face those fears and become a fearless soul without physically dying.

"Listen to this," Steve said as he read from a section called the "Supreme Path of Discipleship." "'Meditation without knowledge, though giving results for a while, will in the end be devoid of true success.' There's a footnote, which adds, 'Or without the guiding teachings of a guru.'"

"We have the knowledge. That quote just says you need to base your meditation and practice on the Buddhist teachings. You keep going back to needing a guru or teacher, but Milarepa makes clear practice, practice, practice will lead to the same enlightened place," I replied as I finished a letter to my parents in Milwaukee.

"I think practice needs guidance. That's what Milarepa is doing for his disciples, guiding their practice," Steve replied.

The next day, the rain fell hard all day, making the short walk to the toilet area and kitchen chilling and unpleasant. Without the ability to go to the roof, we stayed in the sitting room wrapped in our sleeping bags. For a week, the rain did not stop; bundled up, we persevered with our study and practice.

On the seventh night of rain, I was preparing the hash pipe as Steve put on another pair of socks over the ones he was already wearing. He said, "We've reached the end of the introductory material. Tonight we start the actual text, which the lamas read for three days over the corpse. These are the instructions given to the person as he or she passes from one life to the next."

I said, "May this be an auspicious evening as we reflect on our journey in this life and our transition to future lives."

After smoking three pipes, I began, "The obeisance, to the divine body of truth, the incomprehensible boundless light..." I read a person's liberation could be achieved by concentrating on the clear light at the moment of death.

I drifted to thoughts of clear light windowpane LSD. I remembered an acid trip where my body was reduced to molecules, and a bright white light surrounded me. After focusing on the light, my molecules reformed into what I now thought might have been the image of a baby being born. I experienced a natural rebirth akin to the process described in *The Tibetan Book of the Dead.*

Closing the book, I said, "This is heavy material, going through death. Lamas read this to the dying person, 'O nobly born the time hath now come for thee to seek the path in reality. Thy breathing is about to cease.'"

"I wouldn't mind having lamas reading over me as I pass onto the next world," Steve said.

When we completed the text, we began to read the addenda, covering topics such as yoga, tantrism, and initiations.

Early one afternoon, I walked into the sitting room carrying a fresh loaf of brown bread. Water dripped from the hood of my djellaba as I sat down hearing Crosby, Stills, Nash and Young's singing, "We're riding on the Marrakesh Express / Sweeping cobwebs from the edges of my mind / Had to get away to see what we could find."

"Sounds good. Taking a trip to Marrakesh. They make it sound magical and I bet it would be," Steve mused as he sealed the letter to Gerri he just wrote.

I said, "We've finished the book. We can celebrate, get into warm southern weather, and tour parts of Morocco we haven't seen. Let's return to Taghazout Beach and go via Marrakesh."

"Right on, brother," Steve exclaimed.

A few minutes later, he spread out the road map of Morocco he retrieved from the van. We looked at the location of Marrakesh and its relationship to the coast and Taghazout.

"This calls for hash," I said.

"Look," Steve said, pointing to the map, "we can visit the holy city of Moulay Idriss, then we can go to the Roman ruins at Volubilis. From there, a few days in Fez and onto Marrakesh."

As the hash hit, we became enthusiastic, talking about what sites and places we would like to see. When the cassette tape ended, I reached for the player and set it to hear "Marrakesh Express" again. Until dinner, we studied the map, thinking about what supplies we would need for camping on the beach.

"We have plenty of hash, kief, and acid, so we've got the essentials," I said. "We've got *The Book of the Dead* and *The Songs of Milarepa* to read. With the blue tent and the Camper we can each have a living space. I dub this trip our road to enlightenment."

Steve said, "Let's clean the house and pack everything tomorrow. We can take acid the next day and leave the following day."

"Sounds ideal," I answered; even though I wanted to go south, I couldn't resist the suggestion of an acid trip.

Two days later, the house was well cleaned and the sun was shining.

I reached forward and put a tab on acid on my fingertip, saying, "This trip is the beginning of a new chapter in our spiritual development. May it and what follows take us further on the path to enlightenment. May all beings be happy."

As Steve took the other tab, he said, "Life and death are both illusions. May we know this in our essence and use this knowledge for the benefit of all sentient beings."

While waiting for the acid to hit, I picked up *The Book of the Dead* and, opening it at random, began to read, "O, nobly born, whatever fear and terror may come to thee in the Bardo, forget not these words, and bearing their meaning at heart, go forwards… May I not fear the bands of peaceful and wrathful deities, mine own thought forms."

I assumed the lotus posture and, closing my eyes, imagined fireworks exploding in front of me. The molecules of my body were moving and reforming into a perfect Buddha. Through the process of rebirth or transmutation, I became an enlightened being.

I shouted, "I'm the Buddha! I'm Shiva! I'm Christ!" I stood up and waved my arms and again shouted, "I'm enlightened! I'm Buddha, and I'm the Christ!"

Steve stayed on the roof, only coming down once to get water. I remained sitting in the lotus posture, not moving from where I started in the morning.

In preparation for the journey, Steve paid the landlord the fifteen-dollar monthly rent for March in advance. With the Camper packed, we locked the house, hid the key, and drove south. I rolled a joint, a less conspicuous way to smoke than the pipe.

With the Crosby, Stills, Nash, and Young tape in the Camper's player, I said, "May this trip bring insights and fun."

Our first stop was the sacred city of Moulay Idriss south of Meknes, a Muslim holy city and the goal of pilgrims but with restrictions on non-Muslims who could not enter this holy shrine. After our arrival, we viewed the beautiful buildings from rocks above the town and then got in the Camper and moved on. We reached Volubilis, the ruins of a large Roman city, marking the farthest southern expansion of the Roman Empire. As we approached, tall columns appeared out of the mist. Storks migrated to the area to birth their young. I pointed out empty nests on the top of several columns near the small area where visitors could park and camp. Steve paid a two-dollar fee, and we parked for the night. The clouds were now thickening, and a light, misty rain began to fall.

Next morning, Steve said, "Now I'm ready for a magical day in Fez."

Four hours later, we strolled through Fez' extensive marketplace. Shops selling colorful silks and brightly dyed wools as well as a variety of leather products from the local tannery lined both sides of the covered, narrow, cobbled streets. Wearing our djellabas, we didn't attract any attention. On one side of small square, heavily armed soldiers appeared to be hassling sullen-looking students. The negative vibes shocked us. We returned to our Camper and drove back to our parking spot in the campground on the outskirts of town.

Next morning, we got up early and, skipping our morning rituals, drove out soon after sunrise, heading to Marrakesh. After several turns, the road opened into a two-lane highway with the Atlas Mountains rising into the clouds on our left.

During the first hour of driving, we didn't talk until Steve broke the silence, saying, "I'm going to see Gerri in England when our three-month visas expire on April twelfth."

"I'll be in Khemis if or when you ever want to come back," I replied as I mulled over the future.

"I'm drawn to go to India and Nepal to further my meditation and be in a Buddhist land, Katmandu in '72," Steve said. "Why don't you join me and we'll go east together?"

"I've been in Morocco only a year and four months. I'm not ready to leave now. We have the perfect setup to advance on the path," I replied.

We both lapsed into silent thought again until Steve pulled over at a wide spot in the road. We got out and walked to the edge of a steep drop-down, a rocky slope with a burnt-out crashed truck at the bottom.

"Just a reminder," I said, not having to elaborate further about the transitory nature of life and the ever-present possibility of unexpected death. "Right now I'm excited about Marrakesh," I said, knowing I would stay in Khemis and continue my quest whatever Steve's course.

"Marrakesh and then the beach. Let's read a Milarepa story before we drive on," Steve said.

The drive took longer than anticipated and required us to slow down to detour around broken sections. We passed through a hot desolate landscape of rocks and sand until in late afternoon, palm trees appeared ahead. The temperature lowered, and an invigorating coolness hit us as we entered a green oasis where the air smelled of flowers. Birds were flying through the palms, and their calls mixed with the clacking of the palm fronds created a magical atmosphere. After driving past palm groves and crossing a flowing stream, the walls of Marrakesh rose before us. The twelfth-century minaret of the moorish Koutoubia Mosque towered over the city.

Sitting in the Camper, we lit a hash joint and smoked it slowly as a caravan of heavily laden camels passed going toward a gate to the city.

"I already feel how special this place is, and I'm ready to dive into it. Onward," I said.

I spotted a broken-down-looking establishment with an entranceway for vehicles to drive through and park in the interior. I pointed it out to Steve, who pulled inside. Rooms surrounded a central courtyard with a few vans with German license plates parked but most of the spaces empty.

Steve got out and went into a door marked, "Reception," and found an elderly woman in white dress sitting behind a high counter. "*Labas, bon jour*," Steve said in a friendly way.

"American?" the woman replied.

"*Oui*," Steve said. "*Combien por un chamber?*"

After a short bargaining session, we were shown a small room with two single beds. There was a sink and shower but no hot water.

"This is okay and cheap. The van will be safe, and we don't need a hot shower," Steve said as I began unpacking the van.

"Let's get settled and see the famous souk before dark," I responded.

The fading light gave the buildings a reddish glow as we walked one block from our pension to a huge open space. There were camels, goats, donkeys, horses, and mules tended by young boys. The famous desert warriors with raised tattoos on their faces, whose skin was a black-blue color from the dye in the cloth they wore, mingled with people of every hue and costume. Flames from grills made out of fifty-gallon drums were shooting up from a row of food vending stands on one side of the space. A storyteller clapped his hands as he brought his tale to a conclusion in front of a crowd of rapt listeners. We wandered slowly among the people—some moving, deliberately carrying heavy loads, and others strolling, taking in the sights and smells with wonder just like us.

A tribal woman in an outfit of brightly colored scarves sat at a card table. A version of the tarot deck lay out in front of her on the table. She beckoned to us, putting her hand out, and said, "*Floos*," asking for some coins to read the cards.

Not directly responding, I said to Steve, "That's something I can do. I have the tarot deck and I can sit in the square and read the cards for anyone who stops by. Tomorrow is leap year day, February 29, 1972, I'll celebrate by being a tarot card reader in Marrakesh."

Steve didn't say anything as the woman called to us in a language neither of us understood. Obviously, she wanted some money as she pointed to the cards. Annoyed, I took out some coins and gave them to the woman, who looked at them disparagingly.

She put the deck on the table and indicated I should cut it with my left hand while still talking to Steve. "If I offer tarot readings, I might be able to meet some hippie chicks."

The woman passed her hands over the cards, bowed her head, and turned over the top card. "The tower" appeared, depicting a man and woman falling from a high tower, which had been hit by a lightning bolt. The tribal woman looked worriedly at me, said something else in her language, picked up the deck, folded her chair and the card table, and without a further word, rushed away.

Steve got a worried expression on his face, but I said in a joking voice, "I guess I only paid for a one card reading.

"Let's go over to those stands and see what we can get to eat," I said, motioning to the food stalls, where bright Coleman lamps were hung on wires and hot stews were being dished out.

After a dinner of vegetable stew with dried apricots, we returned to our room and lay down. Steve prepared a pipe of hash while I took out the tarot deck and *The Book of the Dead.*

I said, "The tower isn't a card that strikes me as very positive. It's a foreboding of disaster, but at least if it's me falling, there is a chick falling with me."

"You're going to sit in the souk stoned. I'll be your support crew and smoke hash and wander around. I doubt anyone will stop. The tribal woman didn't have many customers," Steve said. "If your idea is to connect with some Western women, I didn't see any of them either." Lighting the pipe, he said, "May you leap forward on the path to enlightenment on your leap year's day in the Marrakesh Square."

The next day, I smoked hash before I left the room. I walked to the section of the market where the women fortune tellers sat at tables. I lowered myself into the lotus posture with the tarot deck in front of me. Wearing my djellaba with my thick beard and long hair untied and spread down my back, I thought I looked like a holy man.

At first I attracted little attention. Steve watched for a while but became bored and left to explore the Grand Souk. Circles of viewers formed around the various performers. A man playing the flute charmed a cobra rising from a woven basket. A storyteller acted out the parts of various animals with such clear gestures it was obvious a camel was talking to a donkey.

A Moroccan man came over to me, wanting to know what I was doing there. Using a combination of English, French, Spanish, and Arabic and some sign language, I communicated I could read the cards. In our conversation, the man learned I was an American, which amazed him. Gesturing with his hands, he pointed and told other passersby, "Look, there's an American sitting in the square." At the same time, the man dropped several coins in the lap of my djellaba. More people started dropping coins in my djellaba thinking I was begging. People crowded around me, forming a circle three or four rows deep. Steve came through the crowd; calling over the bystanders, he asked me how it was going.

To which I replied, "I'm okay, but only Moroccan men are interested so far. No chicks."

"I'll check back later," Steve said as he faded back into the square.

Next time Steve returned, a larger crowd now encircled me as the word spread that an American was sitting in the souk.

Steve had to push his way through the onlookers as he called to me, "You have the largest circle of people in the market."

I did not respond. I was meditating.

A Moroccan man knelt down and invited me to come to his home and have dinner. When he went on to say I could also sleep with his wife, I respectfully declined. By early afternoon, the coins accumulating in my lap made me uncomfortable. I decided to redistribute the money and handed coins to young boys and girls who made up the first row encircling me. This started a near riot as children from throughout the market descended on me and began to push in from every direction. The children were yelling and pointing and grabbing at me with outstretched arms. More and more boys pushed forward, coming closer and closer, and I began to fear they would crush me.

I remembered a scene from a WWII movie that affected me as a boy. American soldiers came to bring food to starving villagers in

Africa. One GI jumped out of the truck and began to distribute cans of food. In the rush to get the food, the natives crushed the soldier to death. This was happening to me. My charitable action created the possibility of being smothered for my generosity. Frightened, I quickly gave out the coins. Having no money left, the excited children continued to surround me. To calm the situation and myself, I began meditating by focusing on a small white stone on the ground in front of me. As I sat motionless, the children drifted away.

Some passersby continued to drop money into my lap, but now I scooped the coins into the hood of my djellaba. In the late afternoon, I stood up, stretched, gathered the tarot cards, and walked out of the souk. I bought a pack of cigarettes at a small stand and went to an outdoor café, where I enjoyed a café au lait and a smoke.

Back in our room, I said the desire to be holy motivated me to give away the money people had put on my djellaba, but it really backfired. Steve pointed out I saved the situation by meditating to calm my own mind and the atmosphere around me.

"Leap year day in Marrakesh, people responded to your holiness and charitable intention," Steve said.

Silently, I reflected on the perception of me as a holy man when my intention was to meet hippie chicks and the day ended with cigarettes and coffee. I questioned my real motives and my genuine devotion to the dharma path. Was I really an embodiment of Milarepa's teachings?

Early the next morning, we left Marrakesh and drove silently for two hours through rugged terrain until we came over a hill where the Atlantic spread out before us. We drove north a short way along the Atlantic, the sound of the waves beckoning us to the beach at Taghazout.

When we arrived at the beach encampment, Steve turned onto a rough dirt track leading up the side of a dune to a campsite overlooking the beach. Steve parked, and I brought out two chairs and, facing west, lit a fat hash-and-tobacco joint.

"Smell the air," Steve said, looking at the shades of blue and green in the ocean waves.

I said, "Let's go," and we both raced down the dune and across the beach and jumped into the cool ocean.

Hitting the water washed away the effects of the dusty ride from Marrakesh. Swimming and floating in the bracing water pumped new life into our bodies. As I swam and played in the waves, two naked women with bronzed tanned bodies came slowly down to the ocean and jumped in. I spoke to one of the women, both of us smiling at each other in navel-high water.

On the beach, I took a towel and said, "We got invited to watch the sunset with those chicks and their campmates on the third dune south of where we're parked. I don't know if my personality overwhelmed her or the fact I told her I had some killer hash."

At sunset, the spectacular colors illuminated the clouds as campers looked to see the green flash at the sun's disappearance. Drums began to beat, and someone hit a gong three times just as the sun disappeared. The evening breeze chilled the air. We accepted the invitation of the Brazilian women and recognized two Brazilian men in the group from last spring. After hugging, they led us to a hollowed-out spot protected from the wind with rugs.

Renaldo brought out a pipe and, taking a piece of hash from a metal box, filled the pipe and lit it. Passing it to me, he said, "Good to see you again. Did you bring any of the good hash you shared at Paradise Canyon last year?"

"Of course," I said, passing the pipe.

Drums were beating louder, and people were moving toward a large campfire in a hollow where three dunes came together. A naked man covered with tattoos was feeding wood into the flames, and a row of men and a few women were drumming. The haunting notes of a flute added rhythm, and people began dancing in a cleared area south of the fire. Most of the women were topless and a few wore nothing but perhaps a necklace or scarf tied around their ankles. Steve and I joined a group standing a bit farther back where a hash pipe and bottles of liquor were going from hand to hand. After a few hits on the pipe, Steve was moving with the group, which had grown to about twenty. The music and drugs created a stoned crowd of hippies radiating peace and love in every direction. Later Steve told me people from France, Germany, Brazil, Canada, Australia, New Zealand, Japan, Holland, Switzerland, some African countries, mostly former French colonies, plus one person with bright-red skin from Finland made up the dancers.

As the night got colder, people drifted away, and we returned to our campsite.

Sitting outside under a star-filled moonless sky, I said, "I'm so glad we took this trip. So much magic, so many adventures. I don't want us to break from our practices. Now we're settled here for a time, let's do our yoga, meditation, and reading."

"Come inside the Camper. I'll put on the lantern and let's read something now. I'm inspired," Steve said.

Inside I took out *The Book of the Dead* and said, "We've read the whole book. We've read most of it twice. Listen to this, 'Because thy body is one of voidness, thou needest not fear. The lords of death too are emanations from the radiance of thine own intellect.'"

Steve said, "Let's bring the teachings to life by acting them out. I'll take acid and lie down in the tent and be the dead person. You read the book as the lama giving the instructions to the person who just died," Steve said. "Living the experience of death seems a proper culmination for our studies."

"Let's see what's happening and figure out when we can see you through the transition from this life into the next," I said as I closed the book.

Walking among the Taghazout Beach settlements I came to the top of a dune. Michelle and Todd's Citroën with the British flag on the bumper meant I'd found old friends. Their beautiful Doberman pinscher, Ute, lay in the shade, and Lola sat a table drawing with colored pencils.

"Good to see you," Lola said.

Ute just picked up her head, looked at the group, and returned to lying down peacefully.

"Great to see you too, Lola, you've grown up this past year," I replied as Michelle emerged from her tent.

She hugged and said, "We were just talking about you, Steve, and Gerri, and we were wondering if we'd see you here again."

"Just Steve and I. We're camped three dunes over, near where we were last year," I said.

"Still got that good hash?" Todd asked as he got out of the tent.

"Sure, come over and smoke some. I've got some kief now. Want to share a pipe?" And not waiting for a reply, I sat down and filled my sebsi.

As I admired Ute, Michelle said, "Best dog in the world. Gentle as lamb with friends and children but alert and ready to show her teeth if anyone ever seems the least bit threatening to us." She nodded toward Ute, who seemed to know she had just been complimented. "We're going to breed her. She's part of a long line of purebred dogs, and we have contact with a registered stud. The pups will go for $500 each, and people are dying to get them because they'll be the perfect dogs."

Ute stood up and smelled me.

"Now she'll know we're friends. You can walk up to our tent at night and she won't even stir, but a stranger, watch out," Lola said proudly.

I patted Ute's head and stroked her smooth, dark fur and said, "Visit our site later and we can smoke something stronger than this kief."

The next morning after an extra heavy night of smoking and partying, I brewed tea and opened *The Tibetan Book of the Dead*, thumbing through it. My eyes lit on the pages covering "The Death Ceremonies." I read how the lama seated at the head of the dead person began the reading of the prayers and incantations over the body without anyone else present. The ceremony continued in stages until the spirit of the dead person was guided into a new birth. This was the ritual we wanted to do.

A short while later, Steve arrived back at the Camper, bringing two large colorful nylon bags full of yogurt, cheese, bananas, brown bread, as well as some treats of chocolate and sesame candy. "We're very low on hash. We've smoked most of what we brought with us. If we don't ration our use, we're going to be dry by the end of the week. No hash, what a disaster," Steve said.

For the next few days, we read Milarepa stories, did our yoga sessions, and meditated each morning.

One afternoon, we were invited into a large circus-type tent, the campsite of a Canadian carpenter and his go-go dancer wife. She was nursing a three-month-old baby. She showed us a new book she received from her sister in Vancouver. She dropped the blue-covered square paperback book in front of us. I stared at the cover with the title, *Be Here Now*, written continuously around a circle and the word "Remember" written on each side facing inward. Flipping it open, there was a photograph of Ram Dass, formerly Richard Alpert, in white pajamas sitting in the lotus posture under a tree with the word, "Om," under it.

Turning to the second page, I read slowly, "'Except as ye be converted and become as little children, ye shall not enter the kingdom of heaven,' and in big letters the words, 'START AGAIN.'"

Four pages later, the mantra, "*Aum Mani Padme Hum*," jumped off the page.

We both independently and spontaneously started to cry with Steve actually sobbing, "The wisdom is out there. We're not the only ones. The truth is here for all."

Be Here Now embodied what we had studied and practiced in isolation for the past year. As part of a worldwide movement with many other seekers, we had tuned in.

With March going by, we needed to return to Khemis to pay our April rent and leave Morocco to avoid overstaying our three-month visas. Steve agreed. He said he didn't feel like going to jail again, especially as a second offender, but didn't think it mattered if our rent was late. We needed to leave Morocco by April 12, nearly a month away.

We experienced great difficulty controlling our hash smoking because whenever we wanted to, we smoked. As our supply dwindled, we forced ourselves to refrain, which made us testy. We sought out other travelers who smoked hash and spent time joining them. Thinking about getting some free smoke, Steve went to the large campsite with a corral of burros. When he returned to our camp, he told me about his conversation with Peter, one of the Darien group we had met last year. Peter said their group, with some additional friends who were flying in from the States, planned to walk into the uncharted mountains east of the beach.

Steve told Peter, "He'd love to go into the mountains," as he'd dreamed about doing an adventure into the uncharted area since last year.

Peter replied, "Join us. I'll check with the others, but I'm sure they would accept you as a fellow traveler. We're going to let Beth, Candy's sister, get a little adjusted. She's coming from Hollywood, and I heard she's a bit out of shape after making a film with Andy Warhol. We intend to start the walk in less than a week."

"I'd be thrilled to join you, and I'm sure I could help out since I've lived in Morocco for over a year now," Steve replied.

"This walk is meant to blow our minds and help us resolve little bumps in the relationships among the old gang. Having you there could be beneficial," Peter said.

When I heard this, I responded, "I don't think we should stay until the burro trip gets going. I see how slowly things go, and we need to return to Khemis for the rent, visas, and hash."

"I'm going on the walk, it's a dream come true for me. I'll take my chances if it's delayed. There's still enough time for me to drive north and get out of the country before my visa expires. Even if I can't, it's worth the risk—those mountains call to me," Steve said.

"Let's do the ritual over your corpse the day after tomorrow. We'll fast tomorrow and prepare ourselves," I said.

The day of our ritual started with Steve taking a tab of windowpane acid and lying down naked in the blue tent on a sleeping bag covered with a thin cloth in the still chilly early dawn. He assumed the yoga posture, shavasana, the corpse pose, on his back with his arms turned upward at his side spread at a forty-five-degree angle from his body and his legs slightly spread. To prepare for the ceremony, I smoked a large bowl of hash, almost exhausting our stash. Entering the tent, I lit several sticks of incense and seated myself comfortably in a cross-legged posture. I read only the text that Tibetan lamas read over the dead body, guiding Steve through the transition from death to rebirth.

As the acid hit Steve, I read, "O, nobly born that which is called death hath come. Thou are departing from this world, but thou art not the only one, death cometh to all." I read steadily, occasionally taking a sip from a bottle of water.

The words I read impacted me as well. I recognized the power of my mind to give form to visions and react to them. The book emphasized the choices of reacting to and interpreting these thought forms. By relying on teachings of the Buddha, the devotee needed not to allow the mental images to overwhelm him

After the visitation of the deities, the effect of Karma and its extreme importance is described to the "mental body" as it moves toward rebirth. "O, nobly born Steve, listen. That thou art suffering comes from thine own karma. It is not due to anyone else's," I intoned.

The Lord of Death based his actions of a person's lifetime by counting evil deeds (black pebbles) and good deeds (white pebbles) as reflected in the mirror of Karma. I uncrossed my legs and stretched. I needed a break and having reached "the process of rebirth," I decided to stop reading and go outside. The sunlight in contrast to the dim interior of the tent initially blinded me. I cut two oranges, which I ate slowly.

When I resumed reading, I noticed Steve's face changed. He glowed with a peaceful smile on his lips. I read on, coming to the series of instructions for closing the womb door and selecting a place of rebirth.

Again, from the teachings, I repeated the admonition, "Lo! All substances are my own mind, and this mind is vacuousness, is unborn and unceasing."

It was just before sunset when I read the last sentence and closed the book. Slowly rising, I remarked, "As a man thinketh in his heart, so he is," quoting Proverbs from the preface to the first edition.

I reflected on my coming life in Khemis by myself. It appealed to me although I'd relish adding a woman. I decided to return to Khemis in the next day or two. The unpaid April rent was occupying my mind, even though I knew a late payment would not really cause any difficulty. More importantly, I wanted to exit Morocco before my three-month visa expired. Besides, we had exhausted our stash of hash, and by returning to Khemis, I could resupply myself. The burro walk into the mountains didn't entice me. Exhausted, I went to the Camper and fell asleep.

We spent the next day resting at the campsite. Steve didn't come out of the tent until 11:00 a.m., and I awoke only a half hour earlier. We ate lightly and spoke little.

Just before sunset, I said, "Let's have a pipe of the last of our hash and sit on the dunes and watch the sunset."

"Okay. I wonder how it will be without any hash or kief to smoke while I wait to go on the trip to the mountains," Steve replied.

"I'm going to hitchhike back to Khemis tomorrow, so I won't be here to share that problem with you," I answered. Watching the sun slowly descend, I said, "Change is the law of the universe. Everything must change. Everything is in a constant state of change. I'll be in Khemis. You'll be on your way to England the next time we meet. You will need to move rapidly if you're going to make the three-month visa deadline. Our time together has been fantastic. May we each find enlightenment."

"Every ending is a new beginning, but there is no such thing as an ending or a beginning. We'll always be connected as we continue on the path. May all beings be happy," Steve replied as he gave me a hug.

Tears formed in my eyes as I remembered parting with Steve.

The sound of a car engine brought me back to Beni. The guards stood at attention on both sides of the gate as the car I saw in the morning drove out. Obviously the well-dressed man did not come from the American Embassy to rescue me.

CHAPTER 11

Love the One You're With

You are the guru. That's what's so far-out. You are your own guru.
—Ram Dass, *Be Here Now*

At times my mind cleared, and the reality of my situation hit me harder and harder. I could have a life sentence as nothing indicated my incarceration would end. Every day not only lice, inadequate food, filthy sleeping conditions but just getting any water or emptying my bowels exposed me to danger.

Thinking about my horrid present reality, I strained my mind as I tried to comprehend the steps that led to my getting put into Beni. As I walked around the yard after breakfast, I sat and racked my brain to get some clarity before the pills took their full effect.

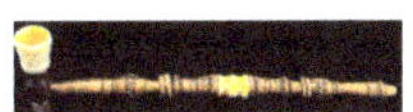

I drifted back to leaving the beach at Taghazout after reading *The Tibetan Book of the Dead.*

At dawn, wearing my djellaba, I walked from the Taghazout campsite to the coastal highway. I carried a small pack and my sleeping bag along with a bottle of water and some oranges. Looking east at the mountains, I thought about Steve's upcoming burro trip and wished him well. I found a spot under a tree next to the highway and began to hitchhike. Very few vehicles passed on the road, but I resolved to stay until sunset. I hadn't hitchhiked during the past year, and I wondered what adventures awaited me.

Not having hooked up with any woman at Taghazout and having been single since Jan left led me to think about how I missed having a girlfriend. My "go with the flow" philosophy accepted whatever happened without hope or fear as Milarepa counseled, but deep down, I did want to connect, and the sooner the better. If desirelessness was a goal of Buddhist practice, this conflict troubled me.

As the sun sank into the ocean, an old truck driven by a middle-aged, bearded man pulled over. The driver called out to me, asking if I wanted a ride to Marrakesh. Even though going inland was out of the direct path to Khemis, I took the ride rather than return to the beach.

As I climbed in, I said, "I'm Fred. *Shukraan*."

The driver put out his hand, displaying his anchor tattoo, and said, "*Soy Aziz, muy bueno*." He was unshaven and dirty, and the cab smelled foul, so I opened my window.

The road inland went through empty barren flat countryside, and after a while, I began to play my harmonica to entertain the driver. I played soulful blues for a long time, which I imagined Aziz would enjoy.

When I paused, instead of applause and compliments, speaking Spanish, Aziz said gruffly, "Play Moroccan music." Evidently, Aziz didn't appreciate my Chicago blues.

After we drove for another hour, Aziz turned off the highway into the desert.

"Where are you going?" I asked, somewhat alarmed.

"I know a shortcut," he replied, but after proceeding to a remote area, he stopped the truck and tried to put his arms around me. He grabbed me around the neck, moving his face close to mine, trying to kiss me.

Being bigger and stronger than Aziz, I pushed him away after a brief struggle. "No!" I yelled.

After I said, "No!" again, Aziz yelled, "*Fuera! Fuera!*" motioning I should get out of the truck. He reached across and opened the passenger door and tried to push me out.

I looked around at nothing but desert and realized staying at this isolated spot could be fatal.

As we struggled in the front seat, I flashed on how a woman being raped might feel. I overpowered Aziz, holding his arms and pinning him down. When I subdued him, I ordered him to continue to Marrakesh. Starting the truck again, Aziz returned to the main road, and we sat silently in the cab's tense atmosphere.

After midnight, at the outer gates of Marrakesh, Aziz stopped the truck, and I happily jumped out. In my hurry down, my sleeping bag snagged on the bumper, and the bag burst open. A cloud of feathers flew into the air. I got out my sewing kit and patched the sleeping bag under a dim streetlight. Sewing the slash left a scar on the bag, serving as a reminder of the emotional scar of the attempted rape. As the adrenaline rush subsided, I got into the bag, and lying on the cold ground outside the city wall, I fell into a fitful sleep.

Next morning, I walked to the main highway heading north and continued hitchhiking home. After two uneventful rides, I reached Khemis. As I retrieved the hidden key and opened the front door, I breathed a deep sigh of relief. I could smell the night-blooming jasmine at the front of the house and stopped to enjoy their fragrant aroma.

After lighting three candles, I retrieved the hash and a pipe. I touched a chunk of hash to the center of my forehead and said aloud in the empty room, "May all beings be happy and at their ease."

The flickering shadows made the poster of Shiva appear to vibrate, sending the message I could relax as blissfully as Shiva. I traveled outside of space and time, transported back a thousand years.

Without consciously thinking about it, I opened to Milarepa's songs at random and read, "Though you renounce your native land, living far away alone, you must still observe the precepts…"

Next morning, the shining sun woke me, and I made couscous for breakfast then mopped both rooms. While the floor was drying, I went up to the roof and did a yoga session in the sun. When I put the mats back, I rearranged the sitting room. I turned a cardboard box upside down and covered it with a bright-colored piece of fabric, creating a table for my notebook, art supplies, and hash paraphernalia-lia. I wrapped the tarot deck in its own special tie-dye fabric. Getting comfortable, I cleaned a *rabita* of kief and smoked a pipeful while I listened to Cat Stevens sing, "Now I've been happy lately / thinking about the good things to come / And I believe it could be something good has begun."

Just then I heard the landlord knocking at the door as he called, "*Hola. Quien aqui?*"

I stood up, covered the hash and paraphernalia with my sleeping bag, and opened the door and responded, "*Hola.* Don Fredrico is back."

The landlord was smiling and said a few sentences in Spanish, which I didn't understand exactly, but the vibes told me he appreciated my return. He asked, "Where's your friend?"

I explained in a combination of Spanish, Arabic, English, and sign language that Steve stayed on the beach and would be back in a few weeks. Going back inside, I brought out the dirhams to pay the April rent.

Taking the bills, the landlord said, "*Gracias and buenos dias,*" and left.

I intended to see the landlord but wasn't sure how to connect with him, but magically, the landlord had picked up the vibes I sent out. Now free of responsibility, I went to the roof where I sat in a half-lotus posture and, facing the sunset, closed my eyes and began to focus on the rising and falling of my breath.

Later in the kitchen, I opened our last tin of sardines and added the odd items left in the pantry. I put together a hodgepodge of leftovers, but obviously, I needed to go shopping.

I knew I'd have to go to Spain soon as my visa was expiring, but I wanted to consult the tarot for any insights about the journey. I cut the cards with my left hand and slowly turned the first card. The four of wands showed people on a boat. The next card showed a peaceful farm scene and made me think it depicted Khemis and the surrounding countryside. The next four cards depicted happy scenes with celebrations, including pentacles cards symbolizing financial success. Halfway through the reading, I turned the major arcana card, the lovers. The reading so far contained positive, upbeat cards. My heart pounded when the lovers card appeared, which couldn't have been a better prediction for my future. After another long hit of hash, I turned the summation card. Seeing the tower changed my mood. This doubly upset me because the tower was the one card turned over by the tribal woman in the Marrakesh Grand Souk. The man and woman falling and the lightning destroying their home seemed to overshadow the other cards proceeding it. The tower symbolized chastisement of pride when attempting to penetrate the mystery of God.

I decided to interpret the reading as depicting the present and the past. The tower referred to Gerri's leaving and now Steve's and the breakup of my home arrangement. I rejected a prediction that put me in hell tortured by fire and having no hope of the torment ending.

I focused on my breathing, repeating, *Rising, falling*, silently to myself. My mind calmed.

When I strayed from the rising and falling, I thought about the lovers and images of attractive hippie chicks flirting with me.

Next morning, I stood on the highway with my thumb out, wearing my full hippie regalia: green velvet bell-bottom slacks, a loose white embroidered shirt, and a fringed suede vest along with my boots of Spanish leather. A seashell I found on the beach of Ibiza on a leather strap was hanging around my neck.

My full beard washed and clean, and my long dark hair in a ponytail with a red hair tie, I thought, *Bring on the lovers.*

A van of Australian men picked me up, and their first words were "You want to smoke some hash before we get to Tangier? We're going on the ferry to Spain and can't have anything with us. It's bombs away."

I meant to shop in Tangier before boarding the ferry, but after my second hit, I knew I needed to go directly to the dock.

When I got out of the van, I tried to compose myself while the Australians said, "See you aboard. We're going to get some beer," and drove off.

Spotting the ticket office, I walked up and bought a seat on the 3:00 p.m. ferry for the two-hour ride to Algeciras. The ferry to

Algeciras cost less than the ferry to Malaga and from there I could take a cheap bus. The big clock on the side of the building read just past noon, so I strolled across the square to a café, where I ordered a café au lait. I looked at the busy exotic street scene so familiar to me. It didn't surprise me to see two donkeys carrying firewood along the side of the road being passed by speeding motorbikes or a soldier ducking into an alleyway and bending over to fill and smoke a sebsi. The sun warmed me as I slowly sipped my coffee and enjoyed the sights. I could see the ticket window for the ferry and watched a few people buying tickets, but my antennae went up when I noticed a young woman with wavy dark hair wearing a loose peasant blouse and flowing skirt at the window. She bought her ticket and was looking around as if she didn't know what to do next.

I walked over to her and said, "Want to join me for a cup of coffee? I'm Fred and I'm on the three o'clock ferry too."

"Good idea. Thanks. I'm Lew and I'm ready to sit down and have something," she replied, flashing a friendly smile.

From her accent, I could tell she hailed from the Midwest, so I knew we'd find a lot in common besides Morocco to talk to about.

We did have a lot to say to each other. Raised in Nebraska, she attended a Timothy Leary lecture at the university and, after his talk, dropped some acid with friends. A month later, she took her savings and flew to Madrid, where she was headed at the moment to get her suitcase, which she left in storage there. Her plan was to return to Morocco, saying she loved the ambiance. She wanted to become part of the thriving Moroccan hippie culture.

By the end of the ferry ride, we snuggled in each other's arms, touching softly and kissing. On the bus to Malaga, I described my home in Khemis, and Lew responded positively to everything I said.

She read the Leary/Alpert guide for acid trips modeled on *The Tibetan Book of the Dead* and said, "I see us connecting on both a physical and spiritual level."

We checked into a cheap pension. My tarot reading was unfolding before me.

Three days of blissful lovemaking followed with slight breaks for meals in working-class restaurants and one shower, which we shared and made love in while the warm water cascaded over us. Lew's openness both to the ideas of Buddhism and every type of sexual activity thrilled me.

She gave me a nice compliment when she said, "Fred, you are a generous lover."

Lew didn't want to leave, but because her possessions were stored in Madrid, she needed to go there to retrieve them.

I drew a map showing her how to find me in Khemis. We parted at the bus station, saying we looked forward to our reunion in Morocco.

As the bus disappeared down the road, I thought, *I'll never see her again. Hippie plans can't be counted on.* Returning to Crosby, Stills, Nash and Young's philosophy, I said out loud to myself, "If you can't be with the one you love, love the one you're with."

Hoisting my pack, I walked to a taxi stand and asked for directions, pointing to Max and Joan's street address. The first driver couldn't understand my request, but the second told me the house was outside of town and difficult to reach by bus and too far for me to walk. He offered to drive me for a reasonable price, so I hopped in. Driving up a steep hill with villas set back from the road, the taxi took me to an area of recently built large homes. The number 22100 was marked by ceramic title at the bottom of a driveway, and the taxi entered and climbed uphill until we came to a circular turnaround in front of a two-story stucco house with an upstairs deck and a patio off to one side.

As soon as I stepped out of the taxi, I heard a scream. Joan shouted, "Fred, welcome, Fred!" from the upper deck as she appeared to be putting on some clothes. I imagined she was sunbathing naked.

The front door opened, and Max came out in his khaki shorts and loose-fitting shirt, well-tanned with a big smile. "Welcome, mate. You must be psychic. We were just talking about you yesterday, and here you are."

Joan rushed out the front door in a scanty bikini and threw her arms around me, saying, "Welcome. It's amazing you're just in time for the celebration. The hash you helped us get arrived safely, and we're throwing a party. You'll be our guest of honor."

They showed me to a large, bright room, where I lay down on the comfortable bed. I looked out the window at the top of a palm tree near the side of the house. Just the luxury of electricity thrilled me every time I turned on the light.

Max and Joan invited me to stay as long as I liked. I looked forward to the adventures ahead.

When the day of the celebration party arrived, I assisted with the elaborate preparations, carrying chairs and setting up folding tables. Max already established a party tradition of putting the tables under a vine-covered veranda so the guests sat facing each other in two long lines. The long table contained bottles of wine, linen napkins, and beautiful ceramic dishes, which Joan told me she bought especially for the occasion. They expected about fifteen guests, including their friends in Malaga, both locals and expatriates and people from a variety of countries, including one person from Turkey who spoke no English. Joan placed a name tag for each guest and some blank ones for others who might show up. Three Spanish women were working in the kitchen, preparing a feast.

I did not join in the predinner cocktails of hard liquor, but I did devour several of the fish tapas. After the appetizers, Joan announced everyone should sit down in his or her assigned seat, marked with a name tag. I found my place and sat down across from the Turk, who just sat with a beatific expression on his face. After the large platters of food came out, one of the women, who had been helping serve, sat down next to me.

I turned and said, "I'm Fred. I met Max and Joan in Morocco where I live, just outside of Tangier."

"I'm Lora, a traveler seeking adventure. I'm from New York and met Joan at a bead shop in Malaga. Glad to meet you," the woman with an appealing Rubenesque figure and curly brown hair said as she reached forward, refilling her glass and mine with dark-red wine. As she put the glass to her mouth, Lora said, "I'm interested in Buddhism. I've taken a number of acid trips, and now I'd like to learn about *The Tibetan Book of the Dead*, which Leary and Alpert used as a guide for tripping. Unfortunately I'm having a hard time getting into it."

I raised my glass and said, "You're talking to the right guy," thinking again about the lovers card and living *The Book of the Dead* on the beach in Taghazout.

"Please teach me, I'm anxious to learn," Lora replied.

I couldn't tell if she was joking or serious as she put her hand gently on my arm.

She was speaking in the language of the Evans-Wentz book, so I replied seriously, "Practice and study. Meditation, hatha yoga, and studying the teachings are the lifestyle for anyone who is truly a devotee and seeker. In the Buddhist tradition, this is the path of the Bodhisattva, a person who wants to attain enlightenment. This is the path I've been taking. I'd be glad to share what I've learned with you."

"I'm so happy to have met you here. Please tell me more," Lora said as she finished her glass of wine and poured herself another.

I described how I just read *The Book of the Dead* aloud as if I were a lama addressing a corpse reading instructions for passing through the Bardo from death in this life to rebirth in the next life.

"Far-out," Lora said.

After the meal, Max stood up and, tapping a fork on an empty glass, quieted the group. "I just want to say how happy I am you are here. We have a lot to be thankful for. One person I want to especially acknowledge is Fred," he said. "Fred played an indispensable part in making this celebration possible."

There was a round of applause with Lora clapping enthusiastically as she turned to me and said, "Our meeting inspires me."

As the group spread out in the large living room, I said, "You want to begin now with some wisdom instead of just making small talk down here? Come with me to my room, and I'll read you a story from the songs of the great Tibetan yogi and Saint Milarepa."

"Perfect," Lora said as she stood up a bit unsteadily having drunk quite a bit of wine.

In my bedroom, we sat on the bed, and I took out the *Songs of Milarepa.* Lora sat close to me.

After I read for a bit, Lora asked, "Do you practice celibacy like Milarepa as part of your devotion?"

"No way. I believe people can have sex in a spiritual way. It's a blast. I'm a believer in free love. You often see Tibetan paintings showing the deities having intercourse with the Shakti, the female deity, seated on the lap of the male with her legs wrapped around him." I dropped the book and reached forward, giving Lora a kiss as our night of lovemaking began gently and slowly.

By morning we felt like an established couple as Lora brought me a cup of freshly brewed coffee in bed.

As I took the cup, I said, "Let's begin a fun-filled dedicated time together. I usually start my day with a hatha yoga routine. We can step out on the balcony in the sunlight, and I'll teach you some asanas."

"Far out. I can share some of my yoga practices with you," Lora said.

Together we did a revitalizing session and afterward took a shower together, making love again.

After a big breakfast, Max and Joan took us on a walk through the nearby park, bursting with Mediterranean flowers in bright reds, oranges, and yellows. Lora pointed out some crocuses and daffodils, and I ran my hand through purple lavender and put it under Lora's nose so she could smell the fragrance. The blissful days flowed together as we explored the area around Malaga. We visited the Abdalajis train tunnel, enjoyed seaside cafés where we drank local wines and ate tapas, strolled through the old town, and walked in the countryside. On our walks, I talked to Lara about the Tibetan teachings in *The Book of the Dead*. Lora's thirst for this knowledge thrilled me. It reminded me of how Gerri absorbed and began to practice the teachings.

One day, along with a group of Max and Joan's friends, we participated in an ongoing project embroidering a cover for their van's spare tire. A friend drew an outline of a landscape in pencil on the tan canvass cover. Each person was asked to embroider a section with brightly colored thread from an array laid out on the coffee table.

I selected light purple and took a mountain for my section. Lora did the sun.

"I want the vibrations of my friends to travel with me," Joan said as she poured wine for the group.

The following week, while we were walking in the country, I turned to Lora and said, "I want to return to my home in Khemis. Would you please come live with me? Let's travel the spiritual path together."

Lora responded by saying, "I was hoping you would ask," and kissed me passionately.

"We'll be lovers and disciples," I said, hugging her.

Three days later, I opened the door to the Khemis house and, bowing in a ceremonial way, made a sweeping gesture with my arms and said, "Welcome to our new home. May your time here be auspicious."

Lora walked inside and, seeing the poster of Shiva on the wall, said, "This is just as I imagined it would be. It just feels like a spiritual haven." She turned and, wrapping her arms around me, gave me an open-mouth kiss.

The next morning, I sat next to Lora as she awoke. I held a glass of water and a small plate with two tabs of acid. "One of my mentors, Eldon, who introduced me to Milarepa, said taking acid is the best way to start a relationship. Let's blow our minds."

Lora sat up and shook her hair into place and, without saying anything, took a tab of acid on her finger, put it in her mouth, and swallowed it with a few sips of water. I did the same. A short time later as the acid hit, I looked at Lora's body and face changing shape. Leading her to the roof, we crawled to the far wall, gently taking off each other's clothes. We flowed together in sweet rapture as we made love on the yoga mats.

Afterward, I led Lora through my usual morning yoga routine, feeling the connection between each breath and each movement. The acid made us hyperaware of our muscles and gave us the ability to make minute adjustments, so I was modeling the exact desired asana posture.

"I can feel my body in a way I never have before," Lora said as she stood after ten salutes to the sun.

At the end of the session, laying on our backs naked in the corpse pose, the acid took us even higher. My mind expanded to the size of the solar system. I was flying among the planets and reached Mars, which glowed red below me. I heard pounding on the front door, and at first I didn't know if I was imagining it or someone wanted to enter the house.

Then I heard my neighbor, Karim, calling, using my Muslim name, "*Ali, Ali, amigos aqui. Ali. Ali.*"

Lora did not move. I crawled to the edge of the low wall surrounding the terrace and, looking over, there stood a man I did not recognize and Lew standing in the courtyard with Karim. Trying to orient myself, I realized Lew must have returned from Madrid and, following my directions, now arrived in Khemis.

I crawled back to Lora and whispered, "We have visitors. I've got to go down and open the door because Karim knows we're here."

Staying low, I hastily put on my clothes as I walked downstairs. I opened the door and said, "What a surprise." After thanking Karim for showing Lew and the stranger to my house, I invited them inside.

"I arrived yesterday in Tangier, and today I hitchhiked a ride with Jacques. He's French and doesn't speak a word of English," Lew said as she leaned forward and gave me a kiss.

"Sit down," I said, motioning Jacques and Lew into the sitting area.

Freaked out, I didn't know what to do but decided getting them stoned was the best course to take. I took out a large chunk of hash, attached the largest clay bowl I owned onto the pipe, and filled it. I passed it first to Lew, who then passed in on to Jacques. As the pipe passed around, Lora came down from the roof, wearing a thin, loose-fitting dress.

She smiled at the visitors and said, "I'm Lora, and I'm living here with Fred." She sat down and joined the circle, taking deep hits on the pipe as it went around.

My mind was spinning. I didn't want to make any explanations. I hadn't told Lora about Lew or my invitation to her, nor could Lew have known about Lora. I decided to continue smoking hash and see how this scene unfolded.

Lora put her hand on my thigh in a gesture of possession and intimacy and said, "We were on the roof terrace enjoying the sun and just about to enjoy other things, but we always extend full hospitality to our visitors."

"I met Lew on the ferry from Morocco to Spain before I met you and told her to visit me if she returned to Morocco, but I never expected her to show up here," I whispered to Lora. Turning to Lew, I said, "You and Jacques are very welcome. *Mi casa, su casa.*"

Lew, seeing Lora and I as a couple, put her hand on Jacques' thigh and said, "This can work out just fine. Let's relax and enjoy ourselves."

Thankful no dramatic confrontation would occur, I enjoyed having the two women's attention. The smoking hash while tripping on acid increased my hallucinations, the faces of my three companions changing from masks of horror into benevolent spirits. Instead of haunting me, the spirits now encouraged and supported me. Lora continued to touch my thigh and smile as she, too, seemed cool with the sudden arrival of the two visitors.

Jacques said "*Je suis si joyeux* (I am so happy)."

Lew moved closer and nestled with him.

We four sat on the mat in silence until Lew finally said, "I've got to pee. Where's the bathroom?"

"I'll show you, I have to pee too," Lora said as she got up and, taking Lew's hand, led her out the front door to show her the place behind the house.

I shook my head as images of sex with both women drifted through my mind. Since Jan and I broke up, until meeting Lew, I had no female companion, and now I had two. "Go with the flow," I said aloud, although I knew Jacques would not understand.

When the women returned, Lora said, "Let's sit on the terrace and sunbathe."

We went to roof where Lora took off her clothes and sat naked. Lew did the same, and we men followed suit. We sat naked in a circle under the warm sun as I prepared another large pipe of hash. I lit it and we passed it around.

I thought about a possible orgy but could tell Lora didn't want to have sex with Jacque. We lay on our backs, letting the sun bake our naked skin, each exploring our own mental drifting, all of us stoned on hash with Lora and I also on acid. Far-out.

As late afternoon approached, I said, "I'm glad you are here. As a special treat, I'm going to make a pot of *bessara* tonight. It's Moroccan soup made with dried split peas, carrots, and onions, seasoned with cumin. I need to walk to the store and get our daily loaf of brown home-baked bread, a perfect complement for the soup." Saying this, I put on my clothes and went downstairs.

The three others remained on the roof.

Lew, Jacques, and Lora raved about the *bessara* and the bread. We divided into two separate couples with Lew and Jacques to sleep in the back room while Lora and I would sleep in the main room after the nighttime hash smoking and reading. Lora acted as a perfect hostess, having helped Lew and Jacques bring in their essential items from Jacques' Citroën. She provided them with candles and a bottle of water.

After dinner, I brought out the hash and pipe and said, "In the evenings, I usually read a holy book. Tonight I can read a Milarepa story, although it won't mean much to Jacques."

"Jacques seems content to smoke the hash while he anticipates the good fuck I'm going to give him later," Lew said as she rubbed Jacques' thigh.

As the pipe went around for the fourth hit, Lora turned to Lew and said, "I feel a little like Jacques probably does, waiting for the moment when he'll be hugging and kissing you. I've wanted Fred inside me since you arrived. Let's skip the story tonight and lie down, so we can get it on. I don't think I could concentrate on the wisdom while my mind and body are directed elsewhere."

Lew didn't respond, but she took Jacques' hand and stood up. "*Voule vous coucher avec moi?* (Do you want to sleep with me?)" she said to Jacques, who awoke from his revelry and said, "*Oui.*"

He also turned to Lora and me and said, "*Merci, merci,*" as he followed Lew into the back room.

Lora spread out the sleeping bag and pillows. She blew out most of the candles and put her arms around me.

I thought, *Righteous*, as I heard groans and moans from the back room. I thought I'd never see Lew again.

Maybe out of sight out of mind isn't always true, but "love the one you're with" works. Going with the flow worked out okay.

The next morning, everyone woke up in a good mood. After a breakfast of couscous with French bread and cheese provided by Jacques, I suggested I lead a walk in the countryside around Khemis. Lora suggested another afternoon of sunning. Speaking French and broken English, Jacques retrieved a bag of onions from the Citroën and said he would make onion soup for dinner as he dropped a hunk of Parmesan cheese on the mat. We agreed Lew and Jacques would spend another night.

Pleased, I said, "French onion soup made by a Frenchman. What could be better?"

The next morning, Lora and I hugged Lew and Jacques as the new couple stepped into the car and pulled out to head south.

As we walked back through the family compound past the well to our house, I said, "Life is full of surprises. One of the things I like about living here is never any forewarning of who will arrive. People have dropped in even though we're a million miles from the mainstream. Life on the 'Hash Trail.' Letters are our only connection to the outside world."

"Cool, but they interrupted the beginning of an acid fuck day," Lora said in a somewhat angry tone.

"Not really. Acceptance, surrender, taking what you see before you as your guru, living as we do teaches and tests those parts of the wisdom. Also, I look forward to many acid fuck days. How about tomorrow?" I replied.

Blissful days passed until on the roof one morning, while meditating, Lora touched my arm and I jerked.

She startled me into consciousness and said, "Do you know where The Rolling Stones cassette is? I can't find it."

Instead of radiating friendliness, I snapped, "Don't interrupt my meditation for anything not life-threatening!"

"How can you jump at me? I didn't think you were meditating. It looked more like sleeping, sitting up to me. You can't snap at me. When you're ready to apologize, come downstairs," Lora said, on the brink of tears as she rushed off the roof.

I returned to watching my breath, *Rising, falling,* as I tried to calm down. I remained on the roof for several hours stretched out under the sun. I felt justified; you should never interrupt a person meditating. Lora should be apologizing to me. I stayed upstairs until late afternoon, by which time I realized I was wrong to snap at Lora, so I went downstairs to apologize.

To my surprise, Lora wasn't there. Her pack and big straw bag were gone. She never said goodbye. A deep sense of loss engulfed me. We connected on the spiritual plane, and we both really liked the sex. Her leaving shocked me, and I didn't know if she went north or south. Oddly, my first inclination led me to think about finding another hippie chick in Tangier.

I thought of the page in Ram Dass' book *Be Here Now* showing people sitting on a hillside and looking at the rising sun above with, in large letters, said, "Making It Sacred." I already dedicated myself to the devotee's way of life. Lora joined it, but my human reaction of displaying anger split us apart. Milarepa taught anger caused falling to the realms below and instructed a devotee to refrain from wrath even in the face of death.

Sad, I rededicated myself to the dharma path. Picking up my sleeping bag, I went up to the roof to do a session of yoga and meditation.

A recurring dream, which depicted a person thrown into a Moroccan prison, haunted my nights. In the dream, the person just sat hopelessly in his cell with no possibility of escape or pardon. I applied this to Steve because I knew he overstayed his visa for the second time.

Every morning, I missed Lora sleeping next to me.

The sound of a car at the gate to the compound grabbed my attention. I heard Steve's voice shouting, "I'm back!" I threw the bolt and opened the door, giving Steve a hug in the doorway.

As we hugged, Steve moved me back inside the house. He turned back toward the door and said, "Look who I brought you."

Lora walked in and gave me a hug and a big kiss. I began getting hard as our groins touched with only a few layers of fabric between us.

When we separated, I bowed and, with a wave of my arm, said, "Greetings, greetings, greetings. Sit down and have a pipe and tell me about it."

"Let's unpack some things from the Camper first. Then I can park it behind the gate. We can sit down for a pipe after we're settled. We've been driving since dawn," Steve said as he turned around and went out the door.

Lora turned and followed Steve outside. I pulled on my djellaba and followed them.

"Leave most things in the van as I've got to get across the border as soon as possible. I'm already three weeks over the three-month visa," Steve said as he put the perishable food in a nylon bag.

Lora brought a sleeping bag, a small backpack, and a large cloth bag, which she took out of the van and carried into the house. I carried Steve's sleeping bag and his backpack.

I sat down and began to fill the hash pipe.

Lora sat down next to me and leaned over and kissed me on my neck and said, "I want us together again. After hitchhiking to southern Morocco, I hiked into the hills near Taghzout. One evening, I saw a group of hippies sitting in a circle, smoking hash. I joined the circle. One of the men was reading from *The Songs of Milarepa.* I said, 'You must be Steve.'" Lora continued, "I joined the burro walk in the mountains, and it changed me. Steve's on a different plane. He says it's like he's on acid in a certain way all the time. I know he can read people's minds."

Steve burst through the door, holding a tray with the fixings for a pot of Moroccan mint tea, and set it down in the center of the floor.

I lit the pipe, which I passed first to Lora, who took it and touched it to the center of her forehead and said, "May all beings be happy and at their ease. Forces of fate have brought us together. May our actions further us along the path." Lora took a hit and passed the pipe to Steve, who reached out eagerly and took a drag without saying anything.

"I am so happy to see you both," I said and passed the pipe to Lora, who touched it to the center of her forehead again and said, "Milarepa's wisdom is supreme." After which she prepared the mint tea.

I noticed how deeply the burro walk affected Steve, his physical being changed and a beautiful aura emanated from him. I wanted to hear the details of his journey, but Steve said little except the group wandered for two weeks with a parrot in a cage, three dogs, a huge tent, six burros, and all the hash they could smoke.

I interpreted Lora's return as a positive omen. I wanted to apologize and express my regret for snapping at her.

As I was thinking these things, Steve turned to Lora and said, "I'm reading your mind," addressing the remarks to her.

A red blush appeared across Lora's face as she replied, "And I'm going to do it too."

"May all beings be happy," Steve replied.

I cleared my throat and began to read, "A woman's role in the dharma, obeisance to all gurus…"

After the story, Steve said, "I need to walk and stretch my legs. I'll go to the post office and store." Putting on his djellaba, Steve picked up a straw bag and opening the door and said, "I need some time alone, so I'm going to walk for a while before I return. Don't worry."

As soon as the door closed, I turned to Lora and, wrapping my arms around her, gave her a hug and kissed her enthusiastically.

"I've missed you inside me," she said. "I feel as if I've come back to a holy place where we can walk the path together."

"Amen, sister," I replied and kissed her again.

Steve did not return to the house until almost dark, by which time Lora and I cut the vegetables for the tagine pot cooking on the charcoals. Lora changed into a flowing flowered dress, and her shampooed hair was spread out loose down her back. She sparkled in the twilight glow. I also washed my hair, which was longer than Lora's.

"Just in time for dinner, typical," I said as Steve put the round loaf of brown bread on the kitchen counter.

"Hope you weren't worried. I sat and meditated. Then I wrote and mailed an aerogram letter to Gerri, telling her I was leaving Khemis and hope to see her soon," Steve said.

After a hearty dinner, Lora said, "I told Fred how we met at your encampment in Ait Bihi. When I saw you reading a Milarepa story, I just said, 'You must be Steve, and Fred sends his regards.' I remember the surprised look on your face."

"Your joining our walk for the last week was auspicious, especially since I could bring you back here," Steve said. "We walked through some rough country but being in those mountains reinforced my belief I can further my quest in the Himalayas. I'm aiming for India and Nepal. It's unlikely but possible I might decide to come back here after I see what happens in Europe."

"You'll always have a place here," I said.

Later Steve read from *The Book of the Dead*, "The dharmakāya of thine own mind thou shall see, and seeing that, thou shalt have seen the all—the vision infinite, the round of death and birth, and the state of freedom."

After Steve closed the book, Lora said, "I'm ready to lie down."

"Me too," I said and followed her to our sleeping area.

The next morning after breakfast, we sat together, relaxing with the dirty dishes still on the mat in front us.

Steve said, "I'm going to leave today. I have to face my fate at the border. I'll drive out via Ceuta. Maybe they won't even check my passport to see when I entered. Then I'll drive to Malaga and go to Max and Joan's. There's no point delaying."

"You're welcome to stay. I feel like I just got to Morocco even though I've lived here almost a year and a half now. I want to use my experience and build on it," I replied.

"I know you, Fred, and Gerri shared this place happily. And we three could share it also," Lora said as she poured herself another cup of tea.

"No, I've already written to Gerri. My visa is expired, and I believe I need further instructions on meditation. We're studying and practicing Buddhism in a Muslim country. I'm sure India and Nepal will be a more supportive environment. You two can have a fulfilling life here without me," Steve said, gathering his sleeping bag and other personal items.

As we stood outside the van, my arms around Lora's waist, I said, "Please, send my love to Gerri. I predict you'll get through the border and have an adventure-filled journey. Send my regards to Max and Joan and tell them Lora and I are here and would welcome a visit if they come south."

Lora put her arms around Steve and gave him a hug and a kiss. "Thank you. May the longtime sunshine shine down on you. May all beings be happy."

I hugged Steve and said, "Life is change. May you prosper on the path. Say hello to Mount Everest for me and never forget, 'There is no idleness in the life of a devotee.'"

Steve looked at us and said, "May love surround you. No hope and no fear, is the accomplishment of enlightenment. I'm sure we'll continue to be connected. I undertake this journey for the welfare of all living beings," and drove off.

I took Lora in my arms and gave her a deep kiss, and we remained hugging for several minutes before we walked back through the Moroccan family compound to our home together.

As soon as the door closed behind us, Lora said, "Let's get naked and go up to the roof and make love."

"Groovy," I replied.

Afterward I said, "I feel our reunion calls for a celebratory acid trip. Tomorrow let's drop acid in the morning and spend a day in the wonderful world of our opened minds and hearts."

"I love to fuck on acid so we can reunite on all planes," Lora replied.

After passing the pipe back and forth several times, we both sat hunched slightly forward, staring at the center of the straw mat. I thought about the recent changes in my life, particularly the beginning of reestablished life with Lora. I wanted to bond with her and have us continue and expand our yoga, meditation, and other spiritual practices. I didn't agree with Steve; I had everything I needed right in Khemis, especially nearly a pound of hash and plenty of acid.

The next morning, I woke up as Lora leaned over me and gave me a kiss. "Thanks for making me comfortable after I passed out last night. In my dream, you and I made a happy family with three children including a pair of twin girls. Several of my cousins have twins. The children were so cute with dark hair and brown eyes," Lora said.

"A nice fantasy for the future, but now I'm focused on the path to enlightenment, and as Milarepa says constantly, family is a distraction and hindrance on the path," I said.

I took out a small box containing twenty tabs of windowpane acid and placed two of them on the cover of *The Book of the Dead.* Filling two glasses with water, I handed a glass to Lora and said, "May this acid bring us closer together. May all beings be happy." I took a tab on my finger and washed it down with a sip of water.

Lora reached forward and did the same.

I picked out a James Taylor cassette and put it in the player as we waited for the acid to hit. We tripped together before, but I believed this trip would be a particularly bonding experience for us. As the words, "I hear a heavenly band full of angels and they're coming to set me free," wafted out of the cassette player, I began to feel the slight turning in my stomach; meaning, the acid was beginning to have an effect. The walls were pulsating while Lora's face changed. She turned into an angel with a look in her eyes of divine compassion.

Lora stood up unsteadily, having trouble getting her balance, but once she did, she smiled and picking up the sleeping bag, walked up the stairs to the roof. When the song "Fire and Rain" began to play, I turned off the player. Taking a bottle of water, I went up to the roof. When I opened the door, the bright sunlight blinded me for a minute, but once my eyes adjusted, there was Lora lying on the sleeping bag, naked with her arms behind her head and her legs spread apart.

She said, "Come here and fuck me, fuck me hard."

I got down beside her and began to touch her breasts gently as they changed shape with the nipples getting hard and coming to a sharper point. She didn't move, keeping her arms behind her head, but her breathing became more rapid. I started to move over her, thinking of our acid trip, when Karim interrupted us, yelling from the courtyard about Lew's arrival. No such distractions now. Days of lovemaking mixed with yoga sessions and daily meditation made our time together idyllic.

After breakfast one morning, as I lit a pipe of kief, I casually turned to Lora and said, "What are you doing about birth control?" My girlfriends had always managed their own birth control.

Lora took the pipe and replied, "Nothing."

I repeated the word, "Nothing?" and Lora defiantly said again, "Nothing!"

"I don't want a child. The way we're fucking, you're bound to get pregnant. There's a million reasons I don't want a child, but the main one is I'm a seeker on the path. A child will interfere with my quest. Yet because of the morality required by the teachings, if I fathered a child, I'd have care for him or her," I said.

"I'm ready," Lora replied. "I'm ready to give life, to bring a new soul into the world. Who knows whom it might be a reincarnation of? With our life here, the next Buddha could be our child."

"At least a high lama," I said sarcastically and was sorry as soon as I said it. "We can get birth control pills in Larache. I know because Gerri got some there. Tomorrow we're going to the *pharmacia*, and we're getting those pills. This is absolutely necessary."

Angry, Lora said, "I guess we can't fuck today," as she grabbed the sleeping bag and a book and walked up the stairs to the roof.

The next day, we hitchhiked to Larache. Lora was dressed in a loose, white robe-like dress with a white shawl over her head. I wore in my brown wool djellaba. A truck pulled over as soon we reached the highway. The driver was a young man from the south, returning home after bringing a load of tomatoes to the Tangier market. He spoke pretty good English; he said he learned by watching an American TV series with Arabic subtitles.

The wall of tension between us hadn't dissipated as we walked the few blocks to the large *pharmacia* in the town main square. Lora seemed light and smiled from behind her partially covered face at the women and children. At one point, she stopped and gave a coin to a young girl who held out her hand. I became upset because I warned Lora not to give to money to any beggars until we were ready to leave town. I did not want to be surrounded by children as I had been in Marrakesh.

At the *pharmacia*, I did the talking to a man in a white coat behind the counter. Several times I pointed to Lora, who stood six feet away with her arms crossed in front of her. After our discussion, the clerk went to the rows of shelves and returned with a package of birth control pills. I paid, took the white bag, and Lora and I walked out of the store together.

"Since we're in Larache, let's have hot showers," I said to Lora, whose mood became much warmer.

She kissed me on the neck and said, "I'll hold the pills. Let's buy some supplies, have a café au lait, and then a hot, hot shower. We'll go home and I'll take a pill, and we can fuck, fuck, fuck."

"Brilliant," I said as I hugged her.

After returning home in the early afternoon, Lora kept her word and she and I fucked, fucked, and fucked afternoon, evening, and night.

We established a yogic routine similar to the one I followed with Steve and Gerri and which I practiced even more strictly when alone. Reading, yoga, meditation, and art projects filled our days along with lots of spontaneous sex.

One morning, I noticed the white *pharmacia* bag lying among Lora's clothes. I bent down to pick it up to throw it out when I saw the package of pills inside. I opened the round plastic container and only one pill was missing, although Lora needed to take one each day. Angry and upset, I marched up to the roof where Lora sat naked, reading a book.

"I was getting a bit lustful myself, guess the feeling was mutual," she said, but when she saw me holding the white bag, she said, "Uh-oh."

"Have you been taking the birth control pills?" I asked, although I already knew the answer.

"No, I want a child. Besides, those pills are bad for a woman's health," Lora said.

"You promised to take the pills. You know why I can't have a child now!" I yelled as I threw the white bag at Lora's feet and turned around and walked downstairs.

A few minutes later, Lora came downstairs, picked out some clothes, put them on, and without saying a word to me, put her possessions into her backpack, filled a large straw basket, and walked out the door, slamming it behind her. I sat on the mat watching her leave and lit a pipe of hash.

As I took the second toke, I reached for my Milarepa book and, opening it at random, read, "To cut off all ties is the best companion. To live alone is to become a friend of deities." *A friend of deities, a friend of deities*, I thought as I took my third hit.

By dinner, I missed holding Lora close.

I put down the pipe as I said out loud to the empty room, "I got the blues." I wanted to capture my sad feeling and decided to express my emotions in a blues song.

I fetched my harmonica and began playing a blues riff. "I got the lonesome blues / my baby done left me and I'm sitting in this cold room / My baby shook me all night long / now I'm alone." I sang several verses and wrote them in my notebook. "My Lora wants a baby / but as a seeker no can do / My Lora wants a baby /but as a seeker no can do / so she had to leave / and now I'm oh so blue." I named the song "Jew's Blues."

I hoped Lora might return, but I made a conscious effort to not think about her. One teaching of the yogic practice emphasized the additional benefits of transmuting sexual energy into energy directed to meditation, yoga, study, and devotion. I thought about tantric yoga, where the energy rose from the centers below the navel, traveled up the spine, and shot out from the top of a practitioner's head, just as the Ganges River shot from Shiva's head in the poster I looked at daily.

I decided to settle into my life in Khemis and add to its comfort. I arranged to buy fresh milk from a neighbor's cow. I boiled it and used to make my own yogurt. I needed to buy vegetables at the weekly souk, and even though one day drifted into another, I made sure to know Saturday was souk day. Once I bought a giant onion and roasted it and cut it into slices and treated it as if eating a steak.

Seeing my reflection in a piece of shining tin outside the post office weeks after Lora left, I was surprised and pleased. With my hair almost to my waist and my thick beard, wearing my djellaba and sandals, I looked like the hermit depicted in the tarot card. Studying the tarot, I knew the symbolism attached to this card, and it applied well to me. I drew a picture of the hermit card and sent it to my cousin, Susan, proudly telling her this is what I looked like.

I smoked very little kief and abandoned the practice of waiting until after dinner to smoke hash. I smoked hash throughout the day, usually starting right after my morning hour-long yoga routine. I didn't take acid, but if the occasion arose, plenty of tabs were on hand. I extended the time of my meditation sessions, and although I had no clock to time my sittings, I knew my twice-daily sessions were running longer and longer. As I concentrated on watching my breath, my mind drifted, but more aware of the drift, I could bring my attention back to my breath more readily. Because meditation time passed easily while stoned, I knew hashish and Buddhism went hand in hand.

Every evening after dinner, I read aloud even though alone. Pouring over the Buddhist teachings and following the path of a true Bodhisattva, I usually passed out early, but the next morning, I would continue my practices.

Not wanting to be forced to leave Morocco every three months, I decided to apply for a residency permit to allow me to remain for a year. I hitchhiked to Larache to obtain my "Permit of Stay," even though I'd have to return to the Royal Gendarmerie, where we tried to apply for residency after our release from the Larache jail in December. I tied my hair into a neat ponytail and dressed as if I were a regular tourist in a sports shirt and jeans. I still had the photos from the last time I attempted to apply. I vowed not to be intimated, and I would not return without residency papers.

At 9:00 a.m., I entered a large room with four industrial-sized desks, metal file cabinets, and the king's photograph hanging on the wall. I approached the front desk and explained to the uniformed officer sitting there I was applying for residency status. With a nasty sneer, he told me to take a seat in one of the metal chairs against the wall. I sat down and began to wait. After an hour or two, I went back to the desk to ask what was happening.

The officer shouted and pointed, "You just wait there!"

I determined I would sit in the station until I got my papers. A higher-ranking officer who I assumed was the commander went in and out of his inner office, and after sitting for hours, I stood up and approached him. The commander completely ignored me as if I wasn't there. I sat down again, thinking they won't get rid of me so easily.

After the lunch break, when the officer at the desk returned, I got up and asked when I could obtain my residency permit. This time, the officer told me to sit in a chair outside the commander's office. Hours passed while I sat in a meditative state until I noticed the office was preparing to close. Finally, the commander opened the door and motioned for me to come in. The commander asked me a series of questions, including date of birth, hometown, and occupation, which I listed as "artist." He asked for five dirhams and gave me my stamped residency booklet just before he walked out and the station closed.

With my mission accomplished, I went to the square and ordered a café au lait.

My yogic patience earned me success, and I thought, *Waiting is full.*

One morning, about ten days later, as I closed *Be Here Now*, a knock woke me from my trance, and I heard a voice I recognized. A soft French accent calling, "Fred. Are you home? It's Michelle avec Todd and Lola."

"I'm here, I'm here," I called out. As I jumped up and opened the door, I said, "Welcome," and hugged each as they entered.

"Good to see you, old chap," Todd said as he sat down and, reaching forward for the pipe and hash, said, "May I? I've been thinking about a pipe of your good hash for the last three hours while we've been driving north."

I relished compliments of my hash, being very proud of its quality, and said, “Sure, go ahead. Welcome. Sit down.”

“Can Lola bring Ute in? We’ll give her some water and bring her mat in, and she’ll just rest. She’s due to give birth in two weeks,” Michelle asked as she sat next to Todd and put her hand out to take the pipe.

“Sure, bring her on a leash. I’ll walk out with you, the neighborhood dogs can be hostile,” I said.

“I’ll get her,” Lola said as I followed her out the front door to the Citroën.

Returning, Ute explored the house and then sat quietly beside Lola, to whom I gave some colored pencils and paper to draw. I got a bowl of water and put it near the front door, and Ute took a long drink.

“Look how well Ute has adjusted,” I said. “I remember what a good watchdog she was at Taghazout. I’m on my own and devoted to staying here. I’ve been thinking I could use a guard dog. Are the puppies spoken for?”

“We want to sell the puppies. If Ute has a normal litter, we would have one for you if you want one,” Michelle said.

“Would you take hash instead of cash?” I said, looking toward Todd.

“Fred, you have the best hash, and I’m glad to trade for a puppy,” Todd said.

“I have a beautiful one-hundred-gram piece I could bring you when the puppies are born,” I said as I thought, *If a man has hash, he doesn’t need money.*

“I’ll write you after the birth. You can come ten weeks later and have the pick of the litter,” Michelle said.

“I’ll hitchhike there to get my pup,” I responded, already thinking about naming my new dog.

As we continued smoking, Todd said, “Want to hear the latest hit by The Rolling Stones? I just got this new cassette in the mail from my London friends. It’s called *Exile on Main Street.*”

Todd reached into his bag and put a cassette in the player and, blasting the music, I heard, "Sometimes feel like trouble / sometimes you feel down / Let this music relax your mind."

The following day, everyone hugged as the three left, saying, "*Au revoir.*"

I patted Ute and said, "Wishing you a good litter. I'll see you and your puppies in about twelve weeks."

The thought of picking up puppies was interrupted by a chilling vision of being put in their car.

I remembered being at their house with Todd on one side and Michelle carefully holding me on the other, loading me into the back of their beat-up old station wagon.

As their car entered the main road, a group of young boys rushed to the car window with their hands out. I handed my dark-blue leather Moroccan coin purse holding my money to one of the boys as we drove away.

As the old wagon lumbered to Tangier, I heard Michelle say, "I'm so glad we're taking Fred to the British Hospital. I'm sure they can help him."

"There's no good alternative in this country for a freaked-out hippie," Todd replied.

When the station wagon arrived at the doors of the British missionary hospital, I remained lying in the back. Michelle and Todd rushed from door to door, trying to locate someone to assist them, but no one responded to their calling and pounding.

"I need help!" I shouted.

Michelle cried, "What can we do? He's deteriorating."

Todd said, "We've got to take him somewhere else. The Moroccan hospital is nearby."

At the Moroccan hospital, we exited the car at the emergency entrance. Outside the entrance, two white-coated male hospital attendants came to greet us.

Michelle rushed forward. Pointing at me, she yelled, "This man needs help! Look at his eyes! He went crazy yesterday!"

With his arm extended, one attendant wouldn't let us into the hospital doorway and, using his body to block us, said, "You're not coming in here."

Michelle called out in French, "This man needs help!"

The other attendant responded in halting English, "No, no, not right place. We take you right place."

As I stood watching this emotionally charged scene, I thought, *What's the right place? I'm an enlightened hash smoker, so it must be somewhere special.* A calm feeling encircled me because I knew "the right place" was just what I needed.

Next thing I knew, I lay in the back of an ambulance with sirens blasting, lights flashing, speeding through the streets of Tangier.

My thoughts returned to the day Todd and family left Khemis, I needed to buy supplies in Tangier. When I arrived in Tangier, I saw three good-looking women standing by the arch at the entrance to casbah.

I walked over to them, thinking, *Just my type.* "Enjoying Tangier? I'm a good tour guide having lived here more than a year," I said to a dark-haired woman with beads around her neck and wrists.

"I live in Tangier too. My name is Sarah," she replied.

"I used to live in a commune here. Are you part of a commune?" I asked.

"Yes, praise the Lord, we live in the British Missionary Compound. We share a house there," Sarah said.

"Are you what's called 'Jesus freaks'?" I asked.

"Yes, we practice Jesus teachings including sex only in marriage," said Sarah as she responded to the energy I was projecting. "Come with me to Hope House, and we can talk more about it."

"No, thanks. I need to do my errands and go. May all beings be happy and peaceful," I said and walked away disappointed.

After leaving the Christians, I walked to the Pension Miami, where Mina greeted me with a hug and offered me mint tea.

Chatting over the tea, Mina said, "It's sad so many Moroccan are so poor."

I said, "I sympathize but I'm very poor too."

Mina replied, "Yes, you Americans may be poor now, but you can always go back to America. Moroccans who live here have no place else to go. Poverty is their life."

I couldn't think of how to reply knowing the truth of Mina's statements. I finished my tea and went to sleep.

The next day, I went from store to store, buying supplies of canned sardines, peanut butter, cheese, toothpaste, and a few *rabitas* of kief, as well as ink refills for my rapidograph pens. I checked the mail at *poste restante*. At the newsstand, the headlines informed me the war in Vietnam raged on.

When I began to hitchhike south, a truck took me part of the way, and I rode the last few miles on the back of a horse. A man riding a big, brown horse stopped and waved for me to jump on behind him. I pulled myself up, and the horse trotted until I tapped the man on the shoulder, asking to dismount at the lane leading to my house.

At the house, I smoked a pipe, put the food in the kitchen, and made a pot of chamomile tea. Drinking the tea, I thought how one by one I slowly used the hundred-dollar bills Max gave me. I wasn't concerned about money because having hash was better than money. I smelled the perfume of the night-blooming jasmine, feeling ready to dive intensely into the Buddhist books.

Midsummer brought memories of my childhood summers on the lake in Nippersink, Wisconsin. I remembered the July Fourth celebrations. There were always fireworks and barbecues, golf, and swimming. My family and friends surrounded me, and I usually enjoyed hot summer romances. I was living alone since early May, and for a moment, my isolation made me feel a little sad. Thoughts of home and friends and family were something Milarepa specifically mentioned in many of his songs, a major reason devotees were distracted from the quest for enlightenment. I needed to push aside my natural homesick feelings.

After a meditation and yoga session, I thought, *I am the hermit. I am the hanged man, surrendering to his fate, accepting all. I am no longer the knight of swords, rushing forward.* I picked up the tarot deck and unwrapped the cloth.

I didn't do a reading but slowly looked through the cards fanned out in my hand, picking out the hermit, hanged man, knight of cups, and the fool. I often thought of Steve as the fool who was wandering free. The last I heard from him, he wrote from England, describing how he and Gerri were going to Samye Ling, a Tibetan monastery in Scotland. I wondered if Steve would find a guru.

I decided to increase my devotion for the month before leaving to get the dog. Physically, I transformed into the hermit. My practice brought me close to the union with the divine the hermit embodied. Becoming the hermit and reaching enlightenment as described in Buddhist teachings merged in me. I was reaching the blissful state of one unified with the universal consciousness.

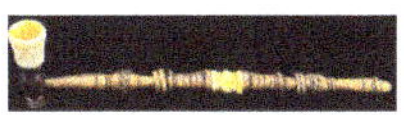

When my recollections ended, instead of feeling calm, I became more agitated than ever. *How did I get from the brink of enlightenment to endless days in this hellhole?*

I got up and walked around the yard, questioning why my Karma brought me here.

CHAPTER 12

Me and the Devil Blues

The mind is madness. Only when you go beyond the mind will there be meditation.

—Sadhguru

As the days passed, I aimlessly wandered the courtyard and sat for long periods with nothing to do. Some days, I just sat against the high wall. The pills made me walk with an off-balance heavy gait as if I was wading through wet concrete. Each morning, I walked around the circumference of the yard multiple times.

My routine consisted of lining up for breakfast and dinner every day and sleeping in the same three-person bed each night. As a trustee in a white coat watched, I took my three pills along with my food. In my first weeks, I happily downed the pills. I credited them with slowing my rushing thoughts and helping me return to reality.

I now trusted the vibes I got from some inmates and approached those men in the yard. I spoke to them in broken Spanish, French, Arabic, and English. Sometimes they ignored my inquiries, but other times I obtained bits of information. I'd asked inmates how long they were here. Some said ten years, others said twenty years. If I asked when they were getting out, I always got the answer, "Never." Several times they told me, "No one leaves here."

I thought the American Consulate would be working on my unfortunate situation. After so many weeks passed, my certainty turned to doubt. What if Michelle and Todd did not go to the consulate because of their involvement with hash? I wondered how to contact the world outside these high stucco walls.

One morning, I noticed a new obviously European inmate not wearing a djellaba. I tripped and fell down as I rushed to approach him.

In English, I said, "Hey, man. What's going on here? Where are we?"

He responded in English, saying, "The police brought me here last night. They told me it is Beni Makada, the prison for the insane. I'm Norwegian, Nils Jorgenson."

"What's your story?" I asked.

He looked depressed and ragged but coherent so far. "I came to Tangier to smoke some hash, but I ran out of money and began to live on the streets. In Norway, I'd get myself arrested so I'd have a few days in jail to get food and a roof over my head. I thought I'd use the same tactic here, so I took off my clothes and ran around the Gran Souk. The police arrested me and brought me here. Now I know public nudity in Morocco equals insanity."

"Guess we should have known. I remember nudity had something to do with my getting here. I ended up being brought here in an ambulance," I said.

Nils gave a choked laugh and said, "I speak good French. I talked to the policeman who arrested me. He said once inside, I'd never communicate with the outside world."

"We're lost and hopeless souls," I responded. The seriousness of my confinement overwhelmed me. "I'm sure someone cares. The American Embassy must protect US citizens. I have friends on the outside," I said to reassure myself.

"Maybe," Nils replied. "From what I've been told, we better prepare for a long stay."

Although I was relieved to encounter someone who spoke English, my conversation with Nils only depressed me further.

Without special occasions or any indication marking a weekend, I couldn't figure out how long it had been since I arrived. I remained among the forgotten. As no one from the United States

Embassy appeared, even my slight hope they would assist me faded. There was no way out. My confinement might be a life sentence. I could speak to Nils, but most of the time, I avoided the Norwegian. Nils always talked about the hopelessness of his, and my, situation. The last time I spoke to him, Nils said he spoke to an older trustee in German, and the trustee told him one only left Beni as a corpse. The Moroccan treatment for insanity consisted of getting the person off the streets and keeping them off the streets, end of story.

"The trustee told me the government did not want to release anyone who would cause additional problems or reflect badly on them," Nils said.

I replied, "I hope the US Embassy will come to my aid."

"Get real. I'd bet anything the embassy doesn't know a thing about your being in here. Who would tell them? Your friends who brought you here? They're drug dealers and users and not even Americans themselves," Nils said.

I replayed this conversation in my mind again and again, and its truth shattered me. I estimated I'd been inside over two months, and no one from the embassy appeared to help. If Todd and Michelle went to the embassy, surely by now someone would have contacted me.

Depressed, I decided I needed to get off the pills. I would stop the pills. Then I could think more clearly about how to gain my release.

By now the inmate handing me the pills at the end of the food line did not pay much attention when I put the pills into my mouth. I easily palmed the pills and pretended to swallow them. I dropped the pills into my pants pocket as I walked away. Proceeding as I usually did, I walked slowly and sat down against the wall and acted as if I was getting sleepy. Pretending to nod out, I sat against the wall, thinking back to the fate of the Argentinean inmate and how helplessly he cried and yelled. Without the calming effects of the pills, it was difficult to concentrate. I knew the daily pills would not leave my system from just one missed dose but decided not to take the evening pills either and see how I progressed.

The following day, I again palmed the pills at the end of breakfast. Now I missed three doses, and the fog was beginning to lift. I sat against the wall, pretending to doze.

I drifted again to the Argentinean, and I thought, Ayudame, Dios ayudame. *What did it mean?*

In a flash, I understood. "*Dios ayudame*" meant "God help me," and I began repeating, "*Dios ayudame*," over and over under my breath. The lice biting my scalp and covering my clothes did not distract me as I repeated over and over, "God help me… *Dios ayudame*." I sat all day in the same spot and repeated the same words until the gong sounded for the evening meal.

When I lay down that night, I could not fall asleep. I went back over the events of my life. *Did I do something evil in a past life and my birth was a punishment? Or was it a test?* I lived the sex, drugs, rock and roll lifestyle. I dealt hash. All night I lay awake, staring at the ceiling and reviewing my misdeeds, plenty to think about. *Did I go insane because of prideful thinking? I could become enlightened without a guru, using the shortcut of hash and acid? Without a guru, maybe I fell into "Yogic madness."*

I remembered a warning from Tibetan guru Trungpa, "We go on deeper and deeper and deeper and deeper until we reach the point where there is no answer. At that point, we tend to give up hope of an answer, or of anything whatsoever, for that matter. This hopelessness is the essence of Yogic madness."

I practiced some of the teachings and ignored others. It's always the Buddha (teacher or guide), the dharma (the teachings), and the sangha (the group of followers and fellow practitioners).

Did my solo effort make it impossible to reach the goal?

Milarepa's guru Marpa told Milarepa to build him a house. When Milarepa complied, Marpa tore the house down and ordered Milarepa to build another before he could receive the teachings. This repeated four times. By continuing to work, Milarepa overcame the bad Karma of his earlier life.

Maybe my confinement in Beni equaled my punishment as a way to burn off the bad Karma I built?

The second morning after I palmed my downer pills, I sat outside in a sunny spot. I remembered my friends Todd and Michelle putting me in the ambulance that drove me to Beni, but I never could remember what happened at their home in El Majaz. During my time in Beni, I repressed this crucial incident. Now a feeling of dread sent a chill down my spine as it came back to me.

Crystal clear memories flooded in as my mind returned to my three months living alone, studying and practicing Tibetan Buddhism and hatha yoga. The practices transformed me mentally as well as physically. My long hair and full beard made me into a physical likeness of the hermit as the tarot reading in Spain a year and a half earlier predicted. My interpretation of the hermit card meant I was nearing the completion of the spiritual journey and close to achieving enlightenment.

I observed myself hitchhiking to pick up a purebred Doberman pinscher puppy from Todd and Michelle. As payment, I wrapped a one-hundred-gram square of hash in a green tie-dyed cloth and tied it with twine. I put the hash into the bottom of my backpack along with a few changes of clothes. I took special care with my boots of Spanish leather, an important part of my hippie ensemble. I polished the boots so they shined like the ocean on a sunny day. I put a white sweat sock over each boot to protect the shine.

A hippie van where I smoked hash dropped me off at a fork in the road near Tangier. Waiting at this rough crossroads area, I felt I'd be vulnerable after nightfall, but as the sun set, a dented old truck came barreling down the road, spewing dust and smoke in its wake. Reaching me, it crept to a stop. The truck sagged as loud clinking and clanking noises escaped its engine as if the truck stopped to catch its breath. About twenty Moroccans sat on benches on the two sides in the back of the truck.

The driver said, "*Entra ven aqui.*"

As I got into the cab, I could see a third man lay on the floor under the dashboard. I rested my feet lightly on top of the man, but neither the driver nor the other man seated in the cab gave any indication this arrangement required explanation.

The driver pulled out, saying, "*El Majaz?*"

I replied, "*Si.*"

And the truck moved ahead without further conversation.

We crept slowly on the curved road, the hash influencing my perception. In the darkness, the starlight cast strange shadows in the surrounding rough, rocky countryside. As the truck rounded a bend, a roll of barbed wire blocked the road. Heavily armed soldiers stood beside it, their automatic rifles pointed directly at the cab. The driver slammed on the brakes and came to a stop as soldiers came forward from all sides. The man hiding under the dashboard pushed his way out of cab and ran off as soon as the truck slowed down. I feared the soldiers would open fire, but they didn't see him race away. Two groups of soldiers shouted harsh orders in Arabic while waving their rifles, ordering everyone out of the truck. We lined up at the side of the road with a machine gun pointed at us from a nearby jeep. An angry officer walked down the line. He stopped in front of each person and, with his face a foot from theirs, screamed in Arabic while two soldiers pointed their rifles at us.

When he came to me, he stopped and, with haughty distain, shouted, "*Pasaporte! Papeles!*" and held out his hand.

I reached inside my backpack and, with shaking hands, took out my passport, saying meekly, "American."

Soldiers grabbed one of the Moroccans from the line and, at gunpoint, dragged him behind the parked military trucks. The officer walked toward the frightened man as he instructed two other soldiers and pointed to me. He indicated by his gestures and rapid Arabic commands that they should go through my backpack. My knees began to knock. I thought about the one-hundred-gram chunk of hash at the bottom of my pack.

One soldier opened my backpack and began taking out each item and inspecting it. First he took out a book then my extra shirt and pants, my toothbrush and soap, looking over each item carefully. Next he pulled out my Spanish leather boots covered by the white cotton gym socks. He started laughing hysterically and called over the other soldiers. He held up the boots, and they doubled over, laughing as if a sock on the outside of boots was the funniest thing they'd ever seen. Holding up the boots again, the soldier threw them toward the backpack and waved me forward without looking further. He missed the hash. I walked slowly to the group that had passed inspection, my heart pounding. The soldiers took their time, completing their searches and interrogations. I waited for what seemed like hours, still scared I would be singled out again as the only foreigner. The men in the line were whispering in Spanish. I heard them repeating the word, "Rey," "king." I also heard the word "assassinate" and thought the king had been killed. After slowly piecing together what the men were saying, I understood the heavy army presence at the roadblock was because of an attempted assassination of the Moroccan King, Hassan II.

Finally, the officer waved his arm at the driver to signal the truck could move on. The remaining passengers reentered and truck drove off. I sat silently in the cab, thinking about the soldier opening my pack, and the hair on my neck rose. We proceeded ahead in silence for about another hour until coming around a sharp curve, the truck pulled into El Majaz.

Noticing we were approaching the town square, I said, "*Aqui bueno.*"

I thanked the driver, and we hugged extra hard because our shared harrowing experience. I lifted my pack and walked down the dark, empty streets, following the directions to Todd and Michelle's house. The sound of the waves and the smell of salt air suggested the Mediterranean's presence nearby.

I knocked softly on my friend's door, and to my surprise, a wide-awake Michelle welcomed me with a kiss as did her daughter, Lola.

Todd gave me a hug. "Welcome, old chap. This is an ideal time. Sit down and have a smoke."

I dropped my pack and sat on the rug-covered straw mat next to a round, brass low table in the middle of the room. Their house resembled mine in Khemis with small windows and a tile floor. The light from kerosene lamps made the shadows jump throughout the room, but instead of the noxious smell of the burning oil, incense made the room smell of patchouli.

"I'm thrilled you showed up. The pups are available," Michelle said in her French/Belgian accent.

I said, "I remember when we met on the beach at Taghazout. That's when I fell in love with your dog, Ute. I love mixed marriages of the international hippie variety. You two are good examples. You're a mix of good food and good drugs." I began laughing at my own remark as the pipe came around to me again.

"I'll brew a pot of mint tea," Michelle said.

"I'd love mint tea," I said. "I just went through a stomach-churning ordeal. Have you heard about the attempt to assassinate the king? Armed soldiers stopped the truck I was riding in from the crossroads. They pointed machine guns in our faces. They searched everything, including my backpack, but by pure luck, they didn't find the hash. I still can't believe I'm not sitting in a prison right now."

"Thank God you got here safely. Your hash is the best and we need it," Michelle said. "You must have freaked out. This amount would get you years in a Moroccan prison."

"Show him the puppies. They're not sleeping," Lola said as she ran into the other room and returned with a basket full of squirming, yapping puppies. "Aren't they adorable?"

Even with my fried nerves, I reached into the basket and picked up one female black puppy already weighing about twelve pounds. "They're the cutest little things. How can I choose just one?" I answered.

Michelle swooshed into the room with the pot of tea and a tray of cups. I looked at her slim body and long brown hair. She was wearing a flowing blue-and-green caftan, swirling as she walked, showing an outline of her breasts as she bent to pour the tea.

Too bad she's married, I thought. *Otherwise, I'd hit on her.* My moral precepts as a Buddhist devotee and my hippie lecherous self, led me in different directions.

"Last time in Khemis, it seemed like your study of the path to enlightenment really progressed. How's it been going?" Todd asked between sips of tea.

With my head spinning from the hash, I replied, "I feel close to achieving yogic powers and completing my metamorphosis into the tarot hermit."

Lola laughed when I said this.

I turned to her. "My psychic powers are near. It's not a laughing matter."

After heavy smoking, Michelle led me to a straw mat in the next room.

Lying there, staring at the ceiling, I couldn't help but replay the roadblock scenario over and over in my mind. *Almost a complete bummer… I escaped by an inch*, I thought.

I clutched the blanket, thinking, *Why did I leave my safe home? Was my journey wise?* After all, *Did the hermit have a dog?* I had never seen one in the tarot drawings.

When I woke up, I opened the door to the next room, where six puppies were wrestling on the floor with Ute watching over them. I didn't yet connect with any of the puppies. Maybe later I'd find my "Victorious Champion," a name I selected because the purebred needed a name starting with the letter *V*. The generations were named in alphabetical order, so *V* followed *U*.

Going to my backpack, I took out the one-hundred-gram piece of hash and gave it to Todd. "The payment for the puppy. Same as we smoked in Khemis."

Returning to the sitting room, Todd broke off a small piece and heated it in the candle flame; he held the smoking piece to his nose and inhaled the sweet aroma as if it was a vintage wine. "Far-out," Todd said. "You've got hash that would satisfy the most discerning connoisseur." Todd lit the large bowl and took a hit before passing the pipe to Michelle, who took a toke and passed it to me.

"I love a pipe before breakfast," I said.

My mind wandered to the recent past, and a feeling of panic crept in. My frightened thoughts mixed with the hash put me in an eerie headspace. I made a concerted effort carrying on. Being a hippie in a Muslim country, stoned on hash and acid, I often practiced acting normal with mixed success.

Maybe it would be a good time to pick a puppy, I thought. I entered the room with the pups and spotted Lola playing with them. "Which one is your favorite?" I asked.

Bending forward and picking up a fat black and brown and white male, Lola replied, "This is my baby. I can really cuddle with him." She wore shorts and a T-shirt with beaded bracelets on both arms and ribbons in her hair. A true "flower child."

Michelle called out, "*Petit dejeuner*."

The four of us sat down to eat steaming bowls of couscous with raisins, dates, and figs.

Looking at the hash nearby, I said, "I'm well on the road to enlightenment and hash has been a great tool in getting me there. It's been a useful shortcut. Can you dig it?"

Todd made a face indicating his skepticism and said, "I smoke hash for fun and to make sex more intense."

Laughing, I said, "I like that part of hash smoking too."

Michelle voiced her opinion, "There are no shortcuts to true enlightenment. Hash confuses my attempts at meditation and distorts reality. I've seen it make people paranoid. I believe in the goals of Buddhist ethical teachings, but I don't fool myself into thinking hash helps me. You do your own thing."

"I'm not fooling myself. I don't need the years of deep meditation because hash and acid are getting me there so much quicker. I feel on the brink of a real breakthrough," I answered, nearly shouting.

"Do you really believe you can get superpowers from smoking hash?" Lola asked.

"The great yogis could walk on water, fly, and appear in two places at once, and I'm close to being a great yogi," I boasted even louder. *I'll show her powers I can achieve*, I thought.

Todd and Michelle continued smoking the hash I brought throughout the day. They seemed to have increased their smoking intensity, and I joined in. I spent some more time with the pups watching them play together. I was narrowing my choice, although it was difficult focusing on them as they blended together.

Away from my home, I wasn't following my regular routine of hatha yoga practice, meditation, and readings from spiritual books.

As the hours drifted by, I perceived the great spiritual teachers reaching their arms toward me.

As I lit the after-dinner bowl of hash, a newer model British Land Rover pulled up to the front of the house. Two twenty-something British men came into the house with a burst of enthusiasm. They wore long hair and looked like they could have been Rolling Stones band members. The hair, the clothes, the swagger, very "British invasion."

Todd hugged each man and said, "This is Tom and Mike, my mates from the London music scene." With a hand pointed at me, he said, "This is Fred, an old Morocco hand that just came over from south of Tangier where he's been living."

Michelle refilled the pipe with my hash. "We hear this can bring you enlightenment," she said with the corners of her mouth turned up. She shot me a wink as Tom filled his lungs with smoke.

After a deep drag, Tom said, "We're on a mission of mercy. We're working for some nice blokes, the Stones. We're here to score proper hash. This is our first stop as, Todd, you're a legend in London for having good hash. You helped Keith in '69 when he was down here. We want you to help us out again."

"I'm still connected to the best hash, mate," Todd said.

"This smells and tastes great. I'm too blasted to even stand," Mike said as he took another hit.

I thought, *I'm the man! I'm the guy they need to see!*

What a gas to be the hash connection for The Rolling Stones. I could see Mick Jagger reaching out to shake my hand and saying, "Jolly good smoke, old boy," as Keith lay on a couch, ripping a hit from my amazing hash.

Both Tom and Mike praised the hash to the skies. I was beaming like a proud parent. As the night passed, we sat silently staring at a candle burning on the table and soon passed out.

After I crawled to my sleeping bag, I lay wide awake on the straw mat, thinking I could broker a big hash deal. With my hands clasped behind my head, I looked up at the white ceiling, imagining my place in the Hashish Hall of Fame. Then paranoia struck. The picture changed to me standing in front of heavily armed soldiers, my hands bound, and a rifle pointed at my face. Instead of laughing, the soldiers were shouting at me. Catching my breath, I tried to reassure myself of my safety.

I thought, *Am I getting in over my head?*

As I fell asleep, I waited for the right time to bring up the subject of a Rolling Stones hash purchase. The enlightened saints still reached out to me, but fear kept surfacing in the stream of visions.

The next morning, the sweet smell of hash clouds wafted into my room. I had slept in so only leftovers from breakfast remained scattered on the table. Everyone was preparing for the day's trip to the beach. I rubbed my eyes, and I began to regain my bearings as Michelle floated by and presented me with the hash pipe. Without eating, I got ready and joined everyone including Ute on the short walk from the house to the beach.

With very few Moroccans anywhere in sight on the wide white sand beach, Ute played, running wide circles in the sand, while Lola sat at the water's edge, looking out and dripping wet sand into castles. As I looked over at Lola, the Hendrix song, "Castles in the Sand," ran through my head, repeating the refrain, "And so castles made of sand / fall into the sea eventually." The group of adults sat in a semicircle, looking at the bright, blue Mediterranean stretching north toward Spain. Even in the blazing sun, the breeze cooled the air and filled it with the smell of sardines.

Tom looked dazed and said, "This beats the fog and rain in London."

"I love the expanse of open sand. Look, we're the only foreigners on the beach, and we have it to ourselves. In Chicago, the shores of Lake Michigan are so crowded you can't even walk without stepping on someone," I said, feeling the urge to run free.

Running at full speed parallel to the water with the wind blowing through my long hair, I experienced release. At a far point, I turned around and ran back to where the group settled. I ran faster than I ever ran before. Fit, trim, and tanned in my cutoff denim shorts, I thought anyone who caught sight of me would see the image of a Greek god. I could run endlessly inhaling the mild, clean air while stoned on great hash.

After my vigorous run, I jumped into the water and began to swim along the shoreline.

With every stroke, I thought, *I am soon to be hash supplier to The Rolling Stones.*

At the same time, Milarepa and the Buddha welcomed me as an enlightened comrade. My mind jumped between dreams of huge profits, obtaining yogic powers and hanging out with Mick Jagger. As I stood up in the water, hallucinatory figures shimmered on the beach.

I gulped for air, thinking, *I didn't take acid, what the hell is going on?*

I whipped my head around in the direction of Lola, who was swimming nearby. Out of nowhere, I experienced mental telepathy with her. As I squinted and placed a hand on my temple, I could clearly hear Lola's thoughts ringing in my head. I developed the ability to read thoughts, an advanced yogic power. I never experienced anything like it. Standing there with waves hitting me, my head and heart pounded. I was in Lola's mind. Across the water, Lola and I were exchanging thoughts. Reading Lola's mind sent my own mind reeling. I couldn't stop the flowing images. I experienced a vision of Shiva walking through a town similar to El Majaz. People were running out throwing red, yellow, orange, and purple flowers in Shiva's path.

At the same time, I surmised Lola could read my thoughts, even though I wanted to stop the connection.

In crisis mode, I thought, *I can't control other people getting into my mind. I need to use yogic techniques.* I began mentally building a brick wall to surround my mind. Visualizing building brick by brick, I wanted a wall to surround me and keep thoughts from getting in and out.

I avoided going near Lola as I slowly walked from the water onto the beach. I sought a secluded spot, hoping this confused acid-like trip would end. It didn't; it only ramped up. Images flew past me that wouldn't stop.

Get it together, I told myself, but the images continued.

I discerned Milarepa sitting in a lotus position with his arms extended, welcoming me into the lineage of the great gurus. Buddha, Shiva, and Jesus were dancing in a circle around me, singing, "You can't always get what you want / but if you try some time / you might find what you need."

Hours passed. I lost connection to my surroundings. Along with the others, I walked back to the house with no recollection of how I got there. At the house, the group started hash smoking again, but I did not join the circle of the passing pipe. The Rolling Stones blasted from the cassette player. "Just as every cop is a criminal / and all the sinners saints / as heads is tails / just call me Lucifer / 'cause I'm in need of some restraint."

I entered the living room and loudly proclaimed, "It's happened, I've achieved enlightenment. As a saint, the rules of society no longer apply to me."

Michelle looked concerned and said, "Cool it, man. Hang loose. Have a hit." She lifted the smoking pipe in my direction.

"People should recognize me," I said, and I pushed the pipe back in Michelle's direction. "Recognize me as the holy person I have become!" I shouted as I ripped off my shirt, dropped my jean shorts, which I wore without underwear, opened the front door, and sprinted down the late-afternoon street. Dashing on the main road with my arms stretched wide, I roared, "I'm the one! I'm Buddha, Christ, I'm holy!"

Naked and barefoot, united with the cosmos, my hair and beard blowing in the warm wind, I ran down the main street of the village. Arab women opened their doors, releasing the pungent smells of dinner cooking, but slammed them in shock as I ran by. Groups of boys seemed to come out of nowhere and pointed and yelled. I didn't understand their words in Arabic, but I interpreted them as "Look at the holy man."

They get it, I thought.

Todd, leading the way, followed by Tom, Mike, Michelle, and Lola were running down the road after me, calling and shouting "What the bloody hell are you doing! Cool it! Stop! Cover yourself!"

At the top of a slight grade, I turned to face them and spread my legs, raised my arms over my head, and I shouted, "Can't you see? I'm enlightened!" My eyes glowed with a crazy Ancient Mariner look.

Now I knew what I'd done to be committed into Beni.

I returned to the present as I heard a gong and noted the men lining up for dinner in the courtyard.

Next morning, I again palmed my pills. I felt lightheaded and somewhat dizzy, but I remembered a reference to "Yogic madness" in the biography of Milarepa. On occasion, a yogi on the path to enlightenment would break from reality. Clearly, I suffered from "Yogic madness."

As I walked slowly to a spot to sit, I was overcome with the need to empty my bowels. I rushed to the toilet area, braced for the smell, and emptied my guts with a gush. Still feeling ill and now with my jeans wet from the urine on the toilet floor, I observed the utter hopelessness of my situation. As I leaned on the wall in my usual spot, looking at the broken glass-topped walls, everyone was weak, sick, and covered in lice. I thought perhaps I already died. Maybe I died in the ambulance when it took me from the hospital and had been delivered into hell. I died and Beni Makada was hell. A sinner sent to hell, the worst place in the universe. Without hope, suffering the same conditions day after day, week after week, month after month, year after year. I died and was condemned to hell for eternity.

As I slouched into a deep depression, an elderly trustee approached me. He motioned for me to get up and follow him. I complied without understanding where we were going. We went into the central building with the trustee walking slowly and silently in front of me. He opened the door to a big gray room, which contained two cell-like cages facing each other about ten feet apart so people could talk but not touch. He opened the cage door and I went inside. As I looked across the enclosure, I saw a brown-haired woman with no makeup and wearing plain old-fashioned clothes standing in the other cage. I had never seen the woman before.

I shouted from behind the wire on my side, "Hello, who are you?"

The woman's reply shocked me. She said in a British accent, "God sent me to get you out of here."

I recognized the woman as an angel, and tears began to roll down my cheeks.

She continued, "God spoke to me and commanded I get you out of here. I will not abandon you."

"Please, get me out of here. I'm in hell," I sobbed. "What can I do to help you get me out of here?"

"Pray," she said.

After the old trustee led me back to the courtyard, I sat down against the wall. I could hardly breathe as my heart was pounding. I tried to control myself by concentrating on my breath, *Rising, falling, rising, falling, rising, falling.* I walked around the yard, going over everything my angel told me. She was a nurse named Anne at the British missionary hospital in Tangier. She said Todd and Michelle came to the hospital over two months ago after my entry into Beni Makada. They met with the nurses and told them an American was thrown into the prison for the insane. Todd said he tried to visit but wasn't admitted. Nor could he contact their friend, Fred, in any way. As Todd and Michelle left, the nurses told them they would "pray about it."

At the missionary's regular Wednesday night prayer meeting, they went through a list of names of people to pray for. The "American in Beni Makada" name came up every week, and last Wednesday when my name came up, God directed Anne to free the American.

I walked faster as I thought about God's intervention. I began to pray out loud under my breath, repeating, "God, get me out of here." I repeated the prayer with vigor, following my angel's instruction.

Anne told me she would contact Beni's administration. This shocked me because I did not know someone within the institution might assist me.

I did not want any problems, so I decided to return to taking my three pills twice daily.

My angel said she would return the following Tuesday. I asked her to bring me a carton of cigarettes, which I told her was used as currency within the asylum. I could use the cigarettes to barter for better treatment by the trustees.

I wasn't sure how many days passed since my angel's visit. I sat everyday against the stucco wall in a semi-stupor, repeating, "God, get me out of here." Although I wasn't clear who I was praying to. Sometimes I said, "Buddha, help me." Every once in a while, I thought maybe a yogic test had been given to me, just as Marpa gave to Milarepa.

I was nodding out when the old trustee again came to me. He led me into the cage. Angel/Anne again stood in the cage on the other side of the space. I could see she brought a basket with bananas, yogurt, a carton of cigarettes, and a sweater.

"Have you prayed?" were her first words.

"Yes, yes, I've been praying nonstop," I replied.

"I've investigated the system," Anne called back. "The only authority in Beni is the Spanish psychiatrist who comes every week on Tuesday from nine a.m. to noon. I'm trying to arrange an appointment for us to meet with him next Tuesday."

My heart leapt. I rocked back and forth and said in a low voice, "What can I do?"

"Keep praying," Anne said firmly. "I am going to try to convince the doctor to allow you to be transferred to our hospital because we speak English and will provide the medicines and support for your recovery."

"I am praying as hard and long as I can!" I shouted back.

When Anne left, the armed guard who stood in the doorway during the meeting took the basket she brought, taking a banana for himself before handing it to me the. The old trustee opened the door. I made a low bow and handed him three packs of cigarettes. Reaching out and taking the cigarettes, my guide smiled broadly and bowed back in a friendly way.

I stopped and peeled a banana, savoring every bite of my first fruit or vegetable since arriving at Beni. I took the wool sweater from the bag and put it on. I needed it as cooler days were coming. Within minutes, lice were crawling all over my new sweater.

At dinner, when I received my portion of food, I gave a pack of cigarettes to the server and two packs to the large inmate in charge of the meals.

The next day, I looked around the yard for Nils, who I had been avoiding. He was standing against the wall.

"I'm going to be transferred to the British hospital," I said as I handed him a pack of cigarettes.

"We'll see" was Nils' response. "If you do get out, please contact the Swedish Embassy as they look after Norwegians and ask them to please work for my release. Nils Jorgensen from Oslo."

"Of course, you can count on me. I'll make sure to let the Swedish Embassy know you're in here. You were right, far as I can tell, the American Embassy never did anything as to assist me."

As Nils walked away, I leaned back against the wall, my mind drifting.

I was keeping track as each day passed. I tried to picture what to expect at the British hospital, but I fell into a drugged sleep before any image appeared.

My release from hell completely occupied my mind. I would explain to the psychiatrist how I was a religious seeker who rejected the materialism of the modern world. Once the doctor understood I had been overcome by uncontrollable thoughts just for a day, the psychiatrist would be sympathetic. I needed to convince the psychiatrist because of the hospital medication that I no longer suffered from the same condition as on my admission to Beni. I knew I wasn't Buddha or Jesus, and I hadn't been sent for a meeting with the king. I knew hash and acid must have played a part in my actions at Todd's, but I still felt ambivalent about their overall value. There was a lot to think about once freed from hell. I would talk to the psychiatrist; surely he would see now I'm saner than the average person here or anywhere.

I prayed, "God, get me out of here. God, help me," throughout the following days.

I kept track of the passing of time, one dinner, one day, two dinners two days. After six dinners, I knew Anne would return the next day. I'd to talk to the Spanish psychiatrist. I went over what I would say, prepared to wow him. The downers slowed my thoughts and movements, but I'd empty my mind of crazy thoughts. The psychiatrist would easily see I'd recovered.

The trustee did not take me on the same route as previously, this time avoiding the toilet area. He led me down a hallway past closed doors. I went into an office with a desk with three chairs in front of it. Anne was standing in the room with another basket of food, a carton of cigarettes on top. No one else was in the room.

"Have you prayed?" she asked.

"Yes, yes, I've been praying constantly since last week," I answered.

Standing next to my angel sent chills running down my spine. I wanted to take her in my arms and hug her even though covered with lice. I was unable to wash other than run water over my hands in the toilet area. Touching Anne would be a mistake, who was scrubbed clean in a spotless missionary dress looking like it came from the 1940s. Her stern demeanor made even trying to shake hands out of the question.

"I've spoken to the psychiatrist, and he won't see you until next Tuesday," Anne said. "When you see him, remember to show him a lot of respect because your future is in his hands."

"Do I have to lie to him?" I blurted out without thinking, upset by the psychiatrist absence for my anticipated appointment.

"Never lie. Jesus said, 'I came not to call the righteous, but the sinners' (Mark 2: 17). God wants you to truthfully face your sins and seek His forgiveness," Anne said in a serious tone. "God has spoken to me, and He will guide your release. Salvation is available to everyone."

The next Tuesday, I paced back and forth in the yard, repeating my prayer, "God, get me out of hell. God, save me."

I walked around the inside circumference of the yard five times when the old trustee walked toward me. I feared the doctor would again not show. Perhaps the anticipated salvation never coming was another torture of hell. The trustee led me into the same hallway as the previous week and opened the door to the same office.

As I walked in, I observed a short, white-skinned balding man, wearing a suit and tie sitting behind the desk. The man had the authoritarian air of a government official. He just nodded his head as he stared at me. He seemed frightened and disgusted being so close to the dirty, bearded, long-haired, lice-covered figure standing before him.

Anne already in a chair said to me, "Sit down here," pointing to one of the hard chairs in front of the desk. "This is Doctor Rodriquez. He is the chief, and only psychiatrist, at this institution. He wants to speak to you. I'll interpret."

As soon as I sat down, the doctor said something in Spanish.

Anne translated this first question, "Why are you in Morocco?

I tried to think of how to answer and. after a pause, said in English, "I came to Morocco to escape the materialism of the United States. I wanted to live a peaceful life in the country and get back to nature. I reject the materialism of American culture. Here, I lived in a little village where I could draw and paint. I'm an artist who is happy living without electricity and pulling water from a well. I enjoyed my simple life."

To my surprise, the doctor spoke up and, in clear English, asked, "You don't want a car and a color television?"

Shocked the doctor could understand and speak English, I replied calmly, "No, that's what I'm getting away from. I want to escape the materialistic world."

The doctor looked at Anne and spoke a sentence in Spanish.

Anne translated, "He says, 'You have not been sane since the day you were born.'"

My heart sank because my fate rested with someone who wanted the material things I rejected. I encountered this attitude before as Moroccans, and Spaniards as well, could not understand a desire to live the very lifestyle they were trying so hard to rise above. I mulled over what to say and decided to be as truthful as possible while omitting the hash and acid. I thought about what Milarepa taught,

"Money and dainties are the devils envoys. Association with them is pernicious. Renounce them and all other things that bind you."

The doctor did not ask me another question, and I sat silently as Anne and the doctor spoke in Spanish. He wrote a prescription on a pad and handed it to Anne and gestured toward the door.

Anne said to me, "Dr. Rodriquez agrees to your release to me. We'll continue your treatment under his direction and return for follow-up visits. He's transferring you to the British hospital. God will help us."

As it seemed, the interview was ended.

I stood up and said, "*Gracias. Muchas gracias,*" and extended my hand to the doctor, who looked alarmed and did not extend his.

Anne guided me out the door. Nothing mattered to me except getting out of this place. I would follow any British hospital rules; I would consent to do anything to escape the hell of my confinement.

Anne led me into another office full of cupboards and filing cabinets. An armed guard took out several sheets of paper written in Spanish and Arabic and pointed to a line where I needed to sign. One place had a space for the date.

I turned to Anne at a loss and asked, "What day is it?"

Anne said, "November 21, 1972."

The paper also contained my admission date, "August 19, 1972." I had been in hell for three months.

After signing the papers, I thought about the things I had with me when I left El Majaz. "Where are my possessions?" I asked, and Anne translated my question into Spanish.

I started to become agitated as the guard looked at the records. He reached into another drawer and took out my American passport but nothing else.

I could sense my rising agitation was troubling Anne who, turning her eyes upward, said, "God, help this man, for he needs your assistance." She said something in Spanish to the guard and, after his reply, turned to me and said calmly, "He says the records show there is nothing to return except your passport."

"Nothing, nothing," I said, trying to calm my voice. "I had a ring made out of beads Lola gave me in Khemis, and I always wore it. I know I was wearing the bead ring in the back of the car when we left Todd and Michelle's. I want my ring back."

Without a word, Anne took me firmly by my shoulders, turned me toward the door, and pushed me out into the hallway. I knew rescuing me from Beni Makada did not mean Anne thought me sane. She only knew I required salvation even if insane. She led me to her car, an older French Citroën station wagon parked just inside the gate. Opening the door, she ushered me into the passenger seat. She drove directly to the barricade, which the guards opened to let us pass.

Anne drove through the streets of Tangier as I stared wide-eyed. The people, the smells, the sounds, the activity and bustle I loved so much brought tears to my eyes.

"Free at last, free at last… Great God Almighty, I'm free at last," I whispered.

The Jugolinija

EPILOGUE

All You Need Is Love

I stood on the deck of *Jugolinija*, a Yugoslavian freighter on the way to New York from Casablanca. In his letter to Allen Ginsberg, Jack Kerouac described crossing the Atlantic on this ship. So along with smoking from the same pipe as Jagger and Hendrix, I am sailing with Kerouac.

I thought of the phrase, "Change is the law of the universe," when I reflected on the physical and mental changes I had gone through.

Lying on my bunk in my cabin, I thought back over the last three years. I lived in a hippie commune and then moved to a village without electricity, drawing water from a well in a Muslim family compound. I studied holy books, doing art, meditation and yoga, smoking hashish and kief daily, and dropping acid on special occasions. I had several memorable love affairs.

I thought I transformed myself into the enlightened hermit, a Buddhist yogi, but when the opportunity arose, I wanted to supply hashish to The Rolling Stones. I then ran through village streets naked and suffered through months isolated in a Moroccan prison for the insane.

Released through the efforts of an angel/Anne and God, I lived with the British missionaries, where I studied the New Testament and joined the Jesus freaks.

What wisdom had I gained from my searching?

Upon my return to the States, I lived with my grandparents in Chicago; during the first month, I hardly left my bedroom. The culture shock of returning to the USA surpassed my shock upon entering Morocco. One night, I braved the city and went out to see a blues band that was playing in a club downtown. At the club, I saw a girlfriend from my college days. We went home together. I moved in with her that night.

DEVOTEE'S PRAYER

May all beings be happy and at their ease!
May they be joyous and live in safety!
All beings—whether weak or strong—omitting none
In high, middle, or low realms of existence
Small or great, visible or invisible, near or far away
Born or to be born
May all beings be happy and at their ease!
Let none deceive another or despise any being in any state;
Let none by anger or ill will wish harm to another!
Even as a mother watches over and protects
her child, her only child,
So should one cherish all beings,
Radiating friendliness over the entire world,
Above, below, and all around without limit.

The end.

Steve and Fred, 2019, Mendocino, California

AFTERWORD

Luckily I'm sane after all I been through... Life's been good to me so far.
—Joe Walsh/The Eagles

As I look back on my adventures of fifty years ago, the lessons I learned then have led to a productive, satisfying life.

My twenty-fifth birthday in Khemis Sahel, Morocco, I celebrated by dropping acid, taking an oath of silence, fasting, doing yoga, and meditating. On my seventy-fifth birthday, I celebrated with friends and family on Zoom.

I live comfortably in the San Francisco Bay Area with my wife of forty-five years.

Our adult son and daughter and their spouses live nearby, each with two sons.

My spiritual quest has continued throughout my life. I returned to my roots, Judaism.

I built a successful career in the eyeglass frame business.

My golf game is as good as ever.

I still love rock and roll.

I smoke cannabis regularly.

And in the end
The love you take
Is equal to the love you make.
(The Beatles)

ABOUT THE AUTHOR

1971 Tangier, Morocco

2022 San Francisco, California

Fred Zola lives in the San Francisco Bay Area.

In the 1960s, he was part of the Haight-Ashbury hippie scene. He dropped acid with the Grateful Dead and Jefferson Airplane. He *almost became the hashish dealer for The Rolling Stones. He witnessed Joni Mitchell sing her song "Woodstock" in public for the first time. He was there when the phrase "sex, drugs, rock and roll" was coined.*

In the 1970s, he went on a spiritual journey around the world, seeking wisdom and enlightenment, fueled by hashish and LSD.

In the 1980s, he began a lifelong career in the eyeglass frame business. The company he is with designs, manufactures, and distributes eyeglass frames to eye care professionals.

He and his lovely wife are celebrating their forty-five-year anniversary. They have a son and a daughter and four grandsons living nearby.

Printed in the USA
CPSIA information can be obtained
at www.ICGtesting.com
LVHW070842270924
791861LV00012B/23

9 781637 845097